ABEL

ABEL

THE TRUE STORY OF THE SPY
THEY TRADED FOR GARY POWERS

VIN ARTHEY

Biteback Publishing

First published as *The Kremlin's Geordie Spy* in Great Britain in 2010
This edition published in 2015 by
Biteback Publishing Ltd
Westminster Tower
3 Albert Embankment
London SE1 7SP
Copyright © Vin Arthey 2010, 2015

ISBN 978-1-84954-969-1

10 9 8 7 6 5 4 3 2 1

A CIP catalogue record for this book is available from the British Library.

Set in Sabon by SoapBox

Printed and bound in Great Britain by
CPI Group (UK) Ltd, Croydon CR0 4YY

CONTENTS

ACKNOWLEDGEMENTS

This is a third edition of my biography of the spy known as 'Rudolf Abel', previously published under the titles *Like Father Like Son: A Dynasty of Spies* and *The Kremlin's Geordie Spy*. Those to whom I remain indebted are Christopher Andrew, Arthur Andrews, Daniel Aravot, John Arnold, Robert Beatson, Calland Carnes, Ray Challinor, Ben De Jong, Vasily Dozhdalev, George Falkowski, Edward Gamber, Oleg Gordievsky, Ron Grant, Keith Gregson, Alex Heft, Maike Helmers, Per Oyvind Heradstveit, Frode Jacobsen, Knut Jacobsen, Lucy Jago, David King, Sergei Kondrashev, Lev Koshliakov, Boris Labusov, Colin Latham, Darren Lilleker, Anne McElvoy, Angus MacQueen, Richard Melman, Penny Minney, Robin Minney, Tom Mitchell, Dan Mulvenna, Melita Norwood, Linda Osband, Helge Ostbye, Chris Pocock, Colin Robinson, Charles Murray Roscoe, Dieter Sevin, Burt Silverman, Barry Stewart, Sean Street, Oleg Tsarev, Andrew Thorpe, John Wallwork and Nina Westgaard. Some people asked me to keep details of their help confidential and I continue to respect their wishes. I remain grateful to Natalia Kovalenko, Yelena Londareva, Oksana Silantieva, also to Konstantin Chistiakov, Maria Fedoseeva, Richard Miller, Nina Schrader-Nielsen and Rachel Viney who helped me find texts in Russian and Norwegian and translated passages for me. Not only did Geoffrey Elliott assist in finding and translating certain Russian material but his financial support enabled me to make my first visit to Moscow.

In my archive and library research I was indebted to Dilys Harding and her staff in Local Studies at Newcastle City Library, Eric Hollerton and Alan Hildrew at North Shields Library, Judith Etherton at the University of London Library, Martin Pegler at the Royal Armouries Museum in Leeds, Tish Collins and her team at the Marx Memorial Library, Lesley Richardson at the Laing Art Gallery in Newcastle upon

Tyne, to Janet Coles and her staff at Bournemouth University Library and to all who assisted me at the National Archives. I am grateful for the help with the illustrations given by Jonathan Wardle, Stephen Murray, Ange Ferguson, Andy Price and Ken Slater.

The research and writing was undertaken when I was employed at Bournemouth University and at Teesside University. I record my thanks to Roger Laughton, John Foster, Su Reid and Chris Newbold. Also at Bournemouth, John Ellis and Julia Taylor assisted me in the application for University research funding that made possible a visit to Moscow in 2001.

There would have been no reincarnation of this work if it had not been for the perceptiveness and energy of Michael Smith at Biteback Publishing and I record my special thanks to him. I am grateful, too, for the editorial support of Jonathan Wadman and James Stephens at Biteback. *Abel* has benefited from new research and I now add Beth Amorosi, Michael Briggs (University Press of Kansas), John Donovan, Mary Ellen Fuller, Alan Myers, Anthony R. Palermo (who was Special Attorney with the team that prosecuted 'Rudolf Abel' in 1957), Mark Palermo and Patrick Salmon to the cohort of those to whom I am indebted.

However, it is important to state that although I have sought and relied upon the help of many, the contents of this book, its speculations and any errors of fact or judgement, errors in translation or transliteration, are my responsibility. And the following persons in particular knew, or will know, this. Trevor Hearing was present at the very beginning of this work and has encouraged and enthused me from the outset. I shall always be grateful. The support and friendship of Nigel West has also meant a great deal to me, and his books *The Illegals* and *The Crown Jewels* have continued to be valuable reference points. Professor David Saunders, who first proved that William Fisher was born in Newcastle upon Tyne, Kirill Khenkin, who was one of Willie Fisher's pupils, and Evelyn, Willie's daughter, responded without fail to my every letter, call and question and I hope that this book will repay a little of the debt I owe them. My wife, Ann, has never complained about the amount of my time that I have put into this work and I would like my readers to know that without her certain support this book would never have been completed.

LIST OF ABBREVIATIONS

AAS   The Anglo-American Secretariat of the Comintern (USSR)
Arcos   The All Russian Co-operative Society (USSR/UK)
ASA   Army Security Agency (USA)
ASE   The Amalgamated Society of Engineers (UK)
BSP   The British Socialist Party
CIA   Central Intelligence Agency (USA)
CPGB   The Communist Party of Great Britain
FBI   Federal Bureau of Investigation (USA)
GRU   Soviet military intelligence (*Glavnoe Razvedyvatel'noe Upravlenie*, Main Intelligence Directorate)
INO   Foreign department of Soviet state security (*Inostrannyi Otdel*)
INS   Immigration and Naturalization Service (USA)
IWW   Industrial Workers of the World
KGB   Committee for State Security *(Komitet Gosudarstvennoi Bezopasnosti)* (USSR)
KI   Committee of Information *(Komitet Informatsii)* (USSR)
MGB   Ministry of State Security (*Ministerstvo Gosudarstvennoi Bezopasnosti)* (USSR)
NKGB   People's Commissariat for State Security (*Narodnyi Kommissariat Gosudarstvennoi Bezopasnosti*) (USSR)
NKVD   People's Commissariat for Internal Affairs (*Narodnyi Kommissariat Vnutrennikh Del)* (USSR)
OGPU   Soviet intelligence service (*Ob"yedinennoe Gosudarstvennoe Politicheskoe Upravlenie*, Joint State Political Directorate)
OSS   Office of Strategic Services (USA)
RCMP   Royal Canadian Mounted Police
RSDRP   Russian Social Democratic Workers Party *(Rossiiskaya Sotsial Demokraticheskaya Rabocbaya Partiya)*

SDF   Social Democratic Federation (UK)
SIS   Secret Intelligence Service (UK)
USAF   United States Air Force
WSF   Workers' Socialist Federation (UK)

A NOTE ON THE FISHER NAMES

Names, the use and the spelling of names, are part of this story about the Fischer family, who were members of the German community in Russia from the middle of the nineteenth century. However, the distinctiveness of the German is lost when the name is transliterated into Russian. It sounds, and is spelt, 'Fisher'. At various times, it was required that the Fishers formally and fully adapted the style of their names to the Russian custom, with a patronymic. Then, family members spent time in the West, where sometimes they had their name recorded in documents in the German fashion, sometimes in the English. Often, they may have settled for the easiest way out when registrars or clerks were completing documents for them. Moreover, there were many occasions in the twentieth century when it was prudent to choose one spelling over the other, usually the English rather than the German.

The father was known as, and usually wrote his name as, 'Heinrich Fischer'; the son tended to write his name 'William Fisher'. Predominantly, I have followed their custom. However, given the subject and the context of the story, Heinrich and William used other names as well, pseudonyms, code names and cover names (see the table overleaf). Willie's wife also used and was known by the English name Helen, sometimes spelt Hellen, as well as the Russian Yelena, occasionally in the diminutives, Yelya or Ilya, but at home she was always called Ellie.

Heinrich Fischer
Heinrich Matthäus Fischer
Henry Mattheus Fisher
Matvei Fisher
Matvei Alexandrovich Fisher
M. A. Fisher
Andrei Fisher
A. Fisher
Genrikh Matveevich Fisher
G. Fisher
G. M. Fisher

William Fisher
William August Fischer
William August Fisher
Vilyam Genrikhovich Fisher

William Fisher's code names
ALEC
ARACH
FRANK
MARK

*William Fisher's pseudonyms/
cover names*
Rudolf Ivanovich Abel
Martin Collins
Emil Goldfus
Andrew Kayotis
Milton

DRAMATIS PERSONAE

FISHER (FISCHER) FAMILY

Aleksandr August Fischer – William Fisher's paternal grandfather, born in Germany.

Evelyn Fisher – William and Yelena Fisher's daughter, their only child.

Heinrich Matthäus Fischer – William's father; Aleksandr and Maria's son; born in Russia.

Henry Fisher – Heinrich and Lyubov's first born son; born in England; William's brother.

Maria Kruger – William Fisher's paternal grandmother, born in Germany.

William Fisher – Heinrich and Lyubov's second son born in England, 11 July 1903.

Stepan Lebedev – Kapitolina's husband (died when Yelena was four years old).

Yelena Lebedeva – 'Ellie', William Fisher's wife.

Boris Lebedev – Yelena's brother; Lidiya's father.

Ivan Lebedev – Yelena's brother, falsely accused of Trotskyism.

Kapitolina Lebedeva – Yelena's mother.

Lidiya Lebedeva – Evelyn's cousin. Their close friendship (they referred to each other as 'sister') lasted into old age.

Seraphima Lebedeva – Yelena's sister; suggested to William that he seek work in the translation section of the Soviet security service.

Lyubov Zhidova – William Fisher's mother.

Vasily Zhidov – William Fisher's maternal grandfather.

Agrafena Zhidova – William Fisher's maternal grandmother.

WILLIAM FISHER'S FRIENDS

Rudolf Abel – William Fisher's closest friend.

Kirill Khenkin – Willie's wartime radio trainee; foreign press analyst for the KGB; defector.

Ernst Krenkel – Served in the Red Army with Willie Fisher; arctic radio operator and explorer.

Willie Martens – Son of Heinrich Fischer's Russo-German friend Ludwig Martens. Willie Martens was a GRU officer, and the families continued to be close friends.

NKVD/KGB OFFICERS

Vladimir Burdin – KGB co-ordinator of the Abel–Powers exchange.

Yuri Drozdov – KGB officer managing the Abel–Powers exchange.

Felix Dzerzhinsky – Founder of the *Cheka,* the first of the Soviet state security organisations.

*Leonid Eitingon (*aka *Colonel Kotov)* – High-ranking NKVD Special Tasks officer; close colleague of Pavel Sudoplatov.

Reino Häyhänen – KGB officer transferred to illegals work as assistant to William Fisher. Defected and betrayed Fisher in May 1957.

Aleksandr Korotkov – NKVD assassin who rose to take charge of the KGB illegals directorate.

Anatoly Lazarev – Head of the KGB illegals directorate at the time of Willie Fisher's death.

Mikhail Maklyarsky – NKVD Special Tasks officer during Operations Monastery and Berezino.

Georgy Mordvinov – NKVD Special Tasks colonel during Operation Berezino.

Aleksandr Orlov – NKVD officer commanding in Spain during the Civil War. Willie Fisher's senior officer during European missions. Defected 1938.

Yakov Serebryansky – Pharmacist, assassin and early *Cheka* recruit who rose to be the first head of NKVD Special Tasks.

Yuri Sokolov – Legal diplomat but KGB *rezident* in the USSR delegation to the United Nations during part of the time that Willie Fisher was illegal *rezident* in New York.

Pavel Sudoplatov – Early *Cheka* recruit who rose to be KGB general. Headed NKVD Special Tasks in the 1940s and '50s and was Willie Fisher's most senior officer during this period.

Mikhail Svirin – Legal diplomat but KGB *rezident* in the USSR delegation to the United Nations, initially scheduled to manage Reino Häyhänen.

NKVD/KGB AGENTS

Anthony Blunt – One of the 'Cambridge Five'.

Earl Browder – General Secretary of the Communist Party of the USA 1930–45; married to Kitty Harris.

Guy Burgess – One of the 'Cambridge Five'.

John Cairncross – One of the 'Cambridge Five'.

Lona Cohen – American-born agent who spied for the USSR in the USA and the UK; married to Morris.

Morris Cohen – Recruited as a Soviet spy in 1937 during Spanish Civil War; service as a member of the 'Abraham Lincoln Brigade'.

Aleksandr Demyanov – NKVD operative in Operations Monastery and Berezino.

Arnold Deutsch – NKVD operative, but also recruiter and case officer.

Iosif Grigulevich – NKVD operative, but also case officer and assassin.

Kitty Harris – NKVD operative, courier and safe house manager.

Donald Maclean – One of the 'Cambridge Five'.

Valery Makaev – KGB illegal recalled from New York in 1951, leaving Willie Fisher in sole charge.

Konon Molody (aka *Gordon Lonsdale*) – KGB illegal, but also recruiter and case officer.

Kim Philby – One of the 'Cambridge Five'.

IN THE USSR

Viktor Abakumov – Beria's deputy. Became head of SMERSH.

Waldemar Abel – Rudolf's brother; commissar, Baltic shipyards.

Andrei Andreev – Politburo member. Friend of Heinrich Fischer.

Lavrenti Beria – Head of NKVD. Stalin's closest ally.

Georgy Chicherin – Marxist revolutionary and Soviet Foreign Minister from 1918 to 1930.

Vladimir Dekanozov – Head of NKGB Foreign Intelligence Department 1938–39.

Andrei Kapitsa – Pyotr and Anna Kapitsa's second son, born 1931.

Anna Kapitsa – Pyotr Kapitsa's wife.

Pyotr Kapitsa – Russian physicist, winner of Nobel Prize in 1978 for his work in low-temperature physics.

Sergei Kapitsa – Pyotr and Anna Kapitsa's son, born 1928.

Vsevolod Merkulov – Senior officer in Soviet state security from 1941 until the early 1950s. Close associate of Beria.

Alfred Nagel – Worked for Moscow stock holding and trade co-operative in the 1920s.

IN THE UNITED KINGDOM

Thomas Baston, Daniel Currie, Adaphus Danvers, Thomas Edgar, Joseph Hogarth, Robert Hutchinson, Thomas Dugger Keast, John Leslie, W. McKie,

Alfred Nagel, John Fyfe Reid – Conspirators and alleged conspirators in the 1907 cartridge cases in north-east England and Scotland.

Fullarton James – Chief constable of Northumberland at the time of Heinrich Fischer's second application for naturalisation as a British subject.

J. B. Wright – Chief constable of Newcastle upon Tyne at the time of the cartridge cases.

IN THE UNITED STATES

Paul Blasco – FBI agent present at Abel's arrest.

Ed Boyle –INS agent, Abel's arresting officer.

Mortimer W. Byers – Trial judge in the case against Rudolf Abel.

Ed Gamber – FBI agent present at Abel's arrest.

Edward Gazur – FBI special agent; debriefed and befriended Aleksandr Orlov.

Thomas Debevoise – Abel's defence attorney; assistant to James B. Donovan.

James B. Donovan – New York lawyer. Defended Abel against espionage charges. Conducted the negotiations to exchange Abel with U-2 pilot Gary Powers.

Arnold Fraiman – Abel's defence attorney; assistant to James B. Donovan.

Harry Gold – LIBERAL spy ring courier; his confessions led to the arrests of David Greenglass and the Rosenbergs.

David Greenglass – Machinist on the US atom bomb project. Spied for the USSR as member of the LIBERAL spy ring. Gave evidence in court that led to the Rosenberg's convictions.

Theodore Hall – Physicist who worked on the 'Fat Man' atomic bomb, and passed secrets to the Soviet Union.

Robert J. Lamphere – FBI agent who was credited with uncovering a number of Nazi spies during the Second World War and Soviet spies during the Cold War.

Francis Gary Powers – U-2 pilot shot down over the Soviet Union in 1960. Exchanged for 'Rudolf Abel' in 1962.

Ethel Rosenberg – Found guilty of passing atomic secrets to the USSR. Executed June 1953.

Julius Rosenberg – Codenamed LIBERAL. Leader of the spy ring bearing this code name. Found guilty of passing atomic secrets to the USSR. Executed June 1953.

Burton Silverman, Jules Feiffer, Sheldon Fink, David Levine, Danny Schwarz – Artists who befriended the man they knew as 'Emil Goldfus' at the Ovington Studios in New York.

Morton Sobell – Engineer and part of the LIBERAL spy ring. Passed conventional weapons secrets to the Soviet Union.

IN GERMANY AND BEYOND

Col. Heinrich Scherhorn – Captured German officer who collaborated with NKVD in the NKVD Special Tasks deception game Operation Berezino.

Otto Skorzeny – Waffen-SS special operations officer, tasked to relieve Scherhorn's troops.

Wolfgang Vogel – East German lawyer who was the initial negotiator with Jim Donovan for the Abel–Powers exchange.

Ernst Wollweber – Seaman, weapons smuggler and early member of the German Communist Party. Head of the East German Ministry of State Security in the early 1950s.

NKVD/KGB CODE NAMES

ARTUR or MAX – Iosif Grigulevich.

BEN – Konon Molody/Gordon Lonsdale.

DACHNIKI – Morris *and* Lona Cohen.

ENORMOZ – The American atomic bomb project.

HARRY – Valery Makaev.

KARL – Willie Fisher's senior officer and Oslo *rezident* in 1934.

LESLI – Lona Cohen.

LIBERAL – Julius Rosenberg.

LUIS – Morris Cohen.

LYUTENTSIA – The exchange of Gary Powers and Rudolf Abel on the Glienicke Bridge.

Max; Aleksandr; HEINE – Code names for Aleksandr Demanyov, NKVD double agent for Operations Monastery and Berezino.

SCHWED (The Swede) – Aleksandr Orlov.

STEFAN – Arnold Deutsch.

VIK – Reino Häyhänen.

VOLUNTEER – Morris Cohen.

PROLOGUE

'THE BRIDGE OF SPIES'

On Monday 19 August 1957, James B. Donovan received a telephone message from the Brooklyn Bar Association. Would he defend Rudolf Ivanovich Abel, the so-called 'master spy' arrested two months earlier and accused of spying for the Soviet Union?

Despite the severity of the charges and the notoriety of the defendant, Donovan took the case. When the trial began, he argued that his client's arrest had been illegal, but despite his best efforts Abel was found guilty. The maximum sentence was death. Shrewdly, Donovan argued for a prison sentence on the basis that there might come a time – should an American spy be captured in the Soviet Union – when the United States would want a prisoner to exchange. Abel escaped the death penalty and was jailed for thirty years.

On 1 May 1960, an American U-2 spy plane was shot down over the Soviet Union. The pilot Gary Powers ejected safely but was captured, tried for spying and jailed for ten years. The Soviet secret service, the KGB, broached the idea of a spy swap – Gary Powers for their own man Rudolf Ivanovich Abel. The man who negotiated the deal on behalf of the US government was James B. Donovan, whose prediction in preventing his client's execution had been so prescient. The negotiations dragged on for more than a year.

Shortly after dawn on 10 February 1962, several cars drew up beside the Glienicke Bridge on the south-western edge of West Berlin, the so-called 'Bridge of Spies'. Ten men got out, all of them wrapped up against the cold in heavy overcoats. The only other people around, 'informed sources' told the Associated Press, were a few Germans fishing in the Havel river. The group of men walked up to the white line across the middle of the bridge which marked the border between West Berlin and East Germany. At the centre of the group was Rudolf Ivanovich Abel.

When they reached the white line, a second group of ten men walked onto the bridge from the East German side to meet them. They were all Russian, bar one. Like Abel, he was at the centre of the group. He was clean-shaven, wearing a dark suit, a heavy overcoat and a fur hat. This was Gary Powers.

There were no expressions of cordiality between the two groups and a good deal of suspicion, leading to a twenty-minute delay whilst the Americans checked that a US student who was also part of the deal had been freed. Only then did the spy swap take place. Gary Powers was whisked away first to the US Air Force base at Wiesbaden in West Germany and on to America to be reunited with his wife and family. Rudolf Abel walked across the bridge, went behind the Iron Curtain and, as far as the West was concerned, disappeared into obscurity.

It was not until after his death in 1971 that it emerged that the Soviet master spy's real name was Willie Fisher. He was born in Newcastle upon Tyne, England, in July 1903. His father was a Bolshevik revolutionary, an associate of Lenin. He fled the Tsar's secret police two years before Willie's birth and settled in Britain. Willie had simply followed in his father's footsteps. This is the true story of the man they called Rudolf Ivanovich Abel.

1

GERMAN-RUSSIAN BEGINNINGS

Willie Fisher's story begins in Germany, where his grandparents were born. His grandfather, Aleksandr August Fischer, was from Sachsen-Altenburg in Thuringia, south-east Germany. Aleksandr's wife Maria Kruger was from Berlin.[1] Noticed by Prince Volkonsky, a Russian diplomat with responsibility in Saxony in the mid-nineteenth century, the couple were offered attractive employment in Russia, in Yaroslavl province, on the Adreevskoe estate owned by Prince Volkonsky's cousin. Here, Aleksandr utilised his skills as a forester, miller and herdsman. He even served as a veterinary surgeon on the estate, possibly beyond, whilst Maria bred and reared chickens.

From the early 1860s the estate was thriving after a period of decline and by the middle of the decade counted a profitable distillery amongst its assets. The atmosphere of growth and well-being at Andreevskoe embraced the Fischers too, because they started a family. Heinrich Matthäus was born on 9 April 1871.[2]

The nearest big town to the Andreevskoe estate was the prosperous upper Volga port of Rybinsk, which linked trade between Moscow and Archangel and, by the Mariinsk Waterway, this part of Russia to the Baltic Sea and beyond. By the 1870s, large vessels were trading between Rybinsk and St Petersburg. The town was also an industrial centre, constructing ships and printing machinery. In the mid-nineteenth century the arrival of the railway from Bologoe, including a new bridge across the Volga, improved Rybinsk's communication network. Aleksandr Fischer befriended a German working on the project, who, when Heinrich was born, became his godfather.

Heinrich was the first of twelve children.[3] The size of the family was the context of a decision which was to make an impact on events over the next hundred years, across three nations and two continents. When Heinrich was only six years old, he already had a number of younger brothers and sisters and his parents, seeing that he was an alert, capable and confident little boy, wondered whether in fact there might be an opportunity for a better future for their son than they could provide themselves. Heinrich's godfather and his wife had no children, so Aleksandr and Maria made an arrangement with the railwayman that he would bring up the boy as his own. Young Heinrich was certainly destined for a better life, but it was a new life away from his natural parents, his brothers, sisters and the home he knew. Neither the godfather nor his wife is named in Heinrich's memoirs, but despite a hard life, the small boy does not seem to have been unhappy in his new circumstances. At the time of this fostering, the godfather had finished work in track construction and had been appointed stationmaster at Medvedevo,[4] where the boy adapted to his new environment. Heinrich was responsible for household chores, cooking and cleaning, gathering and chopping wood. He was also involved in agricultural work: the station had an adjacent small holding with a cow, pigs and chickens, and his godfather took up farming himself for a short whilst. The young Heinrich was becoming versatile and self-sufficient. In addition, he was fascinated by his godfather's first trade, metal working. He observed his godfather at work and by the time he left home at sixteen, he could forge and beat metal, and make metal tools, implements and household utensils, including samovars. The godfather specifically told the boy, 'To learn how to work well, you have to be a thief. Learn how to steal with your eyes. When somebody does something you don't know how to do, keep your eyes open and learn how to do it yourself.'[5]

The other significant gift the boy received through his godfather was his sound formal education. He was enrolled at a village school when he was seven, virtually as soon as he was fostered, and went on to the next level of his education at the Rybinsk municipal school. With the Rybinsk-Bologoe stage of the railway network completed, the godfather seems to have settled in or very near Rybinsk. In his memoirs, Heinrich Fischer takes care in describing his secondary education in the town, valuing it highly. In the Rybinsk school there were three classes, the pupils spending two years in each class. The municipal schools were quite new in this period and fees were payable. It is likely that the young Fischer started this school before he was eleven. Along with other pupils he would have followed lessons in the Russian language, reading, writing, arithmetic, practical geometry, physics, history and geography. Art featured in the curriculum, too, along with singing and physical education. As a German Lutheran, at least nominally, Fischer was excused the religious education classes in Orthodox Christianity that were compulsory for the Russian pupils, and religion was never to play any significant part in his life.

Craft classes were available in the municipal schools if there was community interest and financial commitment, and given the town's recent growth and prosperity, this was likely the case in the Rybinsk school. The Rybinsk school certainly offered a class in book-keeping, which Heinrich took and put to good use by getting a holiday job in a construction company's office. He could have followed up this opportunity and become a white-collar worker, but turned it down. His childhood had not been an easy time for him, but it had given him independence and confidence and it prepared him for the difficulties that were to come. He loved metalwork and had been brought up in the vicinity of a vibrant, growing town, built on river trade and now linked by rail to the big cities. The godfather understood the boy and in a German-language newspaper spotted a metalworking apprenticeship opportunity at the Goldberg plant in St Petersburg, which manufactured printing machinery.[6]

The sixteen-year-old Heinrich Fischer, now beginning to use the Russianised version of his name, Genrikh, who arrived in St Petersburg in 1887 must have been an impressive young man.[*] He had had a good education and he knew it. His level of knowledge and his intellectual skills were far above the average for his age group. He was bilingual, too, speaking both German and Russian. Not only did he have practical manual skills, he already regarded himself as a metalworker: his godfather's influence and teaching had given him

---

[*] See the 'A note on the Fisher names'. In his primary school years, Heinrich's schoolfriends could not pronounce his German name and called him 'Andrei'. Later, it was discovered that he had a brother actually named Andrei, so Heinrich then began Russianising his second name, calling himself Matvei. Some records give him the Russianised name Matvei Aleksandrovich. Other records simply give initials 'A' or 'GM' (Genrikh Matvei) - David Saunders.

that. His experience of agriculture from large estate to smallholding meant that he understood the role of the rural economy. After all, his parents and godfather were Germans. They were skilled in agriculture and although they came to Russia before the emancipation of the serfs, serfdom was not something the family had undergone, even though it was within the felt experience of many living Russians. Heinrich Fischer had no feelings of religious obligation or guilt.

The young man knew Rybinsk as a thriving provincial centre and he arrived in St Petersburg to find this city in a new stage of industrial development. For skilled labour it was a seller's market, and he was able to move from job to job (often using German contacts), earn good wages, extend his skills and advance his career as a metalworker and engineer, all increasing his self-confidence. At the same time he was inevitably drawn into an exciting social and cultural world. In the factories, groups of 'conscious' workers met together to study. There were structured curricula, with participants following classes in the natural sciences and atheism before moving on to political economy and the history and theory of socialism.

Work and politics were the centre, but not the only aspect, of Fischer's life in St Petersburg. He was gregarious and enjoyed women's company, and changed lodgings to be with like-minded, literate, cultured, working people, who, significantly, avoided heavy drinking. In his memoirs, although there is no evidence that he was a prude, Fischer expresses his distaste at seeing drunkenness and debauchery throughout his life. Without being judgmental he remembered, too, from his earliest years, that his natural father often arrived home hopelessly drunk from agricultural fairs.

Back at the municipal school in Rybinsk, he had been employed as a pupil teacher, coaching slow learners. Here in St Petersburg he carried on this work. In the factory, he helped more experienced colleagues who had trouble with their workshop arithmetic or geometry, and on one occasion he was offered a share in some accommodation in return for mathematics tuition. His political links put him in touch with activists at St Petersburg's Technological Institution and it was this group that developed his political ideas and so imbued him with the works of Marx and Engels that within a few months he was teaching the Marxism classes himself. In 1893 Fischer became acquainted with Vladimir Ilych Ulyanov, Lenin, who had come to St Petersburg to take up leadership of the Technological Institution Group.[7]

Each of these experiences was a step in a revolutionary political career. In the early 1890s, Fischer was an active member of the city-wide Marxist group and connected with two interlinked political groupings – the 'worker-intelligent' and the 'student-intelligent' – who were convinced that organised and educated factory workers would be the engine to effect social and political change. He had emerged as a significant political activist and worker-revolutionary.

The inevitable happened. Early in 1894, at Fischer's lodgings, a meeting was held to elect leaders of underground revolutionary cells. An informer was present and the 23-year-old Fischer was arrested and held in prison. Typically, he used his time on remand to study and, as political books were prohibited, he read physics, algebra and trigonometry texts. Continuing to deny any connections with the revolutionaries, he was released from custody.

The authorities were prepared to allow Fischer to spend the rest of his remand outside prison provided he was not in St Petersburg, so he returned to Andreevskoe to help his now widowed mother and seven of his brothers and sisters, who were still at the family home. In his memoirs, Fischer makes no reference to his godfather at this time. Perhaps he too was dead, or had moved away. Or perhaps, now being with his natural mother and siblings for the first length of time since he was six years old, it was the painful rather than the positive aspects of his fostered years that came to the fore and that he wished to forget.

In January 1896 Fischer was sentenced to three years' internal exile in Archangel on the White Sea coast in sub-Arctic northern Russia. Ever resourceful and indefatigable, he made the most of his time. He became active in underground revolutionary groups, went back to teaching and took classes for his comrades in basic Marxism whilst at the same time studying advanced Marxist theory as a pupil in higher level seminars. In his memoirs, published more than twenty-five years later, Fischer noted that his exile in Archangel was well spent. The climate was severe; he had no family and no industrial career to nurture, and he spent his time in political organising, reading and developing himself intellectually.

His sentence was completed in 1899, but he remained 'restricted' for two more years. Denied residence in any large city or university town, he moved to Saratov on the Volga, 530 miles south-east of Moscow, where there was an iron foundry and steel mill and where he could find work. The evidence about Fischer's early life comes primarily from his own memoirs, but in Saratov he was to meet a radical worker who also wrote an autobiography. Semyon Ivanovich Kanatchikov was more of a raconteur than Fischer and his writing gives a flavour of the lives the comrades led, how they interconnected and how they survived. Kanatchikov was without work, still finding his way in Saratov, when he received a visit from a Mikhail Ivanov, who had worked as a metal fitter in St Petersburg and was now working in the railway repair shops at Saratov. Ivanov had got wind of a vacancy for a pattern maker at the steel mill, a job that would suit Kanatchikov.

Kanatchikov was an outsider and needed an entrée with the foreman. 'I've got the connections,' enthused Ivanov. 'We'll go off to the Ochkin area. Ochkin was the landlord of an estate of low-quality housing let to workers. A comrade of ours lives there. His name is Fischer – he's also from Petersburg, under surveillance here. Now he's working at the Gantke factory as a turner, but before that he worked at the steel mill, and he still has connections there. Only hurry; first we'll go to Fischer, and then he'll introduce you to his friend, who will recommend you to the foreman of the pattern shop.'[8] No photographs of Fischer from this time have come to light, but Kanatchikov's description gives us a glimpse of him at the age of twenty-seven or so: 'We were greeted by a broad-shouldered, dark-haired man of medium height, with a big forehead that protruded over his intelligent, calm, sparkling black eyes. It was Fischer.'[9] The two men greeted each other, with Fischer probing Kanatchikov. He wanted to know what his visitor had been imprisoned for, and for how long he was to be exiled to Saratov. It transpired that the two men had mutual acquaintances, and Fischer was positive about Kanatchikov getting the steel-mill job, but suddenly his mood seemed to change:

> 'You've already been in town nearly a month without coming here,' he added, looking at me reproachfully from under his forehead. 'Could those light-minded triflers have mixed you up that much?'
>
> I didn't understand the last sentence and wasn't even sure whether it was addressed to Ivanov or to me. I looked at Fischer with puzzlement.[10]

The moment revealed something of Fischer's character and his politics. He was utterly confident, even arrogant, in his own ability and importance as a worker, a networker and a revolutionary. He saw himself as a man to be taken note of and reckoned with. Ivanov gave a further explanation of Fischer's remark, 'That's his way of casting aspersions on the intelligentsia. He just can't stand them.' This was another factor in Fischer's confidence and self-possession. Although never a university scholar, he was a pupil and a teacher of demanding disciplines in worker educational circles. Not only did he loathe intellectuals, but he loathed the privilege that allowed the Russian elite access to university. In the Marxist debate between the roles of the workers and the intelligentsia in pre-Soviet Russia, Fischer was firmly in the workers' camp.

Fischer's 'sparkling black eyes' were also seen by another comrade, the eighteen-year-old Lyubov Vasilyevna Zhidova, a trainee midwife who had been born in Khvalynsk, a few miles north of Saratov on the west bank of the Volga. Her mother, Agrafena, was a midwife too, and she encouraged her daughter into the profession. Lyubov's father, Vasily Zhidov, was a tailor – the finest tailor in Saratov, it was said – and he was reputed to have made a pair of trousers with stitching so fine that it could not be seen with the naked eye. Lyubov also inherited her father's skill with the needle.[11] The young couple married in late 1898 or early 1899. Fischer's memoirs say nothing of his wife, and Kanatchikov's tell little of her other than that 'the woman' worked as a medical assistant, was a Social Democrat and was an active participant in their workers' group.[12]

The turn of the century was an immensely significant time for Fischer. Not only was he newly married, but his term of restriction spent in custody and then in Andreevskoe, Archangel and Saratov, was almost at an end. What was he to do? He was German and had served a sentence for offences against the Russian state. The authorities made it clear that if he did not leave the country of his own free will, he would be taken to the German border. The thought of this particular exile was chilling, for at twenty-nine or thirty as an ethnic German he was eligible for conscription into the German army. Worse, he might face immediate imprisonment for the avoidance of military service thus far.

The solution to his problem came from another comrade, Aleksandr Ivanovich Khozetsky. Khozetsky, who was also from Moscow and was a metalworker too, had been an exile in Archangel with Fischer, but his subsequent travels had taken him to Newcastle upon Tyne, in the north-east of England. Khozetsky had worked in Newcastle and had contacts with socialists there, so Heinrich and Lyubov Fischer decided to move to Newcastle with Khozetsky. Apart from the safety that England would provide, and an environment which seemed conducive to continuing political activity, Heinrich Fischer already had at least a basic understanding of English. The Fischers left Saratov on 22 September 1901, journeying first to Warsaw, where they stayed until Khozetsky joined them. From Poland, the trio travelled to Berlin and Hamburg, and then by sea to England, where they disembarked in Grimsby before travelling by rail to Newcastle. They reached their destination some three weeks after leaving Saratov.

2

NEWCASTLE UPON TYNE

In 1724, Daniel Defoe wrote:

> Newcastle is a spacious, extended, infinitely populous place. It is seated
> on the River Tyne, which is here a noble, large and deep river, and ships
> of any reasonable size may come up to the very town … They build
> ships here to perfection, I mean as to strength and firmness, and to
> bear the sea; and as the coal trade occasions a demand for such strong
> ships, a great many are built here. In Newcastle there is considerable
> manufacture of wrought iron.

One hundred and seventy-seven years on, this was a Newcastle that
Heinrich Fischer would have recognised on his arrival.

Khozetsky had set the scene and chosen well for his comrade. In
many important ways, Newcastle resembled the towns and cities where
Fischer had spent the first thirty years of his life. Like Rybinsk, it was
a thriving port on a major river, its workforce too including bargemen
and dockers. Both Newcastle's and Rybinsk's marine industries had
begun with the building of wooden ships. Milling and engineering
were amongst the trades that contributed to the economies of both
cities and like St Petersburg, Fischer's second home, Newcastle was a
hub for ocean-going business. Indeed, in the late nineteenth century
and early twentieth century, Russia was importing hundreds of
thousands of tons of coal annually from north-east England, shipped

from Newcastle. Most of this coal went into St Petersburg and then by river and canal to other Russian cities, Rybinsk, Archangel and Saratov amongst them. Newcastle was not St Petersburg, but comparisons could be made. Both were the commercial capitals of their regions, Newcastle's power in this respect dating back to the medieval period, and the neo-classical architecture of Grey Street was also reminiscent of St Petersburg.[1] Marine culture and well-established shipbuilding and engineering industries were common to both. The river, metalwork and engineering were typical of Saratov as well, so it is not too fanciful to think that Fischer felt at home in Newcastle upon Tyne.

However, he was beyond the Russian border for the first time and as well as registering similarities with his previous homes and workplaces, he would have to come to terms with a new culture. Newcastle had been a key strategic site since Roman times. Hadrian built his wall through the city, bridged the Tyne here and guarded his bridge with a fort, Pons Aelius, its site remaining a visible fortification, the Castle Keep, to this day. Newcastle and its soldiers had been active in border battles against the Scots until Scotland's union with England in the eighteenth century. The military tradition remained strong when Fischer arrived here and a significant number of workers were reservists in the armed forces.[2] The need to defend the river crossing, the port and the coast ran deep in the town's sense of itself.

The feeling of town, or 'toon' as pronounced locally, continued even after Newcastle became a city in 1882. Although it had a well-established tradition of civic education, a medical school associated with local hospitals, institutes and societies dedicated to learning, lecture societies and night schools, it had no university, another factor which no doubt appealed to Fischer. Newcastle's industrial successes were evident and celebrated. The proximity of the Tyne and coal deposits had given an economy of shipbuilding, mining and coal trade since the fourteenth century. The movement of the coal wagons from the pits had led from wooden to iron railways, and it was not very far north into the county of Northumberland that George Stephenson developed his first locomotive to move coal wagons. Stephenson's famous engines *Rocket* and *Locomotion I* were built in the world's first railway works, in Newcastle, and before long nineteenth-century Tyneside, and Newcastle in particular, was manufacturing iron ships, hydraulic cranes, engines, munitions, and all manner of heavy and specialised industrial products. For Fischer this was a living textbook of capitalist industrial development. When he arrived, Newcastle was linked to the coast by an efficient suburban railway and the nearer suburbs could be reached from the main streets of the city centre by new electric trams.

There was a downside to this industrial development. In 1901 Newcastle's population was in excess of 215,000. The years since 1870 had seen improvements in social conditions, but housing was still overcrowded and it was only at the very beginning of the twentieth century that Newcastle's death rate fell below twenty per 1,000 annually.[3] Even so, Tyneside towns remained at the top of British lists of death rates (including infant mortality). The reliability and cleanliness of the water supply was improving rapidly and with it public health, but compared to the nation as a whole the north-east region's health record was not good. On his arrival, Fischer was struck by the child poverty:

> Right in Newcastle station, as you leave the train, you are surrounded by a crowd of ragged boys. They are so dirty that you wonder what has happened to England's famous personal hygiene. With trousers torn, shirts sticking out behind and barefoot. We never came across so many of them as on Tyneside. Is there another place in Europe with so many poor children running around the streets? Wherever you look, there are little ones selling newspapers, matches, picture postcards, advertisements, etc. You immediately feel that something is not right here.[4]

His observations of the environment were equally sober:

> Everything was blackened so that you could not tell what material a building was made of. The houses were low, and whole districts had the same style of architecture. I was often astonished that people could manage to find their own homes ... The streets were narrow and dirty.[5]

These inauspicious impressions were not published until more than twenty years after his arrival in Newcastle, and then for a readership that would be sympathetic both to anti-British sentiment and to descriptions of the scourges of capitalism. But at the time, Fischer was not inclined to leave Newcastle. There was so much here that was strangely familiar for him and it was a near-perfect example of the development and ills of a capitalist economy as described by Karl Marx. Given his situation, it might be said that it was a case of 'any port in a storm', but in fact Newcastle and its environs provided everything that was important, and would be important, in his life. He was to spend the next twenty years living on or close to the banks of the Tyne.[6]

When Khozetsky and the Fischers arrived in Newcastle on or just before 15 October 1901, they found lodgings at the recently built 46 Armstrong Road in Benwell.[7] Although it was still outside the Newcastle boundaries in 1901, Benwell was growing fast. Pitmen working the three mines there lived in cottages, but speculative building had begun in the 1880s. The huge Armstrong Whitworth company, manufacturing naval craft and heavy guns at its Elswick plant nearby on the riverside, had seen a rapid expansion of its workforce, from 13,000 in 1894 to 25,000 in 1900. Houses close to the workplace were required, but the development of Benwell was not quite as simple as that. Shrewd developers noticed that investment in land and property in this area would bring a significant return on their money. Sometimes even quite small landlords would buy two or three terraced houses as they were built and make them available for rent. The tenants tended to be from the skilled working elite, an increasingly influential lobby in the locality.[8]

Fischer soon found work as a builder's labourer on the house-building sites close to where he was lodging. Khozetsky was labouring too, but he quickly obtained a start at Armstrong's Elswick works and within weeks had found an opening for Fischer. With the support of English comrades they had somewhere to stay and had employment, initially as carpenters. The names of these first comrades are not recorded, but worker and socialist networking enabled the men to assimilate quickly. Fischer had made the acquaintance of a man who had taken a role similar to the one he had occupied in Saratov. Three weeks after their arrival, Khozetsky and the Fischers moved to new accommodation at 58 Greenhow Place, also in Benwell. By Christmas 1901 the men could be said to have established themselves and were earning decent wages, which they pooled, giving them a total of £3 12s. for a 53-hour week. By early 1902 this had gone up to £3 19s. a week.[9] They were to stay in Greenhow Place for another year.[10]

Although Khozetsky had lived in England before and Fischer

had learned some basic English before he left Russia, they set about improving their rudimentary language skills. They also joined the Newcastle Socialist Institute. However, a speech at the Institute from a German Christian Socialist some time during Fischer's first few months in England moved him to anger. He was so frustrated that he berated the speaker in German. It was a sobering experience, and he decided to postpone any idea of proselytising amongst the English workers until his command of the language had improved. The two men worked hard at their English. At first, they used basic texts for foreigners learning the language and graduated to reading books and articles on subjects that interested them, using the techniques of worker education that they had been used to in Russia. During the working day, they were in continuous contact with the spoken English of their workmates, but this was not necessarily the best way for them to improve their own skills in the language. Native Tynesiders, or Geordies, spoke in dialect or at best in a distinctive accent. Their way of speaking was and remains a statement of regional pride in itself.

The subjects of their workmates' conversations, too, were sometimes impenetrable for additional reasons. Fischer was baffled by conversations about horse-racing with numerical odds, the names of horses and the complexities of British gambling law. Some of his fellow workers were probably illegal bookmakers or bookies' agents. The British obsession with sport was not something that generated a great deal of interest with Fischer, it seems, for his memoirs do not record his opinion of Newcastle's football club or its successes during the first years of the twentieth century. Newcastle United's ground, St James's Park, was a short walk from Greenhow Place, and the matches regularly attracted crowds in excess of 50,000.

As revolutionary socialists Fischer and Khozetsky were more interested in the role of the trade unions in English culture. The two exiles had a range of skills and their industrial upbringing led to friction with their co-workers:

> We were more enterprising in getting the work done. The English workers looked askance at us, since we raised productivity, which according to English trade-union ethics was against them, as the increase in production reduced chances of unemployed union members getting jobs. So we were boycotted even by those Englishmen who had previously fraternised with us and had themselves been frowned on for

doing so. But not one of them suggested that we joined the union for the simple reason that we would report them, and then some brave soul would be dismissed. I would often discuss the question of joining the union with Khozetsky, and we always put it off. After a whilst relations improved somehow, and I myself asked one Englishman whether we would be admitted to the union.

'Gladly,' he replied.

'But why then', we asked, 'did none of you breathe a word of this?'

'Because the union has an agreement with the capitalists not to put pressure on the workers.'

My free will to join solved the problem.[11]

So Fischer and Khozetsky became members of the Amalgamated Society of Engineers (ASE) and tentatively began to develop an Anglo-Russian political debate. They discovered that their new comrades were not ignorant about the Russian political situation and that people in Newcastle had given practical support to the Russian anarchist Peter Kropotkin in the nineteenth century, but Fischer was critical in his analysis of English workers and socialism. He noted the financial, class and intellectual factors that effectively barred English workers from the mainstream of English politics. Shrewdly, he also saw that as England had been the first country in the world to industrialise, its workers were paid comparatively well, which 'facilitated the development of false patriotism and self satisfaction amongst the working class'.[12] Fisher had no personal complaints about the money he was earning, and he recorded his increases in wages as he moved from job to job at the beginning of his time in Newcastle. Tyneside shipyard and engineering workers counted themselves the best paid of their craft in the world. Foremen at Armstrong's saw themselves as an elite, an aristocracy amongst skilled workers. These factors channelled the workers' political energy into trade union objectives of better pay and conditions, rather than into the revolutionary socialism that would change the system at its roots. Fischer was critical, but philosophical.[13] With membership of the ASE and of the Newcastle Socialist Institute, he had the forums in which to debate politics and the platforms from which to launch his own ideas.

Politics was Heinrich Fischer's *raison d'être* and he makes few references in his memoirs to his personal life and none to his wife Lyubov. He does not say if she ever worked outside the home, for example; or what she thought of the situation he had brought her into. But other records do tell us something about her. It is likely that she was newly pregnant when she left Saratov to make the journey across Europe to England in September 1901. Her first son, Henry, was born at their home in Greenhow Place on 18 April 1902. The birth certificate also records his father's first name and surname in its Anglicised spelling, as well as giving an independent record of his occupation at the time, an iron turner. Heinrich gave his first-born son the Anglicised version of his own name, but makes no mention of him whatever in his memoirs.

At some point in the winter, with a tiny infant in the house and when she was pregnant with her second child, Lyubov underwent surgery at the infirmary, a mastoidectomy to relieve a bacterial infection.[14] In December 1902 Khozetsky was also taken ill with appendicitis, but his surgery was too late and he died from the peritonitis which had taken hold. It is recorded that the 28-year-old Aleksandr Khozetsky was buried in unconsecrated ground at Elswick cemetery on 22 December 1902.[15]

If 1902 ended with pain and sorrow in the Fischer household, 1903 saw a new start for the exiles. Heinrich and Lyubov moved to 140 Clara Street, a 'superior class' of house, still in Benwell, and it was here that their second son, William August, was born, on 11 July.[16] Like his brother, William was given an English name that was easily Germanised. Unlike his brother, he was also given a second name, August, after his paternal grandfather. William immediately became known as Willie, the German rather than the English diminutive, to his family and eventually to his friends.

Heinrich was becoming 'established'. He had a good job with a prestigious company and his nearest neighbours in Clara Street were enginemen, machinists and fitters. Although the majority of householders in the street's 260 dwellings were skilled metalworkers, other residents included a surgeon, a schoolmaster (four doors down from the Fischers), insurance agents, miners, boilersmiths, clerks, draughtsmen, a dressmaker, a tailor's cutter and two police officers.[17]

During the last months at Greenhow Place and the first months in Clara Street, Heinrich became more active in socialist politics, both British and Russian. At this time, he travelled to London to visit Nikolai Alekseev, who had been sending him copies of *Zarya* ('Dawn') and *Iskra* ('The Spark'), Lenin's revolutionary journals, which were being printed in Munich. However, the Russian authorities had leaned on the German police and the *Iskra* operation had been forced to move from Munich.[18] Alekseev had found some small print shops in London's East End that possessed Russian type for setting the pages. *Iskra*'s proofs were then to be run off on a machine at 37a Clerkenwell Green, the home of the Twentieth Century Press, managed by the Social Democratic Federation's Harry Quelch, who also edited the SDF's weekly newspaper, *Justice*. Lenin himself came to London in 1902 and, as well as writing and studying in the British Museum Library, he sat in Quelch's tiny office where he corrected the *Iskra* proofs.[*] Heinrich did not meet Lenin in London for Lenin spent little time in meetings of any sort, but there was an opportunity for him to assist his old comrade. Copies of the four-page slim-format *Iskra* were sent to Heinrich in Newcastle, where he arranged for them to be forwarded on to Russia. One English comrade prepared envelopes with printed workplace addresses (letters from overseas to private addresses could attract suspicion) whilst Heinrich and Lyubov ran the journals through the scullery mangle to make them flat, like simple correspondence rather than bulky publications. Other English comrades took on the task of posting the envelopes from different villages around Newcastle each time so as to give a changing variety of postmarks and thus avoid arousing suspicion from the Russian authorities. *Iskra* numbers twenty-two to thirty-eight were printed in London,[19] many of which were sent to Russia from the north-east of England.

Fischer took his political commitments to Russia seriously. As well as smuggling literature, he continued a correspondence with his old comrade from Saratov, Semyon Kanatchikov, keeping him up to date with political developments in Russian socialist politics and telling him about life in England. Fischer had not been able to attend the Second Congress of the Russian Social Democratic Workers' Party (RSDRP) in London in 1903, but one (unnamed) delegate stayed with him en route home after the Congress. Fischer had helped him find a berth on a foreign ship and thus began to forge links with sailors from the Baltic, particularly Latvia. The Newcastle quayside was an exciting place to be and a low-cost leisure attraction for a family

---

[*] 37a Clerkenwell Green is an eighteenth-century listed building. It was once a chapel and is now The Marx Memorial Library.

with small sons. According to Fischer's memoirs, a Russian vessel named *Smolensk* was under repair in Newcastle during 1905 and Fischer supplied the crew with political literature and conversation. The family, including three-year-old Henry and two-year-old Willie, spent a lot of time socialising with the crew on the steamer. Earlier in 1905, Fischer was prominent in the campaign of British protest over St Petersburg's Bloody Sunday. On 9 January thousands of workers and their supporters had marched to present a petition to the Tsar, calling for wage increases, an eight-hour working day and government reform. The authorities responded with cavalry charges and gunfire. Research suggests that some 200 people died and 800 were wounded, but at the time reports suggested that the casualties were much higher, putting fatalities at over 1,000 with 5,000 more wounded.[20] Outraged but aware of the opportunity to proselytise, Fischer addressed a workplace meeting which was reported in the *Newcastle Evening Chronicle*, and within a few weeks he went on to found the RSDRP branch in Newcastle. In August, the branch invited Alekseev to speak at a public meeting, chaired by Fischer at the Socialist Institute, and a collection for the revolutionary fund was taken.[21]

Fischer was also active in English politics, taking every opportunity to engage his fellow trade unionists in political debate. Despite his critical perspective on English social democracy he decided to join the SDF, then Britain's largest Marxist party and which clearly had Lenin's seal of approval, and held office in its Newcastle branch.[22] His suspicion of the British political system did not prevent him campaigning on behalf of the trade unionist Labour candidate for the Newcastle constituency in the December 1905 general election, so as 1905 ended, he could look back on four eventful years in Newcastle, both personal and political. The months ahead would prove to be equally dramatic.

3

GUN-RUNNING

In October 1906 Heinrich Fischer had been in Newcastle for five years and was eligible to apply for naturalisation as a British subject. This he did.[1] The appropriate forms were completed and duly recorded the details of Fischer's birth and parentage. He was thirty-five years old and his sons, Henry and William August, were four years seven months and three years four months respectively. The Fischers were now living at 113 Hampstead Road, still in Benwell, which had been incorporated into the growing City of Newcastle upon Tyne in 1905. On the standard naturalisation documents issued by the Solicitors' Law Stationery Society, four Benwell householders – Eldon Bell, Robinson Firth, John McKay and Michael Winship – all vouched 'for the respectability and loyalty of the said Heinrich Matthews Fischer'. Eldon Bell of the School House, Canning Street, stated that he had 'known and been intimately acquainted with' Fischer for five years and one month, so must have met him within days of his arrival in England. The others gave their personal knowledge and intimate acquaintance of the applicant (or 'Memorialist') as four years eleven months.

On his declaration, Fischer signed that it was his intention to 'continue to reside permanently within the United Kingdom of Great Britain and Ireland', that he had 'no intention of permanently leaving the United Kingdom', and was 'desirous of obtaining the rights and capacities of a Natural-born British Subject'. The full documentation was witnessed by Joseph William Johnston of 171

Clara Street. Although a commercial traveller, an occupation to which members of the lowest social class aspired (in Fischer's estimation), Johnston was active in local socialist circles and from November 1905 a Newcastle City Councillor representing Benwell.[2] Johnston made his declaration 'from personal knowledge received by visits to the residences of the said Heinrich Matthews Fischer during the periods above mentioned'. Arthur Oliver, the commissioner for oaths that Fischer and his referees attended, witnessed and signed all the documents under the date 24 November 1906. The documents were posted and rubber-stamped as received at the Home Office on 29 November.

Part of this application's record is lost, but its progress is quite easy to follow from the surviving documents. When the application was considered, it was noted that there was an error in the residential referee's declaration, giving wrong dates for Fischer's residence at 140 Clara Street, and that the occupations of the referees had not been given. Notwithstanding, the officials agreed to pass the application to the Newcastle Police for their report, and chief constable J. B. Wright was written to on 19 December. The Chief Constable's reply, dated 7 January 1907, confirmed the statements made in Fischer's memorial and in the referees' declarations, and testified that the signatures were authentic. The referees, wrote the chief constable, were all householders and respectable working men. 'As regards the applicant,' he wrote, 'from enquiries made it has been ascertained that he is a respectable man.' The letter concluded, 'Fischer can read, write and speak the English language very well.'[3] The Home Office decided that the application should be granted and returned the documents to Fischer for the 'correction of the careless mistake in the Residential Referee's declaration'. The offending date was altered and initialled by Arthur Oliver. Johnston signed his declaration once more, now dated 8 February 1907, and the amended documentation was received by the under-secretary of state at the Home Office on 11 February. Again there was a hold-up. 'The re-declaration is not identified as it should have been, but for all practicable purposes there is sufficient identification. Send usual letter asking for fee,' was the grudging comment from the permanent secretary dealing with the case. The fee of £5 was requested on 25 February.

This fee was a considerable sum for the Fischers and it was more than a month before Heinrich was back in touch with the Home Office:

113 Hampstead Rd N/cle on T
3/4/07

The Under Secretary of State

Dear Sir

I have the pleasure forwarding you £5.0.0 postal money order for ... a Certificate of Naturalization, which has decided in my favour by the note of yours of 25 February, 1907.

I remain
Your obedient Servant
Heinrich Mattheus Fischer

The letter was postmarked N'castle-Tyne 3.15 PM APL 3 07.

A great deal happened on 3 and 4 April 1907. When the post was opened at the Home Office, it was discovered that Fischer had forgotten to send the £5. 'No enclosure 4/4/07' was written firmly on the front of the envelope in black ink. Two annotations on the back of Fischer's letter record the decision to write back immediately 'pointing out omission of fee'.

As that Home Office letter was on its way to Newcastle on 4 April, another letter was making the journey in the opposite direction; not Fischer's apology and the missing postal order (these were to be sent two days later on 6 April), but a letter from the chief constable of Newcastle upon Tyne:

The Under Secretary of State,
Home Office,
London

Sir,

I have the honor to inform you that yesterday the house of Matthew Hendrick Fischer 113 Hampstead Road, Benwell in this City was searched under a warrant granted by the Magistrates under the Explosives Act.

A man named Stormer or Stronmer who had rented the room at Sunderland where a large quantity of cartridges were found on 31st March 1907 had lodged with Fischer from 28th ultimo.

The search resulted in the finding of about 750 clips for mauser cartridges.

Stormer cannot now be found but as Fischer may possibly be trafficking in arms and explosives for an unlawful purpose, I beg to recommend that the grant of the Certificate of Naturalisation which he has applied for be suspended until the matter has been fully investigated.

I have the honor to be Sir
Your obedient Servant
J. B. Wright
Chief Constable

For Fischer, trafficking in arms and explosives was a natural progression from trafficking in literature. How senior he was in the network to smuggle rifles, pistols and cartridges into Russia is impossible to say, but the project did have some success and can be placed in the bigger picture: the gun-running episode that became known as 'The *John Grafton* Affair' and the world politics of the time.[4]

Russia had gone to war with Japan in February 1904. The British were allies of the Japanese (and there was a significant Newcastle link as a few years earlier battleships for the Japanese navy had been built on the Tyne) and were sympathetic to their cause. Moreover, on its way to engage the Japanese navy in the Far East, Russia's Baltic Fleet had fired on some English fishing boats. But there was a substantial body of British opinion that was supportive of the Russian people whilst at the same time being more than critical of the Russian government. For the Russian opposition, particularly the revolutionaries and their sympathisers throughout the world, the war was an opportunity to be exploited. When it began, the Japanese military attaché in St Petersburg, Colonel Akashi, was evacuated to Stockholm, where he was visited by the Finn, Konni Zilliacus.[*] Zilliacus wanted support for a broad anti-Tsarist coalition, ultimately

---

[*] Konni Zilliacus (1855-1924) was a Finnish patriot and militant and father of Konni Zilliacus (1894-1967); see page 23.

involving militants, liberals and nationalist and ethnic groups, stretching from Ireland to the Caspian Sea. He kept the Japanese link secret, but by early 1905, after St Petersburg's Bloody Sunday, a plan was in place for a cargo of weapons to be transported via the Baltic Sea and the Gulf of Finland and landed on both shores of the Gulf. The guns would be available to arm a people's revolution. Zilliacus shuttled backwards and forwards across Europe and eventually used London as his organisational base, where he could rely on the help of a sympathetic Russian exile of long standing, N. W. Chaikovsky, who took every opportunity to discomfit the Russian government.[5] With Akashi in the background bank-rolling the project, Zilliacus and his inner circle of co-conspirators made use of Father Georgy Gapon, the Russian Orthodox priest who had led the demonstration and march on the Tsar's palace in St Petersburg on Bloody Sunday, which had incensed world opinion. Gapon was a rallying point for supporters, but his arrival in London attracted a team of Tsarist agents, and Zilliacus had to resort to a range of subterfuges to pursue his goal. Using any number of pseudonyms, he met and corresponded with different arms manufacturers and dealers to lure the Russian police away from his preferred supplier. He was well advised in this respect. One of his contacts was Yevno Azef of the Russian Socialist Revolutionary Party, who also headed the Party's combat wing, an autonomous group of killers employing terror tactics and carrying out assassinations of government ministers and other political leaders.[6] Azef had been at a Zilliacus meeting in Paris and kept in close touch with the Finn. In the history of double agents, Azef ranks as one of the most daring and successful. He was also keeping the Russian police briefed on Zilliacus's moves.

Nevertheless, an arsenal of 15,500 rifles, 2,500,000 cartridges, 2,500 revolvers and 3 tons of explosives was eventually ready for shipment to the Gulf of Finland. With the financial help of his wife Lillian, a German-American heiress, Zilliacus bought a 300-ton tramp steamer, the *John Grafton*, to transport the cargo and after further adventures and mishaps the ship arrived off the northern coast of Finland. The rendezvous in the Gulf of Finland, off St Petersburg, failed to materialise – Azef's hand was suspected in this – and the affair ended in disarray with the *John Grafton* scuttled off Pietarsaari on 8 September 1905.[7] Some of the firearms had been landed and survived for use by revolutionaries in Finland and

Russia,* but far more were confiscated by the authorities or were lost when the steamer was blown up.

Zilliacus played a more superior role in this conspiracy than Heinrich Fischer was to play in his, but there are parallels in the lives and work of both men. They both operated on an international stage. Each was committed to the overthrow of the Tsar: Heinrich to free the Russians and to see the operation of a Marxist economy in an international socialist world; Konni to see his native Finland free of Imperial Russian control. Each had two sons and each named his first-born son after himself. Konni Zilliacus Junior became a naturalised British subject and went on to be a British intelligence officer. He was a socialist, joined the British Labour Party and in 1945 was elected MP for Gateshead, the town on the bank of the Tyne opposite Newcastle, barely two miles from the Fischers' first British home in Benwell.[8]

There were other expeditions to get arms into Finland and Russia during 1904 and 1905, including one by the Bolsheviks, via the Black Sea, organised by Maksim Litvinov, who years later was to become the Soviet ambassador in London. But the successes of these ventures and conspiracies were negligible. Still, principles had been established and sources of guns and ammunition had been identified, as well as a network of activists and sympathisers who were prepared to use imaginative enterprises to arm the revolutionaries in Russia. The 1905 revolution in Russia was thwarted and the SDF in Britain, with Heinrich Fischer an active member of its Newcastle branch, was adamant that the Russian ruling class had been aided and abetted by the ruling class in Britain. Accordingly, in the autumn of 1906, the SDF noted that the people of Russia needed support 'to enable them to carry on their propaganda and to arm against their oppressors' and called upon its members to aid their Russian comrades.[9] Fischer was one of about a dozen SDF members in Scotland and the north-east of England to heed the call. Their scheme was more of a guerrilla operation than the grandiose *John Grafton* or Black Sea affairs: firearms were purchased in Germany, shipped to Britain and kept in separate dumps in Scotland and England before being transported to the Baltic in small consignments from ports on the Forth, the Tyne and the Wear.

---

* Paradoxically, the Russians and the Japanese had signed a peace treaty three days earlier, thus ending the immediate Japanese interest in undermining the Russian government.

The contraband consisted of Browning and Mauser firearms (the Mausers probably C96 pistols, M1888 and M1898 rifles) and more than a million rounds of ammunition.* (The Brownings may have been part of an American-bought consignment that had remained in dumps after an earlier gun-running intrigue in 1904 involving Chaikovsky and the British socialist S. G. Hobson.)[10] Fischer wrote of the business in his memoirs and is probably right when he says that the police began to unravel the scheme when boxes of ammunition were found in Sunderland on 1 April 1907. The formal witness statement of a William Hutchinson reveals how the plot was discovered:

> Robert Hutchinson is my son. Between 12 o'clock noon and 1 p.m. 1st April, 1907 my son came into the house and told me something. Shortly afterwards I had occasion to leave the house. In a few minutes I returned. I found the twelve wooden cases produced in my front room. I was suspicious about them and opened one box. I saw it contained rifle cartridges. I gave information to the police. Det. Sergt. Marshall came and took the boxes away.[11]

Robert then had little choice but to tell the police how he had come by the boxes. He had been promised 1s. 6d. a week to store them, he told the police. Their owner was a Daniel Currie, he said, and that evening Detective Sergeant Marshall, accompanied by a detective constable and the suspicious and public-spirited William Hutchinson, arrived at Currie's home. DS Marshall's witness statement outlines what happened:

> I said to him, 'I am a Detective Sergeant and I have found in Hutchinson's house, No. 15 King Street, twelve cases containing a large quantity of explosive cartridges. Do you wish to say how they came into your possession?' At the same time I cautioned him.
> Prisoner said, 'I got them from a German Gentleman. He asked me to get a place to store them. He said they were mechanical toys. He said he was going to open a shop here.' I said, 'Where is the man now and where does he live?' Prisoner said, 'They call him Thomas Denvis.' I said 'Where does he live?' Prisoner said, 'I'll answer no more questions.'

---

* It is said that C96 Mauser pistols were used to shoot Tsar Nicholas II and his family at Yekaterinburg in July 1918.

I brought him to the Police Station and charged him on suspicion of stealing the cartridges.

Prisoner made no reply.[12]

The frenetic activity did not abate. Marshall's witness statement carries on with the events of 2 April 1907:

I saw the prisoner in his cell. I showed him the letter and postal order produced and said to him, 'This letter has been received by your wife this morning. There was also enclosed a postal order for 4/6d. Do you wish to say who this letter is from?' Prisoner said, 'From the man who asked me to store the cartridges. The money is for the storage.'

The letter is dated 1 April 1907 and reads as follows:

113 Hampstead Road,
Benwell, Newcastle,
1st April, 1907

Dear Comrade,
I am just here now and you will find me at the above address. I might go down and see you if necessary.

Fraternally yours,
G. Stromer

The same afternoon I went to this address, No. 113 Hampstead Road, Benwell, Newcastle, and found that a Russian named 'A. Stromer' had lodged there but had left that day.[13]

The Fischers were implicated and cornered.

What might life have been like in their household during these few days in April? Firstly, the Fischers were living in a ground-floor Tyneside flat, a type of house to be found in great numbers in the city to this day. These dwellings were a feature of the region's housing stock, particularly in Benwell. The houses were built in long terraces with ground floor and first floor as separate, self-contained flats, each two-storey building taking up a ground plan of some 150 to 200 square yards, including a back yard. From the outside it would appear that there were two doors to a single house, but one door opened to a flight of stairs leading to the upper flat, the other opening into the hallway of the lower flat. At the back there would be the walled yard or yards with outhouse lavatories and brick shelters for coal. The back door of the lower flat opened directly into the yard with the upper flat's door leading onto a flight of brick or stone steps down to the yard below.

Inside, a standard arrangement would be for a master bedroom at the front of the house, a second bedroom, probably on the other side of the hallway, and a living or dining room behind the master bedroom. At the back of the house was the kitchen with an adjacent scullery. With Heinrich and Lyubov in such a house were their two young sons (Henry was just of school age) and, it would seem, a flow of visitors or lodgers. Indeed, the network of socialist hospitality had supported Khozetsky and the Fischers when they had first arrived in Newcastle; now, Fischer was repaying the debt. Heinrich Fischer's working week at Armstrong's would have been in excess of fifty hours. His political work was paramount, with arms-smuggling the crucial activity at this particular juncture. It is hardly surprising that in such a feverish atmosphere, he forgot to send the postal order to the Home Office. Indeed, it is ironic that a postal order was sent from 113 Hampstead Road, but it was Stromer's 4s. 6d. for Daniel Currie, for storing the cartridges.

Meanwhile, the Home Office was soon finding out about the cartridge affair in quite some detail. The chief constables of Sunderland and Newcastle forwarded reports of initial enquiries, including the first witness statements. 'I expect we shall hear more of the "Newcastle" affair later on,' reads a note in the Home Office minutes of 12 April 1907.[14]

Currie's trial began on 16 April 1907. He was charged with having unlawful custody of 194.4 lbs of gunpowder. This was contained in the cartridges he had stored in cases at a church hall where he was caretaker, and at 15 King Street, Sunderland, the Hutchinsons' house.[15] Currie maintained that he understood the cases, now proved to contain cartridges, had been full of 'mechanical toys'. He had been told this, he said, by 'the German' who was paying him to store the cases. A statement on behalf of the exporters vouched for Currie. The exporters did not wish to see Currie suffer for having acted for them and confirmed that the cargo was in Sunderland prior to onward passage. Neither the press reports of the case nor the witness statements show that the British authorities were concerned about the eventual destination of the cartridges, but the traffickers' strategy can be inferred. Given Russian police surveillance, it would be easier to ship arms and ammunition from England to Baltic Russia than to export such cargo in any quantity from Germany to Russia. There were supporters of the Russian revolutionaries in Germany too, and the German manufacturers would be keen to trade their products. Although Currie was a socialist, this was not considered pertinent to the case. He was found guilty of unlawful custody of gunpowder and fined £20. The cartridges were impounded.

As the trial had progressed, police activity had continued. Even before Currie's case reached the magistrate's court, an SDF member in South Shields had his house searched and from evidence discovered there police began visiting addresses in Scotland.[16] Back in Newcastle, police raided number 42 Leazes Park Road on 9 April. The chief constable, embarrassed at having given the formal confirmation of Fischer's bona fides so close to the issue of the certificate of naturalisation, kept the Home Office informed directly concerning developments in the cartridge case. His letter dated 10 April 1907 to the under-secretary of state reads:

> In a room occupied by Joseph Hogarth, a jobbing tailor, [police] found 25,000 Mauser pistol cartridges and 6,500 Mauser rifle cartridges, and in a room occupied by J. Dugger Keast, an insurance canvasser, 250 Mauser pistol cartridges and 3,500 clips for Mauser cartridges.[17]

Also arrested in Newcastle was the auctioneer Thomas Baston. He had rented a stable to store 85,750 cartridges and had given the Newcastle Socialist Institute as his contact address. At his trial, Baston pleaded guilty and was fined £10. The German manufacturers made a statement on Baston's behalf at the Newcastle trial, just as they had done in Sunderland for Currie, which confirmed that the cartridges were from Germany and were intended for Russia. This onward shipment to the Baltic had been delayed, said the statement, and storage for the cargo had to be found.[18]

Acting on the information from South Shields, Scottish police had arrested John Fyfe Reid for unlawful possession and unlicensed storage of 15,000 cartridges at 112 Port Dundas Road in Glasgow. In Edinburgh, police had watched Thomas Edgar's premises and seen cases of ammunition being delivered, this time from the docks at Leith. With Edgar, there were court appearances for two others, John Leslie and W. McKie. All four of the Scots were fined for illegal storage and saw the cartridges confiscated. Like Currie in Sunderland, Reid implicated a foreigner, naming him as 'Denner', and, also like Currie refused to say more.

When the Joseph Hogarth case came to court in Newcastle, there was 'an interesting development', as the *Evening Chronicle* of 9 May 1907 put it. 'Thomas Dugger Keast, who has been wanted by the police for some time past, made his appearance.' The magistrates allowed the case against Hogarth to be withdrawn. Keast, 'who is of short stout build ... smartly dressed in a light suit', did not speak at his trial. His legal representative, Mr E. Clark, spoke for him.

The prosecutor for the town clerk stated that Keast had rented a room at 42 Leazes Park Road since November of the previous year. He had described himself as an insurance agent and had taken delivery of cases of cartridges as soon as he had arrived. More deliveries came in January 1907 and Keast, telling Hogarth, his neighbour, that he was 'a dealer in German screws', asked him if he would store the boxes. The prosecutor also noted that correspondence had come to the address for an 'Adaphus Danvers'. Keast took the letter, claiming to be Danvers's agent. In court, Keast's representative expressed the view that he and his client were 'quite certain that Danvers does not exist'. As in the Baston case, the accused had no problem in admitting that the destination of the cartridges was Russia. Keast's fate was settled quickly: he was fined £6 and the cartridges forfeited.

The cases in Scotland were decided by the end of June and the saga of the cartridges was over. But it was a *cause célèbre* for the left and some questions remained. What, precisely, was Fischer's role in all of this? In his memoirs he writes of his involvement, being quite explicit about how he graduated from sending illegal literature and then arms to Russia, and his links with the Lettish (Latvian) Social Democratic Party in this trade.[19] The police statements and letters to the Home Office confirm his connection to the events, although it is the Fischer memoirs that state that the police came looking for a young Latvian by the name of Alfred Nagel. (The recollections of other SDF members name an 'Alf', a member of 'the Lettish Social Democratic Party', as the man who managed the consignments of small arms and ammunition.)[20] The police records indicate that they were looking for 'Stronmer', so there may have been more than one German or Lett staying with the Fischers – or it is equally possible that Alfred Nagel was using a number of different pseudonyms. From evidence at the

Keast trial, it could be concluded that Keast and Danvers were one and the same person. Could Fischer himself have been any or all of these people? He was not Alfred Nagel. Nagel was the only one of the conspirators named in the memoirs and this could have been checked back. Other SDF members knew Nagel, and the police were looking for him. Fischer was also well known under his own name as an SDF member in England and Scotland.

It is hardly likely that Fischer was Keast. Although Fischer was living in Newcastle and could have called at 42 Leazes Park Road to rent a room, he would have drawn attention to himself had he done so. There was a report in the *Evening Chronicle* of Monday, 6 May 1907, of a meeting at the Newcastle Socialist Institute on the preceding Saturday evening, which began, 'Comrade Fischer delivered an address upon the revolutionary movement in Russia,' and concluded,

A resolution was passed to the effect that the meeting expressed its heartiest sympathy with the Russian people in their struggle for freedom, applauds those local residents who have been assisting in the transference of arms and ammunition to the revolutionaries, and emphatically protests against the confiscation of the cartridges seized by the Newcastle police. It therefore calls upon the authorities to return the cartridges to their rightful owners.[21]

This was published three days before 'Keast' pleaded guilty to the charge of unlawful possession of cartridges at Newcastle Magistrates Court. The impudence of then appearing in court under an assumed name might have appealed to Fischer, but not the recklessness. There are brief descriptions of Keast, too, the court report describing his short, stout build and another report, in the *Daily Mail*, describing him as 'a man of middle height, somewhat stoutly built, of florid complexion, and with a light moustache'.[22] Such descriptions might fit Fischer at a stretch, but Kanatchikov had described him as a broad-shouldered, dark-haired man of medium height, with dark eyes. The photographs too emphasise Fischer's dark hair and heavy moustache.

Finally, in his memoirs, Fischer is exultant that it was only British comrades who were tried and punished by the courts, not foreign comrades. It might be argued that Keast was advised not to speak at his court appearance so as to conceal a foreign accent. Keast was sought by police initially as 'a Russian Jew'[23] and was later described as 'a Pole'.[24] But equally, Keast's silence could have concealed an English accent: another report stated that the police understood the fugitive to be 'a native of Somerset'.[25]

Could Fischer have been Danvers? Such a thought is worth considering, the shady Danvers being remembered by various versions of his name, including Denvers, Denner or Denvis. Denvis was the 'German gentleman' who made the arrangement with Currie in Sunderland. A man with the name Denvers addressed an SDF branch in Fife in late May or June 1907, after the Sunderland and Newcastle court appearances but before the Edinburgh and Glasgow trials. Fischer had spoken in Newcastle on the issue just a few weeks before, so by this time was well used to public speaking. In May, *The Keel* ('The Organ of Tyneside Socialism') had published an article by 'Thomas Denvers (The Cartridge Owners' Representative)', quoting Bassanio from Shakespeare's *The Merchant of Venice*:

To do a great right, do a little wrong
And curb this cruel devil of his will.

The article then launched into a passionate denunciation of the Tsarist regime and argued the moral cases for armed revolution in Russia and for British sympathisers to support the armed struggle with practical action. It also justified the way the cartridge scheme was managed, as it hindered Russian spies' ability to trail the cargo from Germany to the Baltic via the small shipments from England and Scotland. The argument was similar to the one Fischer had used in his address in Newcastle on 4 May. Perhaps Fischer had provided the material and thesis for the article and had it embellished by the editor. It may be that 'Danvers' and possibly even 'Keast' were cover names available to Newcastle socialists or particular SDF members for use when on active service, as it were. It is more likely that Danvers was one of the names used by Alfred Nagel, who, if he was a free agent from overseas, would have had far greater opportunity to travel across the north of England and Scotland for meetings. He was certainly a key conspirator, from outside the region, making arrangements for the transit of the cartridges, often at short notice.

Other questions remain. The discovery of the cartridges at Sunderland at the beginning of April led to Fischer, but need not have led any further. In his letter to the under-secretary of state dated 10 April 1907, the chief constable of Newcastle wrote that the information which led to the search at 42 Leazes Park Road 'was given to me privately'. Who gave him that information? Fischer expressed the opinion that the double agent Yevno Azef had engineered the whole affair, or had at least penetrated the circle and informed on the plans, just as he had thwarted the voyage of the *John Grafton*. But Fischer was writing nearly fifteen years after the events and also after Azef's death.[26] Did one of the Newcastle comrades turn secret informer? Was Heinrich Fischer the informer, protecting himself, the Russians and the Latvians? If it was Nagel who was the 'cartridge owners' representative' whose statements were used in court, had the police done a deal with him and Fischer to implicate as many Englishmen and Scotsmen as possible, in return for their own freedom from prosecution, and even deportation?

Neither man was prosecuted. And Fischer had the added advantage that his revolutionary credentials were enhanced by the episode. If this particular smuggling scheme had indeed been going on since 1906 then certainly some arms and ammunition had got through. Fischer had achieved stature in the eyes of his British comrades. What he had not achieved was naturalisation.

The Home Office decision was noted on 3 May 1907:

> The whole case of illegal trafficking is somewhat obscure ... and Fischer's share in it by no means clear. But there is no reason why S. of S. by a Cert. of Naturalization should relieve Fischer of any danger he may be in under the Alien's Act.
>
> On 25 Feb. the Cert. was promised in exchange for the fee. The fee was not sent till 8 April – just when the disclosures as to cartridges etc. were taking place. The fee was acknowledged and the case suspended.
>
> Now return the fee saying the S. of S. is <u>unable to issue the Cert</u>. [27]

The fee was returned on 10 May 1907.

4

TO THE COAST

In his memoirs Heinrich Fischer says that after the gun-running episode failed, he moved 10 miles out of Newcastle. However, the move was not immediate. The family stayed at 113 Hampstead Road for at least a year after the last of the Newcastle cartridge trials. It may have been family reasons that kept Heinrich in Benwell, for young Henry had his fifth birthday in April 1907 and would have been due to start school. Heinrich knew the value of a full education and made every effort to ensure that his sons received the best possible schooling. But Heinrich was no sentimentalist, and his first-born was about the age he himself had been when adopted by his godfather. Moving the children would not have been an issue. It is much more likely that politics kept the family in Benwell. In one sense certainly the gun-running had been bungled, but some weapons and ammunition had got through and Fischer had proved to his comrades that he was a significant player in European revolutionary politics. Moreover, Russia remained in the news. Bombs, strikes, railway wrecking, assassinations, arrests, uproar in the Duma, plots against the Tsar, scandalous prison conditions, all were regularly reported in the British national and local press read by the people of Newcastle. The socialists were getting more detailed reports from their own presses and Fischer could get first-hand information from the Russian- and German-speaking crews of Baltic ships that docked in Newcastle. The Newcastle socialists continued to need Fischer's stimulus. Likewise, Fischer himself needed the stimulus of a political reputation.

And in the months following the cartridge case, it was not only international revolutionary politics that exercised him. British local and national events also gave him a platform for political work. Despite his disdain for British trade unionism, which concentrated on wages and working conditions, he was active in his branch of the ASE. At the time of the cartridge affair, engineers in the north-east of England were pursuing a wage claim of 2s. a week and 5 per cent on piece rates, culminating in an eight-month strike. Just as this dispute was coming to its conclusion in the early autumn of 1908, Fischer was involved in a parliamentary election campaign. The death of Newcastle's sitting MP caused a by-election, which was called for 24 September 1908. The Labour Representation Committee was cautious about fielding a candidate against the Liberal, Edward Shortt, but the intervention of the ASE at national level led to the candidacy of Edward R. Hartley of the SDF. As an active member of the SDF, Fischer campaigned vigorously for Hartley but saw his candidate soundly beaten. What is more, Hartley's intervention led to the defeat of the Liberal and the election on a minority vote of George Renwick, the Unionist. In the same month, the employers routed the engineers' pay claim, and the strikers returned to work no better off than they had been at the beginning of the year.

Despite this disappointment Heinrich continued working at Armstrong's in Elswick, but the late autumn of 1908 found the Fischer family living at 39 Eskdale Terrace, Whitley Bay, in the county of Northumberland. It was a significant change in Fischer's life. He was nearer forty than thirty and another phase of his political activity was over. His family was complete: both boys were of primary school age and the Fischers had no more children after Willie's birth in July 1903. But the decision to move to Whitley Bay seems puzzling. It was about 15 miles by road from urban Benwell. The culture, too, was very different; not only was Whitley Bay a village, but it was a seaside resort as well. This, of course, may have been one of the attractions. It was very close to the mouth of the River Tyne and the journey on the new electric suburban railway line from central Newcastle to Tynemouth and Whitley Bay took barely half an hour. It seems probable that the Fischers, like many other Newcastle families, took their children to the coast for days out, particularly in the summer. Changes in the rented housing market, and some concern about the spread of infectious diseases, led to a perceptible change in the occupancy of houses in Benwell in the years just before the First World War.[1] A number of skilled workers moved out of Benwell to other parts of Newcastle, but Whitley Bay itself was also expanding, with an increasing supply of newly built houses for rent. For all these reasons, the Fischers were attracted to Whitley Bay. There was a further reason: it was still Heinrich Fischer's intention to acquire British citizenship and he would have planned as carefully as possible for the success of his next application. A fresh start in a new locality under a different police authority might help.

When Henry and William August Fisher* arrived in Whitley Bay, they were about the same age their father had been at the time of his adoption: Henry was six and Willie was five. For them, Whitley Bay, and more particularly the adjacent village of Cullercoats, was as significant as Rybinsk had been for their father. But whereas it was the industry and culture of a major river that had so influenced Heinrich, it was the sea that impressed itself on the boys. It dominated Cullercoats, Whitley Bay just to the north and Tynemouth just to the south. In the twelve years they lived in the town, the homes the Fischers rented were always less than a quarter of a mile from the North Sea coast. Closest was Cullercoats Bay, its stone piers enhancing the natural protection of Beacon Rock, Saddie Rocks and Crab Hill. The bay accommodated a sandy beach, fishing boats, the Lifeboat House with the Watch House above and the Dove Marine Laboratory, a three-storey building dedicated to the study of the coast's natural history. Just outside the bay was Smuggler's Cave, the inlet used by brandy smugglers in the eighteenth century. A smaller, rockier inlet, Brown's Bay, was located just north of Cullercoats, and beyond this the stretch of Whitley Sands. To the south was Long Sands, a mile-long beach which ended at Sharpness Point. Past the point was King Edward's Bay, looked over by Pen Bal Crag and the ruins of Tynemouth Castle and Priory. On the other side of the crag, an observer would see the tiny bay of Prior's Haven guarded by the Spanish Battery above (named after the Spanish mercenaries garrisoned here in the sixteenth century) and the long North Pier protecting the mouth of the River Tyne.

These four miles of the North Sea coastline, from the mouth of the Tyne to St Mary's Island just north of Whitley Sands, had a dramatic and romantic geography and history. Although by 1908 Cullercoats

---

* Although not exclusively, the boys tended to use the English spelling of their surname; see 'A note on the Fisher names', above. In this chapter both spellings of the family name are used.

had ceased to be a trading port, it still operated as a small fishing port. The fishermen landed their catch in Cullercoats Bay and their women, shawled fishwives in long dresses pleated according to their wearer's locality and station, filled the baskets. Fish were gutted close to the bay and crabs were taken up to the back lanes for boiling. The fish lasses sold from stalls, or on to fishmongers for shop sale in Whitley Bay or inland; other fishmongers sold fish from small horse-drawn carts. (Lyubov recalled the fish man coming along the back lane in his cart. The family cat would become excited and, after she had bought fish, it was Lyubov's custom to leave some pieces on the yard wall for the cat.)[2] The fish lasses were lauded (or lampooned) in folksong or music-hall sketches and they also inspired visual artists. They featured on postcards for the tourists and on the canvases of the painters who came to the village.

The variety of humanity and images in Cullercoats and nearby attracted professional artists as well as amateurs. The watercolourist Myles Birket Foster was born in North Shields in 1825 and drew and painted local scenes. Robert Jobling came from Newcastle and was to become most famous for his paintings with the Staithes Group, but he knew this part of the north-east coast from childhood and later bought a house in Whitley Bay. He remained a member of the Tynemouth Arts Association and continued to paint in the region until his death at eighty-two, at home in Whitley Bay, in 1923. Perhaps the most famous artist to be captivated by Cullercoats was the American Winslow Homer, felt by many at the time of his death in 1910 to be the greatest American artist of his generation. Homer was in his forties when he came to Cullercoats in 1881 and he stayed for over a year, drawing and working with oils as well as watercolours. The fish lasses feature predominantly in his work from this period, but like all the visiting artists he drew and painted the fishing boats, the coastline and the sea itself.

The four houses in which Heinrich and the family lived during their time at the coast were in or near Cullercoats, but three of them had Whitley Bay addresses, and it was Whitley Bay that Willie Fisher regarded as his home town when he talked about his childhood in England. Whitley Bay had been a fashionable resort during the Victorian period and retained much of this character well into the twentieth century. The well-to-do still spent holidays here and the photographs and domestic directories of the period indicate a bourgeois and comfortable neighbourhood. The seaside too made it a favourite location for a retirement home and the electric railway had enhanced Whitley Bay's role as a dormitory town. Although it was the local children who tended to win the summer sandcastle competitions in the early 1900s, it was predominantly the visiting holidaymakers who patronised the donkey rides. The beach began to draw more and more visitors from a greater geographical area and a broader social mix. Day-trippers from nearby as well as Fairs Weeks holidaymakers from industrial western Scotland were amongst those who enjoyed the sea and the booming amusements and entertainments trade.[3]

This, then, was the environment in which the Fisher boys grew up. Willie started school here, probably at the John Street School, which was the nearest to the family home in Eskdale Terrace. As was the custom of the time, he was allowed to be in the same class as his older brother until he was settled at the school.[4] When Willie was six, the family moved to 24 Eleanor Street, a small terraced house with a front door which opened directly on to the flagged pavement. The back yard, with a wooden gate to the cobbled back lane, had an outside lavatory, or 'netty' in local dialect, and a coal shed accessed from the lane by a small shuttered door at chest height. The next move the family made was in February 1913, to 12 Lish Avenue, the most superior of their dwellings yet. Here, they had the yard at the back, but at the front there was a small garden with a low wall and an iron gate opening on to a paved footpath, rather than a road for traffic. The house faced a matching terrace opposite.

It was whilst he was at this address that Heinrich Fischer applied once more for naturalisation as a British subject, this time with success. His referees were friends and neighbours from Whitley Bay: two fitters, a pattern maker, a baker and a florist. On 31 March 1914 Fullarton James, the chief constable of Northumberland, vouched for the accuracy of Fischer's application and his suitability for naturalisation. The Home Office enquired carefully into Fischer's conduct during the seven years since his previous application. A chief superintendent of the Newcastle Police wrote to the Home Office on 11 April 1914, informing them, 'From enquiries made at the Works of Messrs Sir W. G. Armstrong Whitworth and Coy., it has been ascertained that Fischer is still employed by them; he is stated to be one of their best workmen and to be of exemplary character'.[5]

The Home Office persisted in their enquiries about Fischer and clearly wanted specific assurances from Newcastle's chief constable. J. B. Wright was still in office and on 27 April 1914, seven years after he had first written to the Home Office with the urgent information about Fischer's association with gun-running, he was required to write to the under-secretary of state once more:

> I have to state that Henrich Matthews Fischer is stated by his employers to be a man of good character and an excellent workman.
>
> I have no reason to suspect that he has been engaged in illegal trafficking of arms since 1907, neither has the Chief Constable of Northumberland with whom I have consulted on this point, but having regard to what transpired in 1907, if such trafficking was taking place here I would be strongly inclined to suspect Fischer of being concerned in it.

The Home Office deliberated, and the minutes read:

> 28 Apr 1914
> A cautious, and not very conclusive statement, but as Police have nothing definite against him since 1907 I suppose we should ?grant cert.

> 29/4/14
> Yes we cannot refuse a man on the chance that if there was anything wrong hereafter he might be in it.[6]

Fischer paid his fee and his certificate of naturalisation was sent to 12 Lish Avenue on 22 May 1914.

The Fischers were happy in Lish Avenue and a few years later moved to number 18.[7] Their neighbours in these mainly rented properties were skilled workers – a millwright, a plater and a stoneworker, for instance – but residents also included a schoolmaster, an insurance manager and a marine engineer. The Fischers' moves from Armstrong Road, Benwell, in 1901 to Lish Avenue, Whitley Bay, from 1913 had seen them rise from a typically working-class to a typically middle-class community.[*]

---

[*] The house where Willie Fisher was born, 140 Clara Street has now been demolished, but all the other houses are still there, although in a redevelopment the ground floor Tyneside flat at 113 Hampstead Road has become part of a larger terraced dwelling now numbered 111.

Industrial worker and revolutionary socialist he may have been, but now Heinrich Fischer was a naturalised Briton enjoying a comfortable middle-class English lifestyle.

The family photographs from the time confirm the image: proud and loving mother, father confident and content, the sons happy children and gauche schoolboys. Lyubov told and showed her granddaughter a little more about the family's time in Whitley Bay. They enjoyed traditional north-eastern fare, with fish featuring regularly in the family diet. Lyubov prepared breakfast porridge in a distinctive way, baking and grinding the oats prior to serving with hot milk. They ate from blue-and-white willow pattern plates. Christmas was celebrated in the English way with roast chicken, Christmas cake, Christmas pudding and mince pies. Lyubov was a typical English housewife of her class and era and loved her life in Cullercoats. She was in the prime of her life. As well as being an excellent cook, she was a skilled seamstress and dressmaker, making most of her own clothes. She would also make and mend clothes for her husband and sons. She would knit. Her home was well managed and her boys had their tasks: Henry was responsible for cleaning the step and Willie for polishing the brass.[8]

Meanwhile, Heinrich was determined that the boys should have the best secondary education possible, and that meant getting them into grammar school. To have both boys educated at grammar school would have been a financial impossibility, but children with a Northumberland County Scholarship were exempt from fees for . Heinrich pushed his boys hard. Henry was awarded his scholarship in 1913 and, as there was no grammar school in Whitley Bay, he travelled daily to the county school in Blyth, a short railway journey north. But on 29 September 1914 the new Whitley Bay and Monkseaton High School was opened and both Henry and Willie entered the school as two of the twenty-eight scholarship holders in a total of 107 boys.[9] His Majesty's inspectors visited the school in March 1916. Their report provides an insight into the education the Fisher boys experienced, and into Whitley Bay itself at this time. The inspectors commented on the school facilities – classrooms, laboratory, art room, assembly hall and playing field, all shared with the adjacent girls' school, together with a workshop for the boys. Given that Wallsend to the south, as well as Blyth, had County Schools, 'the pupils of the Whitley Schools [were] mainly drawn from the immediate neighbourhood', which was 'a residential area and seaside resort for the populous industrial region of the Tyne'. The pupils, said the inspectors, were 'drawn from a fairly well-to-do class of the population' and they were 'on the whole rather above the average in intellectual ability'.

The curriculum comprised of classes in English, French, Latin, mathematics, history, geography, science, manual instruction (woodwork), physical exercises, art, music and religious instruction. The headmaster was a classicist and was adamant that Latin was studied as well as French. The inspectors were particularly interested in the way science was taught.

All the Science is taken by the Second Master, under whom the boys are receiving a valuable training in thoughtful and orderly scientific method. The course is planned with the chief industrial interests of the neighbourhood kept in view, so that without being definitely technical it will provide a useful basis of scientific knowledge for a boy who looks forward to an industrial career, besides accustoming him to regard a material problem from a scientific standpoint.[10]

Henry was a more diligent scholar than his brother Willie. He took the Oxford Junior Local Examination at the South Shields Centre in July 1917 and passed with first-class honours.[11] He was a gentle boy, well behaved and good with children, friends noted, and his mother's favourite, 'a loving son', Lyubov said. Amongst family and friends it was said that Henry was his mother's son, Willie his father's. Willie was less hardworking at his studies than his brother and in terms of school results felt very much in Henry's shadow. Willie may even have been jealous of his brother, his intellectual gifts and his place in their mother's affections. Nevertheless, Willie had skills and interests in science, mathematics, languages, art and music that can be traced in part to the grounding he received at the high school, but in part, too, to his father's abilities, bents and achievements. His love of music may well have come from his father, for Heinrich played the accordion and was popular at social gatherings. Willie had piano lessons and also learned to play the guitar. He craved a chemistry set but, as might be guessed, this was not so much to help him with his science homework as to create foul smells and frighten the family with explosions. Once he went too far. He was hidden in the cupboard under the stairs and concocted a chemical brew that produced the loudest explosion yet. Unfortunately, his mother was halfway down the stairs at the time and the shock caused her to fall the rest of her descent. It was Willie's last experiment with chemistry in the home.

Boys will of course be boys. Even the dutiful and responsible Henry could stray from the straight and narrow. When Willie was quite small, Henry and a group of friends thought it would be fun to teach the younger boy to swim, and they did it in the time-honoured way by throwing him into some deep water. The result was not a fear of water on Willie's part, but a lack of any desire to repeat the experience, so he never learned to swim. But this did not prevent him from playing near the water, nor did it stunt his spirit of adventure. He and a friend liked nothing better than to try to 'borrow' boats from unsuspecting fishermen in Cullercoats Bay, to row them out to sea and then back without being caught. If they were caught, Willie did his best to get some flowers home to his mother before the enraged fisherman arrived. He brought flowers to his mother – wild flowers especially, but also small posies from the local florist – if he tore or dirtied his clothes whilst out cycling, playing football with friends or playing in farmyards. Lyubov said that whenever Willie appeared with flowers, she knew that there had been, or would be, trouble.[12]

Willie had also become a smoker and the way he managed his habit made for a new bond with his father. Heinrich smoked, and Willie surreptitiously collected the cigarette ends his father stubbed out and from the waste tobacco began to roll his own cigarettes. These he kept hidden in the netty and smoked them behind the bolted door. One day as he felt for his 'tabs', as the locals called them, he pulled out a packet of the branded cigarettes his father smoked. He had been discovered. He watched his father, but Heinrich gave no indication that he had found out or that anything at all was amiss. Later in the day, when they were alone, Heinrich still said nothing, but looked at Willie, inclined his head and winked. The boy learned a lesson about self-control and about communication, and he learned more about the father he admired. For Heinrich, he was beginning to meet and understand his son as an adult.[13] This relationship was to be of support to both over the next few years.

The event that exploded into Heinrich Fischer's domestic and political world came from an unlikely direction. On 28 June 1914, in Sarajevo, the Serb Gavrilo Princip shot dead the heir to the Austrian Empire, the Archduke Franz Ferdinand. Less than six weeks later, Great Britain was at war with Germany.

For the Fischers, an early impact of the war was on Henry and Willie's education. They both started at the new grammar school in September 1914. Masters who would have been expecting to teach them volunteered for the army and joined up. Throughout the duration of the war the school governors were having to deal with serving teachers and appointees leaving the school to fight. As His Majesty's inspectors noted in 1916:

> It is very unfortunate that the whole life of both schools has as yet been spent under war conditions ... the Boys School has lost two Masters for military service, the two vacancies so created, together with another from the growth of the school, being filled by women.[14]

And for north-easterners, the conflict itself was not something that was happening far away on mainland Europe. Not many miles south of Whitley Bay, the coastal town of Hartlepool was shelled from the sea by the German navy on 16 December 1914. This was the first hostile action against Britain in the war and 112 civilians were killed in one morning, two more dying of their wounds shortly after. Hartlepool occupied a position at the mouth of the River Tees estuary similar to Whitley Bay's position above the mouth of the Tyne. Whitley Bay people felt angry and vulnerable. Following the bombardment, the Royal Navy increased its visibility in the River Tyne and off the North Sea coast. There was a significant army presence as well; Whitley Bay and its environs effectively became a military enclave. Just inland, beyond the suburban railway station at Cullercoats, was Marden Farm, where Willie played and rode his bicycle. During the war years, from 1914 until 1918, cavalry and bandsmen were stationed and trained here. Army units were encamped on St Mary's Island and on the seafront at Whitley Bay and towards the end of the war there was a prisoner-of-war camp for captured Germans here, many of whose inmates were not repatriated until well into 1919. The town was protected by searchlights and an anti-aircraft battery, but these did not prevent a Zeppelin bombing raid in August 1916, and although unlike the Hartlepool experience there were no deaths, five people were injured.[15]

However, it was not direct military action or presence that was most worrying to the Fischers but anti-German feeling, which was rife across the nation. Given the Geordie military tradition and fierce patriotism in the region, Heinrich had reason to feel unsafe. Lyubov and the boys were perhaps more anonymous. Lyubov was a housewife and Russian, getting on well with her neighbours in the safe middle-class community in Whitley Bay. With their upbringing and education, the boys were internationally aware and were sophisticated native speakers of English. They spoke 'educated' English, as well as the local accent and dialect. Heinrich, though, was vulnerable. His German name, his accented spoken English and his facility with the German language were evident in the workplace and at socialist meetings from the moment he had arrived in Britain, and his employers and sponsors were less willing to support him once the war started. First, he was sacked from Armstrong's Elswick Works. He was then ejected from another factory and the management had to call for a police escort for his protection as he left. Vulnerable and exasperated, he approached the Russian consul in Newcastle and acquired a document which stated that he had been born in Russia, that he had lived there until 1901 and had never been in Germany.[16] Lyubov and the boys had less need for identification papers.

With the document, Heinrich's situation became easier for some months, but critical once more with the German attack on the *Lusitania* in 1915. A Cunard liner, the *Lusitania* had been built on the Clyde and her sister ship, the *Mauretania*, on the Tyne. They had been launched within a few months of each other in 1906 and both made their maiden voyages to New York in the autumn of 1907. They were the most advanced liners of their time, built to win the Blue Riband. This honorary award was held by the steamship which had the record for the fastest North Atlantic crossing, and the *Mauretania* and the *Lusitania* vied for the prize in the years up to the war. However, the ships had also been built to cruiser specification with a subsidy from the British government, the owners agreeing that the ships would come under Admiralty command in time of war. Now refitted for war, but still carrying civilian passengers, the *Lusitania* was torpedoed by a German U-boat off the south coast of Ireland on the afternoon of 7 May 1915 with the loss of 1,201 lives, including those of women and children.

The sinking of the *Lusitania* caused outrage in Britain, particularly in the north of England and in Scotland. There were marches and demonstrators brandished banners with such slogans as 'Out With All Germans – Naturalised or Not'. German businesses were stoned and ransacked. In County Durham there was rioting involving 7,000 people.[17] At this time, Heinrich had found work at another Tyne shipyard and was ostracised once more, but he was spared dismissal when some workmates spoke up for him. They were working on ships for Russia, and the English workers could see that Fischer got on well with the Russian crews and spoke with them in Russian. In this war the British and the Russians were allies and, although Fischer remained opposed to the prevailing Russian government, the autocracy, as he called it, he was relieved at being able to play the Russian, as well as the international socialist, card.

He maintained all his political links, although his political work at this time was mainly to encourage socialism amongst the Russian sailors. He remained a member of the RSDRP and in UK politics aligned himself with the SDF members who seceded to found the British Socialist Party (BSP), working for the party south of the Tyne, in South Shields, rather than in Newcastle. In 1917, the events for which he had been working all his political life began to unfold. Russia's tottering imperial government finally collapsed and post-Tsarist politics began. Heinrich Fischer was a Marxist and Leninist, but it was not until the autumn of the year that Lenin's Soviets wrested political power in Russia. The new government signed an armistice with the Central Powers but in no way was the nation at peace. Its war began to metamorphose into a civil conflict between the Soviet administration and anti- and counter-revolutionary forces. Neighbouring states, internal nationalities and ethnic groups also took up arms against the Soviets. Given the number of Russian ships that were being built or repaired in the Tyne yards, Fischer saw himself as an agent of considerable influence. In particular, he disseminated propaganda amongst the crews of a fleet of Russian ice breakers being completed at the time.[*]

Willie also played his part. He was still a schoolboy at the time of the February 1917 revolution, which led to the Tsar's abdication. He was in a Tyneside shop when some Russian sailors came in and asked about the Bolshevik literature which was on display. The owner knew the Fischers and pointed Willie out. Willie checked which ship the sailors were from and reported to his father.[18] The sailors were probably Bolsheviks or Bolshevik sympathisers, but it was necessary for Heinrich to have as much intelligence as possible to enable him to proselytise effectively.

---

[*] The naval architect working on the project was Yevgeny Zamyatin, who became better known as the author of *We*, the dystopia that is widely accepted as being a precursor of George Orwell's *1984* (David Saunders).

The war and the revolution were the external forces that were now really shaping the Fischers' life in England, creating both problems and opportunities. Young Henry had his School Certificate,[19] but there is no record of Willie taking the examination whilst at the Whitley and Monkseaton High School. The governors' minutes of 10 June 1920 record the problem of scholars leaving school early: 'pupils should continue in attendance until the end of the school year he or she reaches the age of sixteen'.[20]

For some families, this may have been an economic necessity if they were having to find the money to pay the school fees as well as keeping a fourteen- or fifteen-year-old in food and clothing, particularly in time of war. It had been less of a problem for the Fischers initially as the boys had scholarships, but, even so, Heinrich's experiences of anti-German feeling and sackings from various jobs led to belt-tightening in the Fischer household. Willie's adventurous behaviour, too, meant that he found school discipline more irksome as he got older. As the governors feared, Willie may have simply left the school without taking the examination. Another possibility is that he took the examination and failed. Whatever the reason, it is certainly the case that in 1918, at the age of fifteen, Willie became an apprentice draughtsman at Swan Hunter's yard in Wallsend.* As happened so often in heavy industrial regions, Heinrich did what many fathers did. He spoke up for his son and got him a job in the yard.

---

* David Saunders notes from the Heinrich Fischer memoirs that the icebreaker he was working on was being built at a yard adjacent to Armstrong Whitworth's Yard at Low Walker, which suggests that Fischer himself was working at Swan Hunter's.

5

RETURN TO RUSSIA

From late 1918, as the First World War ended in Western Europe and the Bolsheviks struggled to consolidate their power in Russia, the Fischers were confronted with a number of questions. Should they return immediately and join in the fight for the success of Bolshevism? Should they stay in Britain with Heinrich remaining an agent of Leninist influence? Which would be better for the next stage of Henry's and Willie's education, Britain or Russia? Heinrich Fischer worked hard at solving these problems and strove to achieve the maximum advantage from the options open to him, but he was operating in a new political terrain. His German ethnicity and language had become a burden to him in Britain and he was now nearly fifty years old.

Nevertheless, there was some political good fortune. Whilst the end of the First World War stunted the manufacture of warships and armaments on the Tyne, the Wallsend yard where Heinrich was working carried on doing business with Russia. A succession of ships, particularly for icebreaking in Russia's Arctic seas, came for repair and refitting. Heinrich's political work with ships' companies was at its most intense. He was also in a position to learn something about British naval activity in the Baltic and the Barents Sea that was not available to him in the press. British units had landed in Murmansk in March 1918 to prevent its use as a German base, particularly for U-boats, and to take control of the military supplies stored there, which were originally intended for pre-revolutionary Russian use against the Germans. In the spring of 1918 more British troops had landed in

Murmansk and in Archangel, and were active in making contact with groups opposed to the Bolsheviks. From 1918 onwards, with a relay of Russian ships from the Baltic and the Arctic coming into his yard, Heinrich Fischer was in the right place at a very important time.

Marxists had predicted revolution in the more advanced capitalist economies first. Revolution in Russia was a surprise, although nonetheless welcome. Not only that, the Bolsheviks' success had further enhanced Lenin's world status and for his part Lenin was in a position more readily to advise revolutionary socialists overseas in their strategy and precise tactics. He was not lacking in his leadership and they looked to him for it. For Marxist-Bolshevists in Britain, inspired by the evangelical zeal of their Soviet exemplars, their task was clear. They were to act in the interests of the fledgling Soviet Union and they were to work for the socialist revolution in their own country. Heinrich Fischer's British political activity and alliances at this time found him at the centre of the pro-Soviet tendency. His trade union, now the large Amalgamated Engineering Union (AEU), had as its general secretary the veteran socialist Tom Mann. Taking the lead from the charismatic Mann, the union supported the BSP, and within the party followed the internationalist rather than the 'social' line. (When he retired in 1921 at the age of sixty-five, Mann continued his support for Russian communism and maintained his links with international Marxist socialists, which went back over thirty years.)

Fischer's comrades in the ASE and the BSP were prominent in the Hands Off Russia movement, which grew during 1919 and 1920 in Britain and also in most countries of the industrially developed world. The campaign was driven by the Bolshevist left, but also won support from broader left opinion that opposed any British involvement in Russia. Indeed, the horror of the First World War ensured that public opinion was now very much against more military intervention in Europe. Heinrich knew that this was fertile ground for his agitation. If there was little opportunity for strike action on this issue on Tyneside, he, Willie and Henry at least set about distributing Hands Off Russia literature. Meanwhile, in London, the campaign was operating at a more active level. Sylvia Pankhurst, founder leader of the Workers' Socialist Federation (WSF) and later the militant suffragette, had been to Moscow and brought back funds for Hands Off Russia.[1] Harry Pollitt, a young Lancastrian boilermaker and WSF member, was a prime mover in setting up the campaign and soon became its organiser. Later, in June 1920, he gained a national name for himself when he agitated with London dockers to refuse to load fuel on to the *Jolly George*, which had a cargo of munitions destined for the Polish cause in the Russo-Polish War.[2]

Hands Off Russia and the establishment of the Communist International in Moscow in 1919 were steps towards the formation of the Communist Party of Great Britain (CPGB). This was achieved at a Communist Unity Convention held in London's Cannon Street Hotel on 31 July and 1 August 1920.[3] The 160 delegates were predominantly young, much younger than Heinrich Fischer. The convention was chaired by Arthur McManus, a Clydesider whose Scottish-based Socialist Labour Party was currently amongst Lenin's advisers on the British political situation.[4] Also present were representatives of the BSP, the WSF and the South Wales Socialist Society. McManus became chairman of the new party and the BSP's Albert Inkpin* its first secretary. Lenin's message to the convention, his paper on 'left-wing' communism, nudged the delegates into pursuing a policy of affiliation to the Labour Party and to participate in parliamentary elections, underpinned with trade union activism.

With the CPGB now in existence, the Hands Off Russia campaign became more streamlined. This was the theme of McManus and Inkpin's first circular to their branch secretaries:

> Comrades, the government must be told in plain terms that the workers will not have war against Soviet Russia. It is our duty deliberately to advise the workers not only to refuse all service for that purpose, but to oppose it actively ... Speak boldly and act quickly. Neglect nothing. On the shoulders of every individual member of the Communist party rests the fate of Russia at this critical moment. Let every member, therefore, be a missionary for the salvation of Russia, lest we be branded with the infamy of crushing by our apathy the first socialist republic, and our hopes and ideals at the same time.[5]

Across the country, the Communist Party, empowered to work with trade unionists and the Labour Party, was instrumental in the formation of 350 local Hands Off Russia Councils of Action to support

---

* At the time, Inkpin wrote, 'So far as fundamentals and the general basis of unity – revolutionary mass action, soviets or similar organisations, working-class dictatorship as the weapon for expropriating capital – are concerned, there was complete unanimity. The differences were on the relations of the Communist Party to the trade unions and the Labour Party.' ('The Call', 12 February 1920 [*sic*], quoted in *Weekly Worker*, no. 347, 3 August 2000.)

the work of a national council. For the Communists, the councils were prototype soviets. Two weeks after the circular to Communist branch secretaries, the third issue of the party's journal *Communist* carried a fiery article from McManus:

> The Communist Party is to the Republic of Russia flesh of its flesh and bone of its bone ...
>
> Our work is not for a political revolution with a Labour government, but a social revolution with administration by soviets or workers' councils. Your local Councils of Action have potentialities which should be nourished and developed, and in the meantime we hope that all members will endeavour to act in uniformity with the executive policy, and thus ensure the greatest margin of success ...
>
> Get to your posts! Keep there! And be prepared to respond to such advice as the situation may warrant ... Our watchword for the present should be 'Be active, alert, and ready'.[6]

The campaign was successful, although it is more likely that anti-interventionist public opinion supported by the liberal press was more telling than revolutionary fervour. By the end of 1920, it was clear that the Bolsheviks were the Russian government, and despite the anti-socialist line of War Minister Winston Churchill and others in the British government, overt British intervention in Soviet Russia was ending.[7] The Communist Party was exultant but, less publicly, the Soviet sympathisers in Britain did not find it an altogether welcome occurrence. A softening of the British government's attitude towards the Soviet Union, however slight, was likely to reduce revolutionary attitudes towards the British ruling class. Perhaps even more depressing for those hoping for revolution was the outcome of the economic crisis of the early 1920s. Despite rising unemployment, a revolution did not happen.

Fischer's personal economic situation also worsened. The work on the Russian ice breakers in the Wallsend yards was at an end, and he found employment away from the Tyne, as a fitter and pithead engineer at Seaton Delaval Colliery, just north of Whitley Bay.[8] Whilst there, he found himself 'on the cobbles' once again, during the miners' strike of 1921. Perhaps Fischer could see that the recession following the First World War was leading into a long and inexorable decline in north-east England's heavy industrial economy. Certainly during 1920 and 1921 he was making plans and organising documents for the family's return to Russia, or rather his and Lyubov's return. The boys were British born and subjects of the Crown. They would be leaving their native land.

It was a crucial stage in the boys' education, too. At the beginning of 1921 Henry was eighteen and Willie seventeen. Henry was qualified for university entrance. Willie continued his academic studies whilst working as an apprentice draughtsman. He attended evening classes at Newcastle's Rutherford College and matriculated for entry to London University in the examination of June 1920.[9] If Willie had been less compliant at school than his older brother, it was made abundantly clear to him that he needed to qualify for university. But even when all of this had been achieved, the cost of university places was simply beyond the family finances,[10] particularly at a time of industrial decline and strikes. Surely, though, there would be opportunity for the boys to have a university education in Lenin's Soviet Union, and the plans for the move took shape.

The first task was to obtain British passports. Heinrich and the two boys filled in their application forms. 'FISHER, WILLIAM A., destination Finland, etc.' was issued with passport number 207393 on 21 July 1920.[11] The very next entry in the Foreign Office passport ledger for July 1920 recorded the issue of passport number 207394 to 'FISCHER, HEINRICH M.', whose destination was also listed as 'Finland, etc.'.* The Passport Section was certainly very busy in July 1920. Many hundreds of applications were being dealt with and it was not until the following day, 22 July, that 'FISHER, HENRY' was issued with his passport, number 208253. Like his father and his younger brother, it was noted that he had paid the fee of 7s. 6d., and that his intended destination was also 'Finland, etc.'. No passport record for Lyubov has been found. She had presumably travelled to the United Kingdom in 1901 with scanty documents from imperial Russia. She was not a British subject and had not been naturalised. Her return to Russia was under such documents as she already possessed, and her husband's protection.

In the late spring of 1921 the family prepared for their departure. Lyubov wanted to take as much of her home with her as she possibly could. She treasured her crockery and selected pieces of her very best china. These were packed with settings of her willow pattern dinner

---

* The same ledger records the issue of a passport to The Lady Elizabeth Bowes-Lyon.

service. Heinrich's bone china cup was included and Willie's childhood beaker. Not all of the crockery survived the journey intact, and in Moscow the family glued back together again some of the items that were broken, such as Willie's beaker. Willie himself took brushes, pencils, paints and some of his artwork, including a small folio of paintings, pastels and drawings. The family left their last rented home in Whitley Bay, 18 Lish Avenue, in the comfortable and respectable locality that they had clearly loved, and set sail. Their voyage took them into the Baltic port of Tallinn and they then journeyed by land through Estonia into Russia, to Moscow, a city that they did not know but which was now the Soviet capital. It is said that the Fischers were 'welcomed in the Kremlin' when they arrived in Moscow in the summer of 1921, and this may be true.

The early 1920s were a heady time in Moscow. The diaspora of Russians who had fled or been exiled for political reasons in the previous thirty or forty years of Tsarist rule was returning. To the returnees could be added hundreds of communists and sympathisers from across the world, some coming for congresses and conferences, others to make their homes in what they saw as the land of the future. Harry Pollitt and Tom Mann were there, for the First Congress of the Red International of Labour Unions. Being members of the Communist Party, Pollitt and Mann found themselves co-opted onto the British delegation to the Third Congress of the Communist International. 'The day on which I met Comrade Lenin', said Pollitt, 'was the greatest of my life.'[12] This was the world that the Fischers found themselves in and they were caught up in excitement and celebration that could reach a religious intensity.

They acquired lodgings in an apartment at 12 Nikitsky Bulvar, * a few minutes walk from Moscow's famous Arbat, the haunt of intellectuals, artists, scientists and radical politicians. The boys were immediately given a role in their new world. The returnees, the immigrants and the visitors often had children with them, many of whom, even those with Russian parents, spoke little or no Russian. Between them, Henry and Willie had considerable linguistic knowledge and facility. They were both proficient in English, but from their parents they had basic German and Russian and at school they

---

* Heinrich Fischer gave this as his address on 27 May 1921 (David Saunders).

had learned French and Latin. They were in their late teens and had some confidence and authority about them, particularly as the sons of the highly regarded Heinrich and Lyubov Fischer. Henry, it was said, was 'good with children' and Willie enjoyed art and music as well as the outdoor life. What better than for them to work with children, and this was to become their role for their first weeks in Moscow.

In the summer of 1921, as one of their projects, Henry and Willie took a party of children for a summer camp on the banks of the river Klyazma, a tributary of the Volga, about 20 miles north-east of Moscow. Now, amongst its dachas, flower gardens and vegetable plots, Klyazma village is en route from Moscow's Sheremetyevo international airport. Then, it was a more rural retreat of pine woods and open country through which the river snaked. With the party were thirteen-year-old Rosa Prokofiev and her sixteen-year-old brother Harold. Like the Fischer boys, the Prokofievs had been born in the United Kingdom. Like Heinrich, Rosa's father had been born in Russia but had fled to Britain as a political exile at the beginning of the century. The family had eventually moved from London to Paisley in Scotland, and had made their return to Russia with the Fischers just a few weeks before. The party of children was enjoying a summer holiday, sleeping in huts and in the open, playing and cooking on wood fires, when tragedy struck, an event that was to be the most significant in the Fischers' lives. The Klyazma has the reputation of being a tricky river, with its own tributary streams, eddies, whirlpools and crosscurrents. One day when the youngsters were swimming, one of them was dragged by an undertow and began to struggle and scream in the river. Henry rushed in to help. He saved the child but was sucked under the water and drowned.[13]

The children returned immediately to Moscow, and to the Fischers' apartment. Rosa was with the children. On receiving the news, Lyubov collapsed. 'Why Henry?' she sobbed. Less anguished, she might have asked 'Why not the child who was saved?' or 'Why not any of the other children?' For Willie, who was there, his interpretation of his mother's cry was 'Why not Willie?'. In that same moment, in his own grief, Willie felt most keenly his mother's rejection. He loved Henry, his only brother, and when Henry had most needed his help, Willie, a non-swimmer, was unable to give it. As the family endured their grief, Willie's feelings of guilt were unbearable. There were no old school friends or work mates to offer him support. They were all in the north-east of England. Willie knew that Henry was his mother's favoured son. Henry's death and his mother's rejection hardened something in him. He became more reticent and withdrawn, and was less at ease in his parents' company.

There is no record of Henry's body ever having been found, no official record of his death, no gravestone or memorial. Lyubov was inconsolable, becoming physically ill, and diagnosed as having arthritis she tired easily. From this time she walked with a stick, or carried with her a folding stool with a canvas seat.[14] To assuage the mental and emotional pain, she devoted herself to Communist Party work. The family now had an apartment in the Kremlin and she became social secretary to the Society of Old Bolsheviks, sending the invitations for social events at which she would make the tea.

Heinrich too immersed himself in party work, important official work to begin with, although perhaps not work of the importance that he thought he might have deserved. He may never have accepted fully that his twenty-year exile had excluded him from the innermost circles of Russian revolutionaries and from the *realpolitik* of Petrograd and Moscow, but he did submit himself to party discipline and was assigned to work on the British desk of the Comintern. He also began the first edition of his memoirs, which were scrutinised and edited by the Communist Party publishers and published within the year. In September 1924 he left the Comintern and went back into heavy industry as the manager of a paper mill in Vologda, some 250 miles north of Moscow, where he was liked and respected by his work force.[15] His memoirs indicate that he chose to be a 'worker' once more[16] but the circumstances of his move may have been due more to events than to choice. It was true that he found bureaucracies and the management of them tedious and that he had always been a free-thinking Marxist. Many years later when talk turned to politics in the Fisher household, Willie would recall one of his father's witty political observations. Asked about the difference between a Russian worker and a British worker, Heinrich would reply, 'When a Russian worker has pea soup with bacon, it's a holiday feast. When a British worker has pea soup with bacon, he is almost starving!' That was not a Bolshevik answer. The family mused that perhaps Heinrich never really was a Bolshevik. His private thinking may have been closer to that of the original RSDRP, before the damaging split into Bolsheviks and Mensheviks.[17]

But leaving the Comintern after such a short time was odd, for it was unlike him not to want to be at the centre of political action. Perhaps events conspired to make his position untenable. Lenin's death in January 1924 was a blow to Heinrich. The succession was not one that would be beneficial to him. He had detailed knowledge of the British political scene and knew the senior members of the CPGB, many of them personally. He was associated with Lenin's support of the CPGB policy to engage in the parliamentary system in the absence of British soviets and to seek Labour Party affiliation. So another blow was Labour's defeat in the United Kingdom's 1924 general election. It showed to all that revolution in Britain was in no way imminent. Heinrich's association with the CPGB's parliamentary and affiliation policies were now a burden. The reorganisation of the Comintern in 1924, following its humiliation after the collapse of a planned revolution in Germany in 1923 and the British election result, led to changes. The British section was disbanded and amalgamated into an Anglo-American Secretariat (AAS).[18] Although Heinrich was associated with Ludwig Martens, another Russo-German, who had gone to Britain twenty years before and who had then moved to the United States to manage Soviet trade affairs, his own knowledge of the United States was limited.[19] As he might flounder in the AAS, which was also to be responsible for other English-speaking nations including Canada, Australia, New Zealand and South Africa,[20] the new secretariat was not the place for Heinrich. But there is another, more compelling reason to consider as the trigger for Heinrich Fischer leaving party work for good.

In the early autumn of 1924 the ferocious power struggle following Lenin's death was well underway when Heinrich received news of his old comrade from the Newcastle cartridge conspiracy, Alf Nagel. Nagel had done well in the intervening sixteen or so years. His language skills and knowledge of the import and export business had earned him a significant job. He now worked for Arcos, the All Russian Co-operative Society, which was the London-based commercial stock-holding company set up to promote trade between the Soviet Union and the United Kingdom. However, it was also a cover organisation for Soviet industrial intelligence and links with the CPGB.[21] Nagel had a home in Maly Rozhdestvensky Lane in Moscow and was arrested by security police on the night of 13 September 1924, when his interrogation began. Within days of Nagel's arrest, Heinrich Fischer was working in Vologda, so he was not in Moscow when Nagel was sentenced to death for espionage on 13 April 1925, or when his friend was shot four days later.[22] He returned occasionally to the family apartment in Moscow, first in the Kremlin and later in Marklievesky Street, and also devoted himself to study and to the second edition of his memoirs.[23] He died of pneumonia on 22 March 1935 at the age of sixty-three.[24]

In the years after, Heinrich's family said that he was lucky to die because, as an Old Bolshevik and comrade of Lenin who had spent twenty years in a foreign country, he would have been accused, interrogated and murdered in Stalin's purges. Meanwhile Lyubov survived, saved, it was said, by her illness.[25] Heinrich had made significant contributions to socialist and communist politics in Russia and Britain, but it was his surviving son Willie who would become the better known.

6

RECRUITMENT

In the autumn of 1921 Willie Fisher possessed all the components to make him into *Homo sovieticus*, and then into a spy. He had absorbed his father's teaching and his father's example. Throughout his life, he mentioned proudly the fact that he had been 'born into a worker's family' and that his father had been in the vanguard of Russian social democracy led by Lenin in St Petersburg in the 1890s.[1] It should be assumed that Willie himself was a member of a trade union before he left England. He had been active in the Hands Off Russia movement and, if not a member of the BSP and the CPGB himself then he was of their culture, had seen them in formation and had met and knew some of their members. He may have remembered the police raids on his Newcastle home when he was a small child and, given his father's political activities, it is likely that police surveillance continued after that. Certainly the police had to report on his father during Heinrich's second application for British citizenship. Willie's political sophistication had developed from an early age, for he had learned from his father how systems and politicians operated and he had been drilled into maintaining personal and political discipline.

Even more than his father, Willie had the advantage of knowing from childhood an advanced economy and the class system. He had the felt experience of an upbringing in a heavy industrial culture from the moment of his birth. Whilst Heinrich had been born into an agricultural community, his son was born in the north-east of England, where the Industrial Revolution had begun. Before Willie was born, and when he was growing up, his father had worked as an engineer in shipyards and later at collieries, and Willie himself had gone to work in the shipyard, albeit in a technical white-collar job. Not only that, but Willie had been born and brought up in the class-based society that was Marx's model. Willie's father, 'the old man', as Willie often referred to him,[2] spent the first thirty years of his life in Russia and had his first experience of industry and politics in a cruder class system which was barely out of the feudal era and which was industrialising only haphazardly and often under non-Russian management. Willie had also seen the anti-German feeling that had burst upon his father during the war and had drawn from this that communism alone would protect the worker against prejudice and imperialist attitudes. An internationalism, an 'anti-war ideology' based on Marxist-Leninist discipline, followed.

Willie Fisher, then, was already a rudimentary Soviet citizen when he arrived in Moscow and although people were being attacked in the streets and food was scarce, his discipline was such that he could cope with whatever Russia threw at him. Many Westerners who found themselves marooned in the Soviet Union sought the help of their embassies to get home. Harold Prokofiev could not deal with life in Moscow and managed to find his way back to London,[3] but Willie Fisher's political apprenticeship had prepared him for the Soviet era. Henry's death, too, shaped him and prepared him for his life ahead. Like his father, Willie had shrewd political antennae, which directed his survival instincts in the Soviet state, and he coped by compartmentalising his life. He was a good friend to those who knew him, witty company too, but he was also reserved and self-disciplined. In particular, he found it difficult ever to speak of his brother and when Henry was mentioned, Willie would retreat into himself. His feelings towards his mother were now proper rather than affectionate. In these respects he was lucky in the Soviet Union, immune to what was called bourgeois sentimentality. He was of mixed German and Russian blood and his native language was English, but he was able to confer his patriotism or his 'nationalism' on the Soviets.[4] In his early years in the Soviet Union and as his jobs and workplaces changed, like all citizens he was required to provide the *curricula vitae* that the bureaucracy demanded, citing, amongst many other details, family background and worker credentials. Later when he was formally employed by the state security and intelligence service, the Ob"yedinennoe Gosudarstvennoe

Politicheskoe Upravlenie, the OGPU, a boss who was scrutinising the sheaf of these documents took him to task:

> 'In this document you say that you're German. Here you say you're Russian. Here British. What *are* you?'
>
> 'I don't know what I am according to your rules. I'll be whatever you say I am.'
>
> 'You're Russian.'[5]

What Willie Fisher really thought is simply not known but, as far as the Soviet Union was concerned, William August Fisher became Vilyam Genrikhovich Fisher. Family and friends, however, continued to know him as Willie.

From the moment he arrived in Moscow, he stepped ever deeper into the Soviet system and the system deployed him, hid him and covered his tracks. His KGB-sponsored biography has him working as a translator for the Comintern in the early 1920s, probably under the auspices of a security office that would shortly become the Inostranny Otdel, the foreign intelligence department of the Soviet security services.[*] But it is more likely that until he came of age in 1924 he was working with and for the party youth organisation, the Komsomol. Who was controlling the Komsomol leaders was of no particular concern to Willie. It was to the Komsomol that Willie and Henry were answerable at the time of the camp on the river Klyazma. At the end of the summer of 1921, not long after Henry's death and four months after his arrival in Russia, Willie was apparently working at a shipbuilding institute in Moscow.[6] In the autumn of 1922 he was in language work once more, continuing as a translator and interpreter learning new languages in a specialist institute, where he remained until August 1924.[7] There is also a suggestion that at about this time he started an art diploma at what is now the Surikov Arts Institute in Moscow, but never completed the course. This is perhaps closest to the truth, for given the fact of Alf Nagel's arrest and execution, it may have been that Willie embarked upon an art diploma but was advised or required to withdraw from the course, and that this time in his life is carefully obscured.

In an autobiographical fragment published towards the end of his

---

[*] Dmitry Tarasov's official biography has him working in this role from 1920, when he was actually still living in the United Kingdom.

life,[8] Willie gives but a few short paragraphs to the period 1921–26 and barely mentions his employment during these years. There is no word of his mother or his brother, but he does tell of his father's credentials as a worker and a follower of Lenin and he writes of early years 'abroad'. He romanticises his political activities in the Komsomol from 1922, taking part, he says, in agitprop work in Khamovniki, a district in a loop of the river Moskva about 3 miles south of Nikitsky Boulevard and the Kremlin. The autobiography includes his own political credentials for his readers, his bosses and colleagues, for he notes that he resisted Trotsky's attempts to influence young people and was even involved in fights with groups of Trotskyites. He testifies that it was at this time, too, that his interest in radio began. An internal report on Willie Fisher in the late 1930s states that he was actually a radio technician between August 1924 and August 1925,[9] although Willie himself describes his interest as purely amateur at that time.

It is probable that his interest in radio had begun in England. In 1906 a wooden radio mast was erected on the north-east coast, at Cullercoats, at a site known thereafter as Marconi Point, and it received its first message in December of that year from the *Helen Bloomhaven*, a vessel out of Hamburg and bound for Newcastle.[10] This was two years before the Fishers arrived in Cullercoats so the mast was not only a significant landmark but in full use when the Fisher boys and their friends were playing at the coast in the years that followed. Later, Willie studied physics at a grammar school that specialised in applied science and he continued his academic and technical education in his evening classes at Rutherford College. He became professionally aware, too, of developments in ship-to-shore communications through his work as a draughtsman at the shipyard. His opportunities for practical activity as a radio enthusiast in his mid-teenage years might have been limited, though. Amateur radio licences in the UK were withdrawn at the beginning of the First World War and the authorities took possession of licensed radio equipment. Amateur radio did not begin again in Britain until 1920, just months before the Fishers went to Moscow. However, Willie states that his involvement with practical radio began in Moscow. He constructed rudimentary spark transmitters and detect receivers, dismantled old doorbells for wire and scrounged crystals of galena or carborundum for the detectors. With friends, he collected scraps of silver paper and cardboard for the capacitors the detectors needed and searched far and wide for the delicate wire essential as the cat's whisker.[11] The fun and inventiveness that emerge from these recollections evoke Willie the boy – with the bangs and howls from home-made radios matching the smells and explosions of the chemistry set – rather than the serious and bereft young man of the early Moscow days. It is not surprising then that when Willie was called up into the Red Army at the age of twenty-two, he was drafted into a radio battalion. His two-year military career, which found him stationed for the most part in Vladimir province, about 130 miles east of Moscow, was uneventful, but he learned a great deal from it. Initially he found that he was contemptuous of his officers. They were ignorant, he felt, from working-class and peasant families, and their education consisted of little more than a few years of primary school. He was thus incensed when he saw a note on the CV that he had to complete when he joined the army: where he had written that he had received secondary education in England, there was a pencilled scrawl in the margin, 'Illiterate in Russian!'[12]

The junior officers and NCO gave their recruits a hard time. Willie resented this and was not a compliant soldier, behaviour that would come back to haunt him in the 1930s, when his bosses appraised his career. Reflecting on his time in the Red Army many years later, he made himself out to be more understanding of his commanders. After all most of them, he noted, were veterans, heroes of the civil war. He paid tribute to them as such and acknowledged that their harsh discipline had been a correct policy.[13]

He enjoyed the camaraderie of the army and talked often of the friends he made in his unit, one a soldier by the name of Yermoleev and another named Liengnick, the son of a German Swiss revolutionary who knew Willie's father.[14] Willie naturally sought the company of articulate, educated comrades and also those who were not ethnically Russian, or who took an international perspective. He was friendly with Ernst Krenkel, a member of the Russian-German community, who was to make a name for himself in the 1930s as a geographer, geologist and polar explorer. Krenkel was the chief radio operator on the *Chelyuskin*, which sank in the Arctic in 1934, and it was his signalling which guided the rescuers to the stricken crew. Also in the 1930s he established the first long-distance radio link between Franz-Josef Land and the Antarctic and was the radio operator on Ivan Papanin's 1937 Arctic expedition. Krenkel was honoured as a Hero of the Soviet Union and was an exact contemporary of Willie's as they had both been born in 1903. They were to meet again in the 1960s and, although Willie had been able to follow Ernst's career with interest and pride, Ernst had no idea what Willie had done with his life.

Also friendly with Willie were the actor Mikhail Tsarev, who was to become a People's Artist of the Soviet Union, and a lad from Moscow named Volodya Rass. In October 1926, just a few weeks after Willie had completed his time in the Red Army, Volodya threw a party at his family's Moscow apartment. Tatyana, Volodya's sister, a music student at the Moscow Conservatoire, was there and brought her friend and fellow student, Yelena Stepanovna Lebedeva. At the end of the evening, Willie tentatively asked Yelena if he might walk her home. She accepted his offer and they arranged to meet again.[15] Now demobilised and looking for work, or 'taking some time out', he said, 'to rest', he spent as much time as he could with Yelena before he started work as a radio technician at an army research institute in January 1927.[16] At the conservatoire Yelena was learning the harp. The Lebedevs' apartment had a piano and as Willie read music, loved music and had been a pianist since his childhood, he sometimes played. 'Why don't I', he suggested one day, 'teach you harmony?' Despite having been taught the piano by a Moscow Conservatoire gold medallist who had retired to Ostashkov, Yelena found harmony difficult, so Willie courted her at the piano keyboard.[17]

Yelena was twenty and had been born in Ostashkov, on Lake Seliger. The town looked to St Petersburg and western Europe rather than to Moscow and was famed for its eighteenth-century architecture. During the eighteenth century it became known as 'the Second Venice' because of its location in a landscape of interconnecting lakes close to the source of the Volga, some 300 miles north-west of Moscow. Kapitolina Ivanovna Lebedeva, Yelena's mother, had had eight children and Yelena was the youngest. Her first child, Lyudmila, had died in infancy and when her second child, another daughter, was born, Kapitolina also named her Lyudmila. The superstition that a second child given the same name as the deceased sibling would also die came to pass, and so she named her third child Serafima, and the child survived. Another daughter, Klaudia, and two sons, Boris and Ivan, followed. Between the births of the two sons another daughter, Yelena, was born, but this child too was to die, of diphtheria, in childhood. Kapitolina and her husband, Stepan Mikhailovich, thought that their family of four surviving children was complete but Kapitolina fell pregnant once more. She was some twenty years younger than her husband and had a lover, a Polish count, who was the father of the child. Her last child was unwanted and, invoking the curse, Kapitolina named her Yelena. But the unwanted baby survived, to become her mother's most loved and loving child.

Stepan, a doctor, died when Yelena was only four and Kapitolina, a trained obstetrician and physician, continued in her profession, supplementing her widow's pension with an income from her own private medical practice. The older children found work in Moscow, and Yelena and her mother moved there in 1916, living with Boris, who was employed as a driver. Yelena had not finished her secondary education in Ostashkov, but she craved an arts education and once in Moscow she began studying with the Bolshoi Theatre Ballet School. She was on the way to realising her ambition to be a ballerina when, in 1924, she fell badly on stage during a rehearsal and damaged a kidney. Unable to dance again, after convalescence she found a job in industry for a short whilst before entering the Moscow Conservatoire as a student of the harp. Away from the conservatoire she was also doing well at her lessons in harmony. There was no doubt that she and Willie enjoyed the music and each other's company, but Willie behaved as a demanding teacher rather than a sweetheart. Yelena was at a loss to fathom his feelings. She confided in Tatyana Rass: did her brother Volodya know whether Willie had feelings of affection for her? Tatyana had no idea.

In early April 1927, whilst they were sitting at the piano, Willie earnestly took Yelena by the hand and asked her to marry him. She was bewildered. 'But … do you love me?' she asked.

'How do I know if I love you right now?' he responded. 'It is something you realise with time. Russians love to love everything. They love apples. They love paintings. They love dogs. I like being with you. In England married people love each other and they love their children. And the children love their parents. It's how it is. Your character is soft and warm. I'm the opposite. But we'll make a good couple. We'll complement each other. It will be good for us to be together. And then when we're married, we'll find out if we love each other. But I think that we will.'

Willie's experiences had left him repressed emotionally. To acknowledge feelings, let alone express them, was difficult, but what he lacked in an expressed passion for her, Yelena made up for with compassion for him. She was also intrigued. As a foreigner, there was something exotic about him. He was different from the Russian boys. She thought that perhaps his quite extraordinary proposal was the result of a carefully constructed masculine vanity on his part, and that he was hiding his genuine feelings of love for her. When he visited, his greeting would often be a snapped 'How many hours have you practised your harp today?'. All these feelings and experiences excited and fascinated her. She kept him waiting for a few days and then accepted his proposal. Kapitolina was happy with Willie Fisher as her future son-in-law. He was gentle, respectful and well mannered. He was also educated, articulate, loved the arts, and had scientific knowledge and modern technological skills. He had served in the Red Army and, as a member of the Komsomol, he could be expected to receive full party membership before long. All of these factors were relevant for a widow contemplating the marriage of her youngest daughter. He could and would protect Yelena in a dangerous and uncertain world. Kapitolina and her sons trusted the young man and the whole family liked him.

But although Willie had met his future mother-in-law, Yelena had not met Heinrich and Lyubov. She was to meet her future father-in-law first. Heinrich travelled from Vologda without Lyubov on this occasion and liked Yelena immediately, but he thought it prudent to prepare the young woman for her meeting with Lyubov. ('Lyubov wore the trousers in that marriage,' said Evelyn.) 'My wife is the perfect housewife,' said Heinrich. 'Make sure everything is just right when she visits.' The result was that Yelena was scared to meet Lyubov, worried that she would not be thought suitable. She cleaned the flat and put a vase of flowers on the table. When Lyubov came in and saw the flowers, she cried, 'Where's Henry? Henry has been here!'

'No,' said Yelena, frightened, 'I put the flowers there.'

'You have been sent to me to replace Henry,' said Lyubov, and turning to Willie she continued, 'If something happens now, I shall have a daughter and not a son.'[18]

Willie was hurt and humiliated, and the rift that had occurred with Henry's death widened. In his pain and anger, he never understood that he was like his mother.[19] He had inherited much of her character and personality – order, cleanliness and attention to detail – and he had tried to emulate his father because his mother loved and respected Heinrich so much. If he could be like his father, Willie had subconsciously deduced, his mother would love him. But opposites attract. As well as being her first born, Henry had been like Heinrich – he even looked like his father – whilst Willie was temperamentally like Lyubov, something he had never recognised or acknowledged. One result of marriage would be an escape from his mother, and the day that was chosen for the wedding, at a civil ceremony in Moscow, was also significant. As the Bolshevik government had adopted the Gregorian calendar on 1 February 1918,[20] 22 April 1927 was actually also Heinrich's fifty-sixth birthday. True, knowing the Fisher family's careful management of their finances, perhaps the decision to have the wedding and birthday party on the same day was so that Heinrich could save a day's holiday and save the cost of another return journey from Vologda as well as saving on catering costs, but nevertheless it was the opportunity for special celebration which showed Willie's particular devotion to his father.[21]

In less than six years in the Soviet Union, Willie Fisher had had an adventurous time and, apparently, six jobs, but he took his obligations as a married man seriously and realised now that he needed to find a job with prospects, a career. His sister-in-law Serafima suggested that the translation section of the Soviet security and intelligence service, the OGPU, would be a good place for him to work; she had contacts there and would recommend him.[22] When he wrote about the time himself, however, he put it this way, with no reference whatsoever to his marriage or his family:

> After I was demobbed I rested for a whilst and then I started looking for a job. I had two offers: one was in a scientific research institute and the other was in the foreign department of the OGPU. I was attracted to the first because of the work in radio technology, but the other promised the romance of working in intelligence. Friends said that with my knowledge of languages I could serve my country better. They persuaded me to accept the OGPU offer.[23]

Willie's file actually has him working at the radio research institute from January to April 1927 and joining the OGPU the day after May Day 1927.[24] From a worker's and a bona-fide Leninist family, with Komsomol membership, Red Army service, experience as a radio operator, fluent in languages (one CV even has him studying Hindustani in 1924) and a knowledge of the United Kingdom, Willie Fisher's credentials were impeccable and he was ideal intelligence officer material.

His recruitment, when he was still only twenty-three, brought Willie Fisher into a Soviet service elite. One of Lenin's first acts after the October revolution in 1917 was to form the *Vserossiiskaya Chrezvychainaya Kommissiya po Bo'be s Kontrrevolyutsiei i Sabotazhem* – the All-Russian Extraordinary Commission for Combating Counter-revolution and Sabotage, or Cheka, whose first head was the Pole Felix Dzerzhinsky. Dzerzhinsky had been subjected to imprisonment and internal exile in the 1890s and early 1900s, and in October 1917 was a member of the Military Revolutionary Committee, where his idealism and ruthlessness brought him close to Lenin. As well as being appointed chairman of the Cheka, he was made Soviet Commissar for Internal Affairs. It was he who embedded the notion and the metaphor, the *organs* of state security into the consciousness of the Soviet Union, calling his Cheka 'an organ for the revolutionary settlement of accounts with counter-revolutionaries'.[25] It was under his leadership that the 'Red Terror' which followed the attempt on Lenin's life in 1918 was unleashed. Not only were White Russian counter-revolutionaries arrested and shot, but also supporters of the Revolution, including liberals, socialist revolutionaries and Mensheviks. As Dzerzhinsky said after the murder of the Tsar and his family:

> The Cheka is the defence of the revolution as the Red Army is; as in the civil war the Red Army cannot stop to ask whether it may harm particular individuals, but must take into account only one thing, the victory of the revolution over the bourgeoisie, so the Cheka must defend the revolution and conquer the enemy even if its sword falls occasionally on the heads of the innocent.[26]

Despite his austere character and manner, Dzerzhinsky did little to control the excesses of his more ill-disciplined and fanatical soldiery, but his role in the revolution was secure and in 1922 the Cheka became the OGPU, which incorporated state security and intelligence services. Between 1917 and 1991, when the Soviet Union came to its end, the Cheka sustained its founding principles through eleven reorganisations and name changes, acquiring its final and best-known abbreviation in 1954 – the KGB. Its officers received their salaries on 'Chekists' Day', the twentieth of each month, to commemorate the founding of the Cheka on 20 December 1917.[27] From the beginning, the Cheka was the viscera, the organs, of the Soviet Union.

Willie Fisher was to serve in these organs through nine of their eleven phases. At first, as well as working on languages and reading and filleting books, newspapers and documents emanating from the West to provide reports and briefings for his bosses, he was also involved in more direct counter-revolutionary operations. On one occasion, White agents threw a bomb into the reception area of the OGPU headquarters at the Lubyanka. The resulting explosion broke a few shelves and damaged an office, Willie witheringly recalled. All units were mobilised to track down the bombers. One unit, much to Willie's disappointment not his own, cornered a bomber and shot him in a firefight. In 1928 there were more rumours of civil war and hoarding became rife. Silver coinage disappeared and OGPU units were deployed to root out the secret hoards. Now a unit leader, Willie was ordered to take his team to search a village outside Moscow. At the end of a long day he was supervising three of his men as they hunted through a church building and presbytery. They found nothing. A frustrated young recruit started yelling abuse at the priest and leapt on to a stack of firewood, throwing the logs and planks into the yard and calling upon the Devil to rebuild the stack. Willie and the two others joined in. One of the planks split and coins cascaded into the yard. The unit collected up the cash and turned the scene over to a specialist OGPU team, which went on to discover more coins and hidden treasures.[28]

Whilst his daily work was a mixture of duty and routine, his home life was happy. Yelena continued her study of the harp and the newlyweds continued their duets at the piano. Ellie, the diminutive favoured by her family and the name by which Willie now called her, completed her studies at the Conservatoire in 1929, but she did not seek orchestral or theatre work immediately because she was pregnant. It was not an easy time for her. The Fishers loved animals and their first dog, an Alsatian, Volushka, had twelve puppies that summer. Willie was often away and as she attempted to house-train them, Ellie had to manoeuvre the pups from the Fishers' first-floor accommodation, through the flat of their neighbour, a Party official, to the yard below. Willie and Ellie's first and only child, Evelyn, was born on 8 October 1929. Willie chose the name Evelyn because it was an English name, although in public it was Russianised to Evelina. 'It would have looked very out of place with all the Daryas and Maryas at school,' said Evelyn. The Russian diminutive Lina was never used at home, always the English Evelyn.

Willie was still not relaxed with his mother, but Evelyn's birth did mean that Lyubov was a more regular visitor to Willie and Ellie's flat. Lyubov also got on well with Kapitolina and, with other members of the extended family often there too, Willie could avoid having a great deal to do with his mother. Another factor which helped Lyubov was that her grandchild was a girl. She talked to Evelyn about the family's home life in England, the little cat, the crockery they used which she had brought to Russia, the houses they lived in, and so on. She cooked the food that they had enjoyed in England and for New Year (as agnostics, the family did not celebrate the Christmas festival) she made mincemeat for mince pies and a Christmas pudding. Conversations in the home were often conducted in English, and Lyubov spoke to her granddaughter in English as well as in Russian, thus continuing the cultured, multilingual atmosphere of the Fisher household. Ellie, too, became more Anglicised, sometimes using the Anglicised version of her name, Helen.[29]

The fact that Willie was now a father as well as a husband increased his value at work. A wife and a small child were excellent cover for an agent, so in 1931 Willie's training for his first overseas mission reached its final stages. His bosses calculated that it would not be necessary to create a false identity – in fact the young child would make this dangerous – but the British passport Willie had travelled on to get to Moscow in 1921 was due to expire in a few months. The OGPU was developing its techniques in the forging and recycling of passports and could have supplied documents, but aside of the family considerations, his particular case gave the OGPU an opportunity to test Willie and also to undertake some research into the British passport service and its application procedures. He was therefore sent to the British consular office at 46 Varovskov Street to apply for a new passport.[30] He used his own name, William Fisher, and told the consul a story, which, although close to the truth, used elements of fiction to outline his motive. In his native language, he explained that he was a British subject and that he had come to the Soviet Union when he was seventeen. His parents had gone to England as exiles at the beginning of the century, he said, and had lived in Newcastle and Whitley Bay, where he had been born and gone to school. They had been socialists in England and he and his father had worked in the shipyards on the Tyne. The family had returned to Russia to be communists in the Soviet Union. For him, Willie then said, it had been a disaster. He had been promised a university education, but his hopes had been dashed. He had ended up miles away in Vologda (which of course he knew from his father's work there), a dull and primitive place. The locals loathed him because he was British and because his Russian was poor. There was no work worthy of his skills and he was reduced to labouring. All this, said Willie, perhaps basing his story on the Prokofievs as much as on the Fishers, had led to blazing rows with his parents. He wanted to go back to England, but they did not want him to go. They were not happy here, either, but could not face humiliation and admit that they had made a wrong decision. They had to stay, and wanted their son to stay, too. 'My British passport is lost,' said Willie. 'I think they've hidden it so that I can't leave them.' Willie than explained that he had 'come to Moscow' and, using his British birth certificate, had acquired residency papers. These documents would expire very soon and he needed a British passport so that the authorities would allow him to reside in Moscow until he could leave the country. The consul examined the documents, sympathised with Willie's predicament and prepared a letter, which could be shown to the Soviet authorities. The letter recorded that William Fisher had applied for a British passport and that in the consul's opinion he was entitled to one; however, the application had to be referred to London for approval.

On 6 August 1931 his new passport, number 445470, was issued in London and arrived in Moscow for him before the end of the month.[31] With this, Willie was equipped for his first overseas mission. Now with the code name FRANK, he received his final briefings. He was treated to the traditional Chekists' dinner at a Moscow safe house and his Communist Party membership was confirmed. At the beginning of September Willie Fisher, accompanied by his wife and daughter, left for Leningrad on the night train from Moscow. From Leningrad they would travel on to Helsinki and Stockholm.

SCANDINAVIAN MISSION

Willie Fisher was back in western Europe, a little over ten years after he had first arrived in Moscow. His destination was Oslo, where he was to learn his first lessons as a Soviet illegal in the field. His tasks were initially simple and basic but they were integral in a new OGPU system masterminded by the Soviet Union's most important intelligence strategist in the West, Aleksandr Mikhailovich Orlov, code name SCHWED, 'The Swede'.

An assessment of Orlov's career shows how the organs of the Soviet Union worked and grew, and how the persons and personalities at the top of the Soviet system impinged on each other. Orlov's role, responsibilities and actions gave the context to much of Willie Fisher's work not just on this first mission, but over the next twenty-five years. Of course, Orlov was not his real name, but it has become the name by which history knows him. He used, or was known by, at least seventeen other names during his life, but he had been born Leiba Lazarevich Fel'dbin in Bobruisk, Byelorussia, on 21 August 1895.[1] His family was Jewish and, although it was necessarily dormant for many years, he always put great store by his faith. His father was in the timber business and during the recession at the beginning of the First World War sought work in Moscow. The teenage Leiba (his friends called him Leon, or Lev) went to the Lazarevsky Institute and then to the Law School at the University of Moscow. In 1916 he was called up into the Imperial Russian Army. The abdication of the Tsar a year later meant that Orlov was now eligible for officer training, an opportunity previously denied to Jews, and he took his chance with alacrity. Also in 1917 he joined the RSDRP and espoused Marxism-Leninism. When the October Revolution took Russia out of the First World War, the 22-year-old Orlov became head of the Information Service of the Supreme Finance Council, but bureaucracy bored him and in the civil war of 1918 he became a military officer once more, but this time in the Red Army.[2]

In 1920 he was serving on the Polish front, in the thick of the Russo-Polish War, and it was at this time that he had his first experience of guerrilla fighting and counter-intelligence work. His successes got him noticed by Felix Dzerzhinsky,[3] who saw to it that Orlov joined the ranks of the ever-expanding Cheka. He served in Archangel as head of counter-intelligence, but late in 1921 was officially back in civilian life and continuing his law studies in Moscow. Still an undergraduate, Orlov was appointed to an assistant's post in the Soviet Supreme Court and contributed to the drafting of the Soviet Union's criminal code. When he graduated at the age of twenty-eight, Dzerzhinsky had him installed in the highest echelons of the OGPU's Economic Directorate.

Like Lenin, Dzerzhinsky was obsessive in his work. In 1924, in addition to his roles as head of the OGPU and Commissar for Internal Affairs and Transport, he was appointed chairman of the Supreme Council of National Economy. The OGPU and the national economy were thus in tandem and, at the earliest stage, Orlov was involved in ploys to get European and American money into the Soviet economy. Denied full diplomatic status, the Soviets established trade missions in the West – Arcos in Britain, Handelsvertretung in Germany and Amtorg in the United States – and included OGPU personnel amongst their staff. Then, just after seeing these operations set up, Orlov was suddenly despatched to the Black Sea coast, where, he was put in command of OGPU guerrilla troops. He worked in concert with Lavrent Beria, regional OGPU chief in Georgia, who would become, thirteen years later, the boss of the OGPU's reorganised successor, the NKVD.[4] In 1926, now married and with a young child, Orlov's first major posting outside the USSR was to Paris. Here he had the documents of a Soviet diplomat and was part of the official trade delegation, although at only thirty-one his true role was as chief of the 'legal' intelligence *rezidentura* at the embassy in Paris, which was a major centre for Soviet intelligence activity in western Europe.[5] Paris hosted a significant community of White Russian émigrés, which had to be watched, and the city was a terminus for agents coming to the West from central and eastern Europe. In the mid-1930s it was to become a holding and clearing centre for communist volunteers and agents going into Spain at the time of the civil war.[6]

In 1928 Orlov was transferred to Berlin, again as a diplomat, part of the Soviet trade delegation, through which he engaged in legal business dealings with German industry and commerce whilst at the same time managing industrial espionage and spy networks. Orlov's rise in the Soviet intelligence system continued. In the spring of 1931 he was recalled to Moscow, this time to head the Economic Department for Foreign Trade of the OGPU, where he had been an assistant only seven years before. Back at the Moscow Centre Orlov's experience in western Europe was put to good use. The penetration of Soviet spy networks in Germany and Great Britain in particular had led Orlov to argue that Soviet espionage should in future be centred on illegal rather than legal *rezidenturas*. Throughout 1931 Orlov travelled across western Europe consulting with and briefing the heads of the legal *rezidenturas* on the new policy. The illegals needed to be placed and safeguarded and they needed secure communications systems to receive and relay orders and also to report back through the organisation.[7] Radio communications and the passing of coded messages via 'dead drops' were key elements in this innovative and sophisticated intelligence infrastructure.

The Centre kept Orlov on the move throughout the early 1930s. He was sent on a semi-legal three-month foray into the United States, where he was ostensibly engaged in a project to buy American cars, although he may also have been setting up a method for recruiting agents.[8] After this mission he criss-crossed western Europe and was the illegal *rezident* in Paris from July 1933 until April 1934, when he was hailed by a Soviet defector in a Paris street. He covered his tracks, but was withdrawn immediately to become, between July 1934 and October 1935, the illegal *rezident* in London.[9] Here again, a chance meeting with someone who had known him in Vienna necessitated a premature departure, but in his fifteen months based in London he achieved monumental successes. Although the recruitment and running of the five Cambridge spies, Blunt, Philby, Burgess, Maclean and Cairncross, were primarily undertaken by others, it was Orlov's philosophy, theory and management of Soviet espionage and its personnel in these places at this time that ensured the existence and success of the ring.

As a child and as a young man, he had had the opportunity to understand and absorb Jewish, Russian and Soviet culture, and he used this understanding to learn quickly the cultures of the cities and nations where he was posted. Later in his life he recalled the theory behind the targeting of individuals for agent work in the West, particularly in England:

In spite of all the efforts expended by Soviet intelligence officers to help their informants attain promotions in government service, the results were spotty and far from satisfactory. Only in the 1930s did one of the chiefs of the NKVD intelligence hit upon an idea, which solved this particular problem as if by magic. He succeeded because he approached the problem not only as an intelligent man, but as a sociologist as well. This officer took account of the fact that in capitalistic countries lucrative appointments and quick promotion are usually assured to young men who belong to the upper class, especially to sons of political leaders, high government officials, influential members of parliament, etc. To them promotion is almost automatic, and it does not surprise anyone if a young man of this background, fresh from college, passes the civil service examinations with the greatest of ease and is suddenly appointed private secretary to a cabinet member and in a few short years assistant to a member of the government.

Accordingly, in the early 1930s, the NKVD *rezidenturas* concentrated their energy on recruitment of young men from influential families. The political climate of that period was very favorable for such an undertaking, and the young generation was receptive to libertarian theories and to the sublime ideas of making the world safe from the menace of fascism and of abolishing the exploitation of man. This was the main theme on which NKVD *rezidenturas* based their appeal to young men who were tired of a tedious life in the stifling atmosphere of their privileged class. And when the young men reached the stage when their thinking made them ripe for joining the Communist Party, they were told that they could be much more useful to the movement if they stayed away from the Party, concealed their political views and entered the 'revolutionary background'. The idea of joining a 'secret society' held a strong appeal for the young people who dreamed of a better world and of heroic deeds.

A very important part in influencing the young men was played by idealistic young women of various nationalities, who already had a smattering of Marxian theory and who acted as a powerful stimulus, which spurred the young converts to action. Having been brought up first by governesses as sissies and later sent to exclusive private schools, they were charmed by these daring Amazons, and their intellectual associations with them often blossomed into romances, which frequently culminated in marriages. These young men hardly regarded themselves as spies or intelligence agents. They did not want anything for themselves – least of all money. What they wanted was a purpose in life and it seemed to them that they had found it. By their mental make-up and outlook they were reminiscent of the young Russian Decembrists of the previous century, and they brought into Soviet intelligence the true fervor of new converts and the idealism which their intelligence chiefs had lost long ago.

The NKVD intelligence no longer worried about attaining promotions for their charges. These came automatically, and the NKVD chiefs looked forward with great anticipation to seeing some of the new recruits in ambassadorial posts a few years hence.[10]

Although he mentioned no name in his book, Orlov let it be known that he was the 'chief of the NKVD intelligence' who had the idea, inaugurated and developed the policy.[11] His henchmen and protégés, Arnold Deutsch, Ignaty Reif and Theodore Maly, saw to it that the Cambridge ring, recruited and run to his own classic theory, would be the most successful and most damaging to Western interests of all the Soviet intelligence initiatives.[12]

'The Swede' was not in Stockholm when Willie, Ellie and Evelyn Fisher travelled through in 1931, nor was he in Oslo when the family arrived there for Willie to begin more than three years of OGPU work in Norway under the code name FRANK. But the OGPU operations and cover options policies in western Europe had been shaped by Orlov. Using the technique that he had been tested on when he acquired his new passport in Moscow, Willie presented himself in Norway as an English family man, with his Russian wife, a former ballerina, and his little daughter who was now a toddler. He established the family in a ground floor flat, number 18A Damfaret in Golia, a modest district to the east of central Oslo and soon became known as a radio enthusiast.[13] With business as his cover, this urbane Englishman traded in radio components and had a workshop for manufacturing pieces of radio equipment, which he sold to radio amateurs and to specialist concerns in and around Oslo, even overseas. This trade was close to his actual role, which was primarily to establish clandestine radio reception and transmission points to receive radio signals from the Centre and pass the decoded messages to agents and contacts in Norway and beyond.[14] Socially, Willie sought the company of cosmopolitan, international and community-minded families through which he might tap into the socialist and trade union world and then into the overt and covert world of communists and their fellow travellers. This enabled him to install and hide radio equipment in the homes of communists and their sympathisers, and children of Norwegian party members of the time recall having to 'be quiet' when 'Uncle Fisher was in the attic, fixing his radio'.[15] Transmitting was a dangerous option at this stage, but still used, and coded replies were also sent via dead drops or even by post.

Domestically, this was the happiest of times for the Fishers. They consolidated their own unique family life, away from their in-laws, away from the privations of daily life in Moscow and away from the pressing political realities of the Bolshevik Soviet state. Socially, of course, every relationship Willie and his family made had the potential of being exploited for the cause, but each could still be enjoyed for itself. They became friendly with their landlords and neighbours at Damfaret 18B, the Mohrs, who had two young children, Per and Nina, who were just a little older than Evelyn, and the families often partied and picnicked together. Evelyn inherited her parents' love of animals and plants and the Fishers' home was never without pets or flowers. Another of the families they knew, the Engleberts, part Russian, part Norwegian, were florists who had a nursery just outside Oslo. Not only did the Fishers get their flowers from the Engleberts, but also a dog. When the Engleberts' guard dog, a boxer, had a litter from a bull mastiff, they gave a home to the surviving puppy, which grew into a large, daft dog they called 'Grock', after a famous clown of the time.[16] Grock was affectionate towards the family's other pet, a cat, Vashinka, and did not chase the hedgehog which Ellie enticed into the garden with saucers of milk. Ellie also ran ballet classes and this added to the favourable profile that the Fishers enjoyed in the community, for the displays the young ballerinas gave were put on for audiences of parents at the local high school. On one occasion Crown Prince Olav attended one of these events and was photographed with the youngest of the dancers, Evelyn.[17]

There are few declassified documents at all from Willie's file and none from the first eighteen months of his time in Oslo, but there is every likelihood that, as well travelling under the cover of his radio business in Norway, Willie also travelled overseas at this time. OGPU officers needed training and experience in negotiating border controls. It was clearly second nature to Orlov and it was important that his cadre developed these skills. Significantly, the management of passports ('boots', in the Chekist's argot) and cover stories ('legends') was the subject of a witty and anecdotal speech that Willie made to his KGB colleagues on the 'Fiftieth Anniversary of the Great October Socialist Revolution' in 1967.[18] He spoke of one comrade who had to travel on a Persian passport, having no knowledge of Farsi or Arabic; and another posing as a Hungarian who, when faced with an invitation to meet a Hungarian nobleman at a house party, drank himself into oblivion and took to his bed until the guest had left. Willie's earliest missions would have been less exotic, but it is not inconceivable that he was in Denmark in October 1932 as part of a team to monitor Trotsky's visit and to report on individuals who met with Trotsky.[19] Orlov was involved in trade, and the Soviet Union was desperate to catch up with western technology, so Willie could use his cover to visit trade fairs and exhibitions throughout Europe.

Willie's own British passport was a priceless asset and it is likely that his bosses would have wanted his United Kingdom entry and exit tested as soon as possible. Willie's friend Kirill Khenkin has always thought that Willie was in England in the early 1930s, and that he went to England in the company of Orlov on a mission to lure the Russian physicist Pyotr Kapitsa back to the Soviet Union. His evidence for this was from conversations with Willie in the 1940s, when he inferred that Willie 'had been involved in the Kapitsa business', although in the 1960s when Kirill brought up the subject once more, Willie avoided making any further comment and the subject was dropped.[20] If Willie was involved in a plot to inveigle Kapitsa into returning to the Soviet Union, as his remarks to Kirill implied, the theory deserves testing.

Pyotr Leonidovich Kapitsa is regarded by many as the most eminent Russian physicist of the twentieth century. The son of a military engineer, he was born in Kronstadt in 1894 and in 1912 was admitted to the Petrograd Polytechnic Institute. His studies were interrupted by the First World War, during which he saw action as an ambulance driver on the Polish front, but he returned to Petrograd in

1916 to continue his education. He graduated in 1919 and remained at the institute as a teacher. He was charming, popular and highly regarded by friends and colleagues. In the influenza epidemic which swept the world after the First World War, the young scientist lost not only his father but also his wife and two young children. In 1921 the Soviet Union was sending a mission to renew relations with academic institutions in the West and to purchase scientific instruments and supplies. A. F. Ioffe, his departmental head, thought that a trip overseas away from the scene of his loss would be good for him and arranged for him to join the delegation.

The mission was a success in all respects and the delegation leaders, recognising that Kapitsa could gain useful experience and knowledge in the West, looked for opportunities for their colleague to stay in England. The young Russian physicist was also popular with his hosts and Ioffe, still sensing that time away from Russia would help assuage Kapitsa's grief, introduced him to Ernest Rutherford at Cambridge University. Rutherford was impressed and gave Kapitsa a research post at the Cavendish Laboratory. Kapitsa thrived in this environment, demonstrating such originality and panache in his research that Rutherford invited him to stay. His output and achievements were prodigious. He found methods for obtaining strong magnetic fields and techniques for researching the magnetic properties of metals. Then he turned his attention to low temperature research and devised apparatus for liquefying hydrogen and helium.[21] At the same time he was being awarded scholarships, fellowships, honours and promotions: in 1923 he received a three-year Clerk Maxwell scholarship; in 1924 he became assistant director of magnetic research at the Cavendish Laboratory and in 1925 he became a fellow of the Royal Society. In 1926 he remarried. His bride was Russian, Anna Krylova, daughter of Aleksei Krylov, the mathematician who had led the delegation to the UK in 1921.[22] They had two sons, Sergei and Andrei, and the family moved into a new home, 173 Huntingdon Road, Cambridge, a house which actually became known as Kapitsa House, retaining that name (and spelling) to this day and at which, from the early 1930s, visiting Russian scholars have stayed.

Kapitsa's successes were the foundation for Rutherford's application to the Royal Society to build a laboratory specifically for magnetic and low temperature research, and the Royal Society Mond Laboratory was opened in 1933. Professionalism and gregariousness matched Kapitsa's intellectual eminence. Each of these was evident at his research seminar, The Kapitsa Club, which met informally at Trinity College on Tuesdays and drew physicists from across the world to speak on and debate research findings. It was here, for example, that James Chadwick presented his discovery of the neutron and John Cockroft his research on accelerating charged particles.

In 1934 Kapitsa went to the Soviet Union and was prevented from returning to the United Kingdom. Was he enticed to go back? (Indeed, at this time, as Stalin was consolidating his power, there was a policy of enticing artists to return to their homeland. The film director Sergei Eisenstein was one target of this policy.)[23] And did Willie Fisher play a part in that enticement? Kapitsa, a believer in free scientific work and in international collaboration, was Russian through and through but he was also at home in England. C. P. Snow was to write of him:

> Peter Kapitsa Rutherford's favourite pupil, contrived to be in good grace with the Soviet authorities and at the same time a star of the Cavendish. He had a touch of genius: also in those days, before life sobered him, he had a touch of the inspired Russian clown. He loved his own country, but he distinctly enjoyed backing both horses, working in Cambridge and taking his holidays in the Caucasus. He once asked a friend of mine if a foreigner could become an English peer; we strongly suspected that his ideal career would see him established simultaneously in the Soviet Academy of Sciences and as Rutherford's successor in the House of Lords.[24]

But as Kapitsa holidayed annually in Russia, why should Willie have to lure him to go there? From their conversations, Kirill inferred that Willie, who had had a technical and scientific education himself, found employment in a laboratory at Cambridge, or contrived to be at meetings with Kapitsa, and introduced himself as an Englishman who had lived and worked in the Soviet Union. Willie's task, surmised Kirill, was to tell Kapitsa that life and scientific work in the Soviet Union were fine.[25] But there was no need to do this for Kapitsa knew full well what life and work in the Soviet Union were like, and he was quite happy researching in Cambridge and travelling to the Soviet Union when he wanted to. Nevertheless, there does seem to have been a plot to ensure that Kapitsa returned to Russia and stayed permanently. In July 1931, the peripatetic Ioffe was with the Soviet delegation to the Second International Congress of the History of

Science and Technology, being held in London. It has been claimed that the Old Bolshevik Nikolai Bukharin, the former leading theorist of the party, was also with the delegation, allegedly with secret orders direct from Stalin to persuade Kapitsa to return permanently to the USSR.[26] It is conceivable, if the Kirill Khenkin theory is sound, that this was an occasion when a chance meeting with Willie Fisher, another 'Russo-English scientist', could have been contrived. But according to Dmitry Tarasov, Willie had no British passport until August 1931, a month after the conference, and did not leave Moscow for his first mission until September.[27] Not only that, he was untried and untested in overseas work and is unlikely to have been have been risked at such an early stage.[28]

However, in 1934 Stalin did achieve his objective. Kapitsa made a 'routine visit' from Cambridge to Moscow, together with his wife. (This 'routine visit' has also been described as 'participating in a congress of physicists', his 'usual holiday', a 'holiday' and 'a scientific conference'.[29] In fact, it was both holiday and conference.) As summer moved into autumn, Anna returned to Cambridge to Sergei and Andrei, who were being looked after by her mother. When the conference came to an end, Pyotr Kapitsa was simply not allowed to return to the United Kingdom. It is hard to believe that Willie Fisher could have had any major operational role in this, assuming that he was working in Norway and that he was on his first mission. But there is another perspective. It is certainly a requirement of anyone involved in espionage that they be discreet and circumspect with the truth, and for Willie this discretion and circumspection was a matter of honour. He makes a point of it in the first paragraph of his own short autobiography:

> Considering the nature of my profession, I think that it is understandable that some parts of my biography will be left out ... but even though there must inevitably be some mystery about my life it does not mean that the following facts are false in any way. I prefer not to tell everything, rather than to tell lies.[30]

Rather than lie to his friend, he would have been evasive with the truth. As is clear, for this particular Russian vacation, Pyotr and Anna Kapitsa took a long holiday together, leaving their sons at home in Cambridge. They travelled by ship to Norway and then by car through Norway and Finland, arriving in Leningrad at the beginning of September.[31] From his Oslo base, Willie might have had orders simply to monitor the Kapitsas' journey, checking their departure from the United Kingdom, confirming their arrival in Norway, and reporting dates and times of their stops on the journey. He might even have posed as a British engineer or physicist journeying to the Soviet conference. Whatever he may have said to Kirill, he avoided telling him a lie.

Whether or not Willie Fisher was involved in 'the Kapitsa business' at this stage, 1934 was a tense and busy year for him. His specific radio communications mission continued, but his friends and neighbours in Golia had become a little suspicious. How could Mr Fisher enjoy such a good lifestyle whilst he seemed to make so little money from his radio business? 'There's something not quite right about him,' one of them said.[32] Willie had also attracted the attention of a Norwegian military officer, Major Klingenberg, who was curious at the amount of interest in Norwegian defence installations and technology that this Mr Fisher was showing.[33] The Fishers stayed in touch with the Mohrs and other friends in Golia, but they left Damfaret 18A and moved to fashionable Bygdøy, the small peninsula jutting into the Oslo fjord where the Norwegian Maritime Museum and elite estates of the Norwegian well-to-do were to be found. Whilst Evelyn enjoyed the beaches and flowers of Bygdøy, visits from her friends from Golia and the company of new playmates, her father continued his radio work at home and at the facilities he had prepared elsewhere in Oslo and beyond, but his mission was coming to its end.

The declassified messages between KARL, the Oslo *rezident* and Willie's senior officer, and the Centre from 1934 concentrate on what seem to be mundane matters such as organising the payments into Willie's bank account so that they would look like payments from occasional work, rather than a sinecure. But the move to Bygdøy showed even more clearly that the Fishers were living beyond their visible means and this, together with the attentions of Major Klingenberg, led to the last declassified memo from Willie's time in Norway. Dated 16 December 1934, it informed KARL that the Centre wanted their man back in Moscow no later than the beginning of January 1935, their pretext being that the Norwegian authorities were unhappy with Willie's work permit.[34] The Fishers bade farewell to their friends, saying that they were returning to England. The Mohrs assumed that they would take the journey by sea from Bergen, but

Willie surprised them by saying that they would take shorter sea crossings to Denmark and then, after an overland rail journey south, across the English Channel from Calais to Dover. 'I don't travel well by sea,' Willie told them.[35] So the Fishers departed and, complying with the Centre's orders, travelled through Germany to arrive back in the Soviet Union at the very end of December 1934.

8

HOME AGAIN – MOSCOW AND LONDON

During Willie Fisher's absence abroad, the organs had metamorphosed once more. When Feliks Dzerzhinsky died in 1926, control of the OGPU passed to Vyacheslav Menzhinsky, the first deputy chairman. Whilst Dzerzhinsky had been cast in the same mould as Stalin and was a close ally in his bid for power in the mid-1920s, Menzhinsky was a less imposing figure, more a cultured administrator than a ruthless chieftain. His health was not strong either, and for all these reasons he tended simply to follow Stalin's orders and requirements. Menzhinsky's death in 1934 led to two changes. First, leadership passed to Genrikh Yagoda, formerly second deputy to Dzerzhinsky, a harder, more vicious and more operationally experienced figure than Menzhinsky. Next, the organisation Yagoda headed was called the *Narodnyi Kommissariat Vnutrennikh Del* – the People's Commissariat for Internal Affairs, the NKVD, which from July 1934 included the administration of all state security.

For the first few months of 1935, Willie was back at the Lubyanka being debriefed following his Norway posting, and in the Chekists' jargon he was 'parked' in an internal service department, the training department in his case, until the time came for his next posting abroad.[1] Meanwhile, there were significant happenings in his family life. It was a bitterly cold winter and his father had found it difficult to cope with Russian winters after his time in England's kinder climate. With lungs weakened by years of smoking, Heinrich did not survive the pneumonia he contracted in 1935 and died peacefully in the early spring. Willie was devastated.

As ever, he showed no emotion. To do so would show weakness, and to weaken in response to the loss of his father in particular would be tantamount to a betrayal of his father's memory. His father was disciplined and had been his guide and political mentor, the yardstick against which he could measure his own political knowledge and discipline. Heinrich Fischer was the archetypal worker-revolutionary, part of the armed struggle. He had lived Marxism-Leninism and he had the foundations of experience and knowledge on which to base a continual and living analysis of the Soviet Union's political and economic development. With his father gone, there was no one from whom Willie could now learn in this way. Although his paternal blood link to the pre-revolutionary period had now gone, he knew that some of the techniques and language that he now used in his own daily work had been used by his father thirty and forty years before. *Konspiratsiya* (security, cover, 'need to know' and tradecraft)[2] had been second nature to his father. From him, Willie knew the importance of travel documents and passports, and how to get them, and he treasured 'the old man's' stories of the methods of smuggling literature and arms. He had also learned from him the wiles and tricks of political leaders and departmental bosses and how to deal with them. He had learned music from him, as well as how to cook and the importance of languages. Above all, his father had taught him how to survive. Heinrich had left him a great legacy, and it was one that Willie would honour. His favourite photograph of his father was taken in Russia in the early 1930s, the now white-haired worker scholar looking up from his writing, alert and magisterial. Willie was in Moscow when the second edition of his father's memoirs was published in Moscow shortly after his death.

Heinrich had been baptised into the Lutheran Church, in Yaroslavl in 1871, but his funeral was a secular affair, a cremation. The day was more than a little difficult for Willie and Ellie as Evelyn had caught scarlet fever on her journey back to Moscow. She was quite ill and had been taken to hospital. But Ellie's extended family was supportive. Her mother Kapitolina, now into her sixties, was still fit and active. In the days after Heinrich's death, the support Willie, Ellie, Evelyn and Lyubov received from Ellie's siblings and mother was to become important in the lives of all of them and to their future. The two mothers-in-law, both now widows, liked each other and got on well together and their friendship developed. Kapitolina lived with her children, now as often as not with Ellie and Willie, who were settling into a communal apartment in Vtoroi Lavrsky Lane in Moscow's Trotsky district, and visited Lyubov. Willie's own relationship with his mother when she was widowed remained no more than proper. 'There was no relationship,' remembered Evelyn. But for Evelyn herself, the strongest memory of this time was of her friendship that developed with her cousin Lidiya, her uncle Boris's daughter. As old ladies they still referred to each other as sisters, which they had felt themselves to be since childhood. They stayed together at Boris's or Willie's apartment and in the summer were able to go to Lyubov's dacha. The government had presented the dacha and its small plot of land to Heinrich and Lyubov, as Old Bolsheviks, a few years before.[3] It was 13 miles or so north-west of Moscow and reached by taking the train from the Yaroslavl station, alighting at Chelyuskin and then turning into Kuibyshev Street from Starye Bolshevik Avenue.

Parked at the Centre, less than eight years after his own induction, Willie found himself training a new generation of rookies, one of whom was Kitty Harris.[4] Like Willie, Kitty was from a cosmopolitan background and took socialism learned in a Western culture into the service of the Soviet Union. Her parents were Russian Jews who had emigrated to the United Kingdom in the late 1880s, and Kitty was born in London at the turn of the century. Her father, Nathan, was converted to socialism in England but, when Kitty was eight, the family emigrated once more, to Canada, and Kitty was brought up as a Canadian in Winnipeg. At twelve she was working in a cigarette factory and at seventeen she was a garment worker. A trade unionist from the start, Kitty's union membership and political commitment led first to Workers' Party membership and then, as part of a pattern in the Western world, the WP became the Communist Party of Canada. Kitty's party work took her to the United States and thence to the office of Earl Browder, National Secretary of the Communist Party of the United States of America. Browder married Kitty in the mid-1920s[5] and, irritated by squabbles in the upper echelons of the American party, grabbed an opportunity to take on international trade union work in China. With Kitty he travelled via Moscow to Shanghai, where Kitty was talent-spotted by the Soviets and, after a series of missions for the organs, was eventually brought back to Moscow for specialist agent training.

Willie was a hard taskmaster. Although Kitty was an able linguist and showed some skill in tradecraft, the theory and much of the practice of other demands on the agent – photography and radio work – seemed quite beyond her. Her fumblings with the camera wasted film and hundreds of prints. She used the wrong exposures; on occasion she even forgot to take the lens cap off the camera. Called in to see Willie, she wept with frustration. Willie painstakingly showed Kitty where and why the mistakes were occurring and was absolutely clear about what she should do. Invoking Rousseau, he told her, 'Real education comes less from knowing the rules than from doing the exercises. Go and do more exercises.'[6] His own command of his scientific and technical knowledge and his self-discipline made it difficult for him to empathise with his pupils. At home, Lidiya would take advantage of this aspect of his character.

'Uncle Willie,' she would say, coming to him coyly with some mathematics homework, 'I don't understand this. Will you show me how to do it?', whereupon he would put down whatever he was doing and carefully explain the formula.

'You see?' he would ask.

'No. I still don't understand it.'

Again Willie would take Lidiya through the theory of the numbers and symbols, showing her how to solve the problem, and Lidiya, knowing precisely how far she could stretch her uncle's patience, would feign her lack of understanding until the moment he was about to explode. At that point she would run away laughing, 'I knew how to do it all the time!'[7]

It was with women and children that Willie was an impatient teacher. He could not hector or bully them like he could men and, as he had not had a sister, he had not observed how his father might have related to a daughter. It was his male pupils who were to record their admiration of Willie as a teacher, mentor and comrade. It is not known what Kitty thought of Willie, but he made an important contribution to her preparation for work in the field. Although Kitty was competent in sending and receiving the Morse code and could strip down and reassemble a radio set, she was unable to comprehend the basic radio theory needed, for example, to assess the aerial lengths required in different locations and situations. At first Willie was baffled, but then he realised that Kitty had no comprehension of simple arithmetic.[8] Before she could go a step further, she had to stop for remedial arithmetic lessons, and her radio theory continued only after she had mastered multiplication (including multiplication tables, which she had never learned in her fragmented primary education), division and logarithms.

Willie's next posting came in the summer of 1935 and again Ellie and Evelyn travelled with him. The Centre may well have wanted to send Willie abroad again earlier, but Evelyn's illness affected their plans. A family man had good cover. This time the mission was to England, where Aleksandr Orlov was the NKVD's illegal *resident* in London. Again the family travelled under their own names with Willie's British passport, and arrived first in the Belgian ferry port of Ostend, where they stayed for a whilst.[9] A stay in Ostend, it was reasoned, would give an opportunity to check that Evelyn, now an inquisitive five year old, was reacclimatised to life in the West before her father's real work started. Orlov, who had himself arrived in England via Ostend and Harwich barely a year before, was in a position to bring Willie over for initial reconnaissance before the family arrived to live a little whilst later. Yet again the declassified documents cover only a short period of Willie's time in England, from 14 February 1936, more than eight months after his posting to the United Kingdom began, so more speculation is required to detect the primary objective of the mission. Once more, the Kapitsa story may hold a key.

Pyotr Kapitsa had been in Moscow since the autumn of 1934, prevented from returning to his wife, children, work, colleagues and laboratory in Cambridge. Another Russian physicist, Georgy Gamov, had refused to return to the Soviet Union after the 7th Solvay Conference in Brussels in October 1933, and Stalin's revenge, paranoia and obsessive ideas about the politicisation of science was ensuring Kapitsa's captivity in his own land. In Britain, Ernest Rutherford expressed his concern to the Soviet ambassador Ivan Maisky, warning of the danger to scientific relations between the two countries. Maisky replied by explaining the necessary contribution of scientific workers to the First and Second Five-Year Plans: '[Kapitsa] has now been offered highly responsible work in his particular field in the Soviet Union, which will enable him to develop fully his abilities as a scientist and a citizen of his country.'[10]

Another Soviet government source was quoted as saying, 'We do not believe that Kapitsa, once he got back to Cambridge, would ever want to come back here, or anyhow if he didn't we couldn't compel him. We badly need our good scientists just now. Why not send us a few good English scientists?'[11]

Kapitsa himself was angry, bereft and bitter. For him, science was utterly apolitical and he simply wanted to get on with his work and to be able to travel freely between Russia and England. He seethed to a friend that he felt like a raped woman who would have given herself for love.[12] At the same time, he corresponded determinedly with friends and colleagues, but particularly with his wife Anna and their two sons, Sergei and Andrei, at the family home in Cambridge. To his wife, he poured out his innermost thoughts and feelings. He was aghast at the management of science that prevailed in the Soviet Union, yet he still professed himself a socialist. He was humiliated by the squashing of originality in research and development in favour of rushed copying of Western hardware and techniques. He raged at the bureaucracy that assumed disloyalty on the part of everyone and held up the simplest of requests. 'What in England is done by a telephone call, here requires hundreds of papers.'[13] But after the best part of a year had passed, Pyotr Kapitsa began to accept the inevitable. His research energies were at their peak and he was doing nothing, so he finally agreed to take on the directorship of the new Moscow Institute for Physical Problems.[14] Despite the tense Anglo-Soviet relations (recently aggravated by the Metro-Vickers affair of 1933, when six British engineers working for the electrical company in Moscow were arrested, charged and tried for spying), negotiations began for Kapitsa's equipment in the Mond Laboratory, for creating very high magnetic fields and very low temperatures, to be purchased, packed and shipped to Moscow. On the British side, Cambridge University conducted the negotiations; for the Soviets, it was a governmental, not an academic, matter. In the early autumn of 1935 a sum of £30,000 was agreed by the university for the sale of Kapitsa's equipment to the new Moscow Institute.

There are no declassified documents to prove Willie Fisher's role in the shipping of the equipment, but it does seem more likely that it was this phase of the Soviets' Kapitsa operation that Willie took a major part in, rather than a plot in 1934 to trap the physicist in Moscow. Willie's genuine interest, knowledge and, at the Centre, day-to-day work in technology, mathematics and science equipped him to deal authoritatively with technical apparatus. His Russo-British credentials and his awareness of the two cultures were second to none in the service. There is other circumstantial evidence to indicate Willie's work at this time. Based initially in Ostend, Willie would be travelling into England via Harwich. The Harwich–London and Harwich–Cambridge journeys were quite short and he would be able to shuttle, watching the negotiators and the laboratory itself. London, Harwich and Ipswich too were the nearest ports to Cambridge and the most likely ports from which the laboratory equipment was shipped. The Soviets ensured that the machinery was split into three loads shipping from separate ports to guard against seizure should the British government get involved and try to stop the sale.[15]

The Fishers moved from Ostend to London in the autumn of 1935 and took up residence at 56 Queensway, W2. It was a three-storey dwelling of blackened yellow brick, on the corner of Inverness Place, and almost opposite the Bayswater Underground station on the Circle and District lines. The landlady had the ground floor, accessed by a door in Inverness Place, and the Fishers entered their first and second floor flat from a door directly on the bevelled corner of the building. 'There was a door where the corner should have been,' remembered Evelyn. Their kitchen and living room were on the first floor and the two bedrooms on the second floor. Evelyn liked it here. Just over Bayswater Road to the south were Kensington Gardens, the Serpentine and Hyde Park, and it was here that the Fishers walked their dog, Mickey, and fed the swans. Along Queensway in the opposite direction was the dome of Whiteley's department store. Six-year-old Evelyn loved Whiteley's, particularly at Christmas time, when it was brightly lit and decorated and her father took her to visit Santa Claus. From an operational point of view, 56 Queensway was quite close to the Soviet embassy at 5 Kensington Palace Gardens, but the NKVD was quite confident that Willie could not be tainted by anything that was illegal. He was a British subject legally married to Ellie and carried a British passport in his own name. There had also been a period of four years for the NKVD to detect any British counter-intelligence surveillance of Willie and had found none.

Meanwhile, Sergei and Andrei Kapitsa were seven and five years old. Until Pyotr's detention in the previous year, the Kapitsas had spent all their family life in England and Sergei was now at a primary school in Cambridge. Anna was at a loss as to what to do for the best when Pyotr failed to return. His letters painted a bleak picture about his working life in Moscow, but he was less forthcoming about other aspects of Russia in the mid-1930s. Anna wanted to know about health care and schools for her small sons. Kirill Khenkin interpreted Willie's veiled remarks as an indication that he had actually worked at Cambridge and encouraged Pyotr Kapitsa to return to the Soviet Union*, but a more likely role given Willie's posting in 1935 was, as well as ensuring that the laboratory could be transported from Cambridge and reassembled in Moscow, overseeing the return of Anna Kapitsa and the children. It was certainly in the interests of the Soviet authorities that the family was together in Russia, for the physicist was in despair and his research was at a standstill.[16] The Soviets eventually achieved their goal and the family was reunited in Moscow in January 1936.**

During this time, Willie Fisher's work was being overseen by both the legal *rezident* at the Soviet embassy in London and the illegal *rezident*, Aleksandr Orlov. On 10 October 1935 Orlov received a message from the Centre, 'Lotti must leave for the south.' It was his signal to abandon London immediately and return to Moscow.[17] Orlov had been spotted again, in the very London rooming house where he was renting a bed-sitter in the guise of an American company director and refrigerator salesman with the name William Goldin. A widely travelled, multi-tasked, gregarious intelligence officer, however gifted, is always vulnerable, and this time Orlov had been greeted by his old English teacher from Vienna. The man would have known that Orlov was not an American, even that he was actually a Soviet citizen, for Orlov had been travelling on a Soviet passport when he was in Vienna at the time they knew each other previously. Orlov left his lodgings immediately, booked into a hotel and alerted the Centre via the usual London illegal *rezidentura* link through Copenhagen. The moment his orders arrived, he left London and was back in Moscow by 29 October.

Willie was kept in London, perhaps still involved in the later stages of the Kapitsa affair, but his illegal control passed to the extraordinary Arnold Deutsch, the NKVD case officer whose intellectual and cultural grasp exceeded that of all his contemporaries. Codenamed STEFAN, the Czech-born Deutsch moved to Austria with his parents in 1908, when he was four years old. He was a clever child and his crowning academic achievement was the award of a PhD with distinction by the

---

* See pages 74–7.

** The full details of this episode are still classified, but apart from the family letters, some of which have been published in Russia, there are other illuminating observations. Sergei Kapitsa, now like his father before him a famous scientist, recalls something of his dual cultured home life as a child: 'I knew Russian right from the beginning of course, because we always spoke Russian in our family [but] when we did something naughty and things were running into deep water, my mother switched over into English. That [meant] we were in trouble!' (http://www.pbs.org/redfiles/rao/catalogues/trans/trac/trac_kapi_1.html)

University of Vienna in July 1928 when he was just twenty-four.[18] His thesis was on the chemistry of silver salts, but his university studies also encompassed physics, philosophy and psychology.[19] Deutsch was twenty when he joined the Austrian Communist Party and, like many Jews and Christians of the period, jettisoned his religious faith in favour of communism. Just after the award of his PhD, he married and he and his wife, Fini Pavlovna, became politically active.

As Deutsch began his secret party work in Vienna, he joined the German psychologist Wilhelm Reich's sexual politics movement, which was exploring human sexual behaviour through linking the theories of Freud and Marx. Reich reasoned that sexual repression mirrored political oppression.[20] Deutsch too made the connection and argued that the result would be fascism. Not only did the work with Reich give excellent cover for Deutsch (Reich was establishing birth control clinics in Vienna, for example), it also provided him with insights that would inform his future work in the Foreign Department of the NKVD. Like Earl Browder and Kitty Harris, Arnold and Fini Deutsch shared political commitment and service for Soviet intelligence. In 1928 Deutsch was with a party delegation to Moscow and assigned underground Comintern work when he returned to Vienna. In 1932 he was summoned to Moscow and prepared for an assignment to Greece, Palestine and Syria. A year later he was in France working on 'technical tasks', including photography, and was also under orders to make contact with fishermen on the French coast with a view to developing a network of radio links via fishing boats, for use in time of war. It is certainly possible that this was an element of the work that Willie Fisher himself was doing out of Oslo between 1931 and early 1934, when there is a gap in his record.[21]

Meanwhile in February 1934, Deutsch was posted to England. He worked first for the acting NKVD illegal *rezident* Ignaty Reif until June 1934 and then for SCHWED (Orlov) until August 1935. At this point Deutsch was recalled to Moscow for leave and training, and it was also the time that Willie started work for Orlov in England. When Deutsch returned to London in November 1935, it was as *rezident* and as Willie's boss.[22] The contact between Deutsch and Fisher was really little more than a footnote in both their careers, certainly in the declassified documents, the oral history of Soviet espionage and the Chekists' mythology. Deutsch's contribution remains very much his role in the recruitment of the Cambridge Five. He had known Edith Tudor Hart in Vienna and recruited her; she in turn recruited Kim Philby.[23] Tudor

Hart was one of those 'daring Amazons' referred to by Orlov in his *Handbook*. Although Orlov was the officer who developed the theory behind the recruitment of the Cambridge Five,[24] Deutsch is believed to have been the instigator of that theory.

The recruitment of the Cambridge Five was masterful. Four of them – Philby, Guy Burgess, Anthony Blunt and Donald Maclean – were of that upper-middle-class, public-school-educated group that saw office and influence in British society as their right and responsibility. The Scot, John Cairncross, was brilliant intellectually. They were all pessimistic about Britain's will to defeat unemployment and fascism and all attracted to Communist Party membership. Deutsch's work with Reich had convinced him of the crucial relationship between sex, politics and youthful idealism, and his assessment of the Five's sexual preferences and psychology suggested to him that they could channel these and be ideal covert contributors to the Soviet cause. Blunt was a homosexual aesthete, Philby was a promiscuous heterosexual and Maclean was bisexual. Cairncross was heterosexual and a libertarian. His history thesis, *When Polygamy Was Made a Sin*, quoted George Bernard Shaw: 'Women will always prefer a ten per cent share of a first-rate man to sole ownership of a mediocre man.' Cairncross regarded himself as one of the ten-per-centers.[25] Burgess was a flamboyant and predatory homosexual. His recruitment would seem to have posed the greatest risk, yet Deutsch's understanding of Burgess's psychology, the psychology of those who mixed and worked with him, and the social psychology of the time, made Burgess one of his most useful recruits. Deutsch's own cover as a postgraduate student at London University gave him an entrée to English academic culture, and Willie's journeys to and from Cambridge would have given him opportunities for observation and the delivery and collection of signs and messages.*

Willie's own sexual psychology was mundane. He was a much more restrained character than any of the Cambridge Five, and a declassified report from STEFAN to the Centre dated 14 February 1936 included some observations of his charge. There were six points in the message and three of them were of a personal nature. The correspondence, said STEFAN, included letters for Lyubov and Kapitolina, and 'the Party subscriptions due for himself and for his mother'. STEFAN

---

* The KGB Veterans CD-ROM does not link Fisher with the Cambridge Five explicitly, but it does include pictures of Burgess, Maclean and Philby in the gallery of officers and agents associated with him.

also noted that Willie was asking questions about money. KARL had also referred to money issues when Willie was in Norway. Money, it seems, was a never-failing concern for Willie, and recalls his father's interest in financial matters. Heinrich had kept scrupulous records of his earnings in Newcastle, as well as noting in generic terms the cost of grammar school and university education. What makes Deutsch's note significant, however, is that he suspected that this time it was '[Fisher's] wife' who was bringing up the matter.[26]

The Fishers left Queensway early in 1936 and moved to a much more modern residence, a flat in the new Rivermead Court in Fulham's Ranelagh Gardens close to the exclusive Hurlingham Club which at that time was England's premier polo club, as well the most fashionable private club for tennis, cricket and croquet. Like the earlier residence, it was close to bus and rail routes; in fact because the nearest station was Putney Bridge, Evelyn remembered the flat as being in Putney, and whilst she enjoyed stepping up from the river to the flats, the goldfish in the tiny raised pond, the spring flowers and crocuses in the communal garden and going to a local nursery, her mother and father were re-establishing themselves once more.[27] Willie continued as an Englishman under his own name and made Ellie out to be a Pole. His cover was as an artist, but for the Centre he was a radio operator for the illegal *rezidentura*. The receiver was constructed by the middle of February and the messages were being passed on from 1 March. However, this job lasted barely three months for, with no apparent reason, 19 May 1936 found the family back in Moscow and Willie parked once more.

The family returned to their apartment on Vtoroi Lavrsky Lane.[28] Evelyn went to 'The English School' in Moscow until her American teacher left the country and the school closed, and her mother found work as a harpist in a children's theatre.[29] After her return from London as a six-year-old, Evelyn Fisher would not travel out of the Soviet Union again until she was well into her thirties. Her father was presented with his NKVD lieutenant's epaulettes on 19 November 1936, which no doubt coincided with his promotion to head of the training school for illegal radio operators.[30] Here he encountered Kitty Harris once more. She had been referred by the Centre for radio retraining, but had never passed out as a fully fledged NKVD radio operator. She qualified for radio operation only in emergencies and did get posted to western Europe for agent duties again. When she arrived in Paris in 1937, she received a letter from Willie, a book, some notes and a gift: an electric plug from the radio training room. From a distance he revealed something of his sense of humour and bashful chivalry, and showed that there were no hard feelings. But it was another circumstance in 1937 that was to have a much more significant impact on Willie's life: Rudolf Ivanovich Abel was appointed to radio training duties in Lieutenant Fisher's section.

The two men hit it off immediately and their service comradeship developed into a close friendship. They were an unlikely pair. In his mid-thirties Willie was already balding. He remained reserved and introverted. Although nearly 6ft tall, he seemed almost embarrassed by his height and walked with a stoop, coming across to his students as a scholar rather than as an NKVD man of action. He succumbed easily to colds, which inevitably led to sinusitis, and for much of each winter his daily tasks would be punctuated by the dabbing of his nose with his supply of handkerchiefs. By contrast, Rudolf was an extrovert. He had blond hair and striking good looks, and was physically fit and confident. Rudolf commanded attention by his very presence and was good in groups. Willie, on the other hand, tended to find that people were drawn to him as individuals. Their personalities were complementary and they laughed at the same things. Rudolf respected Willie's intellect and learning, which Willie was only too happy to share. There were other elements in Willie's regard for Rudolf. Willie certainly enjoyed good, adult male company, which Rudolf provided, but even more, Rudolf was only eighteen months older than Henry would have been, and to some extent he replaced Willie's lost older brother. Moreover, Rudolf was a Latvian, a Lett. The Letts, often visiting seamen, had been Heinrich's staunchest Russian-speaking comrades during the years on the Tyne. It is likely that the Russian language spoken by visitors to the Fishers' Tyneside home when Willie was a child was actually spoken by Letts, and the boy knew that his father liked and trusted Letts. Willie, it was said, spoke Russian with a Lettish accent.

Rudolf Abel had been born in the Latvian capital, Riga, on 23 September 1900, the son of a chimneysweep.[31] He had left school at fourteen and gone to work as a delivery boy, which took him to the quayside a great deal and occasionally by sea to Petrograd. In 1915 he decided to remain in Petrograd and started attending evening classes to improve his education. In 1917 he joined the Russian navy and aligned himself with a Red faction, becoming a Red Guard early in the

Revolution.[32] At first he was a stoker on minelayers and minesweepers in the Northern Fleet, and continued on the minesweeping of inland waterways during the civil war, but his potential was noted by his officers and he was sent for radio training. Within months he was commanding radio units in the Soviet Arctic. In 1926 (whilst Willie was doing his Red Army service), Rudolf was delegated as part of the naval attaché's section to radio work in the Soviet consulate in Shanghai, and a year later was recruited into the OGPU. Rudolf Abel and Willie Fisher became Chekists in the same year, although Rudolf had become a married man two years before Willie, when he married the Russian Aleksandra Antonovna Stokalich in 1925. Aleksandra was with Rudolf in Shanghai and remained with him during his first OGPU posting as an INO cipher clerk at the Soviet embassy in Peking. Here they stayed until the Soviets and the Chinese broke off diplomatic relations in 1929. Rudolf's file then merely says that he was 'abroad' until 1936. The file also shows he spoke German, English and French as well as Russian, although publicly he only spoke Russian.[33] The implication is that he continued as a cipher clerk somewhere in SCHWED's territory during the early 1930s.

Not only did Willie and Rudolf get on well, but so did their families and they spent a good deal of time together in the summer of 1937. Willie's lack of ease with small children was compensated for by the Abels, who were to have no children of their own. 'Uncle Rudolf was calm, happy and good with children,' remembered Evelyn.[34] An ability to relate so well to children was another attribute of the deceased Henry. Having Rudolf around when Evelyn and Lidiya were on their holidays meant that Willie was more relaxed, some more of his guilt was assuaged and everyone was happy. Domestically and at the training school, 1937 was a good year for Willie and Rudolf, but 1938 was to prove very different.

9

THE GREAT PURGE

It could be said that Stalin hit the Fishers first, rather than the Abels. Heinrich's departure from political activity in 1924 coincided with the rise of Stalin after Lenin's death, and when Stalin made his move for total domination of the Party and the country in the mid-1930s, Lyubov lost her job as social secretary when the Society of Old Bolsheviks was wound up. The murder of the Leningrad Party boss, Sergei Kirov, in December 1934 had eliminated a senior Bolshevik whose popularity at the 17th Party Congress earlier in the year had so threatened and enraged Stalin, once Kirov's patron. After Kirov's death, Stalin manoeuvred his secret and triumphant attack on the Leninists whilst at the same time invoking the sanctity of Lenin's memory, so finally bending the party to his will. Lyubov had only recently lost her husband, but widowhood, departure from the Kremlin and particularly her poor health may have spared her from imprisonment and saved her life. She was out of sight and out of mind during the frenetic power struggle, although Willie may have harboured concerns that his mother's record would be held against him and this too would have deepened the rift between them.

But it was the Abels who suffered more harshly once the Great Purge began. A conspiracy led by Trotsky, Zinoviev and Kamenev had infected the party throughout the land, it was alleged.[1] Rudolf's older brother Waldemar had risen in the party hierarchy and was a commissar in the Baltic shipyards when he was arrested on 10 December 1937 and charged with involvement in a coup against the state. The case moved swiftly to trial and a guilty verdict was delivered on 11 January 1938. Seven days later Waldemar and 216 others were shot and buried in a mass grave in Leningrad. Rudolf Abel was immediately investigated. His record showed that his wife was from an upper-middle-class family, for his father-in-law had been a landowner during the time of the Tsar. The ink of the paragraph stating that his brother had been executed for treason was barely dry when Rudolf was called in by his department head and dismissed from the service.[2]

Willie's dismissal came right at the end of the year. He arrived for work on the morning of 31 December 1938 to be told that his services were no longer required and that he should leave immediately. He was given no reason, but no doubt assumed that his birth overseas and his father's forty-year association with Leninists were the incriminating factors. He would also have wondered about his contact with other intelligence officers, not just Rudolf, but also his old boss Aleksandr Orlov.

After departing London in the autumn of 1935 and leaving Willie in the capable hands of Arnold Deutsch, SCHWED continued to oversee the work of the Cambridge spies and to maintain an influential role at the Lubyanka.[3] In the spring and early summer of 1936, after Willie had arrived back in Moscow and was training radio operators at the Centre, Orlov was also at the training centre, teaching recruits the techniques of intelligence and counter-intelligence and preparing a textbook from his lecture notes. The late summer and early autumn of 1936 was a busy period for him. In August he was chosen as one of the senior NKVD 'observers' at the show trial of Kamenev and Zinoviev. In order to watch the defendants and their reactions more closely, he chose to sit in the courtroom itself rather than in the special lounge overlooking the proceedings, which had been reserved for the NKVD's monitors. But he had little time to reflect on or analyse his observations, for within days he was posted to Spain to be the covert NKVD chief there on a mission which had political intelligence, police and military objectives. He would be responsible for creating and maintaining an intelligence service for the beleaguered Spanish Republican government and for training international communist guerrilla troops. In Spain, Orlov had what might be described as 'a good war'. He did indeed establish an intelligence service for the Spanish Republicans and ensured that it could be exploited by the Soviets. A close senior associate, Colonel Kotov, ran the guerrilla training camps, a model of their type, and Ernest Hemingway visited the camp at Benimàmet near Valencia in 1937, using what he learned in *For Whom the Bell Tolls*.[4] Beyond his defined role, Orlov was achieving success in other spheres. Alternative Marxist groups – Trotskyite groups in Stalin's mind-set – were sidelined and their leaders compromised or eliminated.[5] Then in an audacious operation, and under Stalin's orders, Orlov organised the shipment of the Spanish government's gold reserves to Moscow, ostensibly for the duration of the war and safekeeping, but in reality it was theft from an ally.

Initially, it might have seemed advantageous for Willie to be seen as SCHWED's protégé; however, not only was the Republican cause in Spain unsuccessful, but before the war ended Orlov defected to the West. With his wife and young daughter, he arrived in the Canadian city of Quebec on 21 July 1938 and soon went to ground in the United States. The world became aware of Orlov's existence only after Stalin's death, when an article on the secret crimes of Josef Stalin, written by Orlov, appeared in *Life* magazine on 6 April 1953. According to Ed Gazur, Orlov's confidant, the events which led to Orlov's defection began on that day in the summer of 1936 when he had looked into Zinoviev's eyes in the Moscow courtroom. Zinoviev, Kamenev and their fourteen co-defendants were executed within hours of the guilty verdict being delivered on 24 August 1936. Orlov, a lawyer, was subsequently to discover that within a week of these death sentences, 5,000 political detainees were summarily executed in contravention of the Soviet legal code that he had helped draw up. Whilst in Spain, he also learned of the purge of the Red Army's most senior officers. This, he realised, was in parallel to the party purge. Stalin now felt able to take revenge on those Red Army officers who had outshone him during the civil war, but Orlov's informants had another perspective: they had evidence that they believed showed Stalin to have been a double agent in the early part of the century, backing both sides and in the pay of the Tsar's secret police, the Okhrana. Red Army generals were apprised, but before a coup could be attempted Stalin had the officers arrested in the summer of 1937, charged with 'spying' and shot.[6] NKVD head Genrikh Yagoda, who had carried out the political purge, was himself replaced in 1936 by Nikolai Yezhov and tried and executed in 1938. Then Yezhov was tasked to purge the NKVD from 1936 and gradually Orlov learned of colleagues being arrested, imprisoned, tortured and executed. When he was recalled to Moscow in 1938, he knew that he was in mortal danger and activated his escape plan.

Safe in Canada, Orlov put the last pieces of his safety mechanism into place. Ensuring that they would arrive on the appropriate desks, he immediately wrote two letters, one to Stalin and the other to Yezhov. In the letters he was quite specific, demanding that his mother and his mother-in-law should remain free and unmolested. If either of them should come to any harm, as revenge for his defection, he would see to it that his record of Stalin's terror would be published immediately. So that there should be no doubt as to what he would do, he provided a list of Stalin's crimes for the recipients to read. In the letter to Yezhov he included an appendix giving details of the OGPU/NKVD operations in Europe that he had been responsible for, or privy to. If he and his family remained safe, Orlov wrote, he would reveal nothing.[7]

For his part, Willie only knew that Orlov had defected and that those associated with 'The Swede' would come under suspicion. In fact, the declassified record – the *spravka*, or 'fitness report', which preceded Willie's sacking – is a skeletal, circumstantial document and does not mention Orlov.[8] The record states that Willie had been 'checked' and that he had never been in any trouble with the police, although his difficulty in coping with Red Army discipline is noted. He had apparently been in contact with Berlin and with 'English people'; in fact, an informer had reported that Willie had been 'visited by two Englishmen'. It was also alleged that an 'enemy of the people' had seconded him to INO work in 1930. More incriminating, however, was the note that in 1926 he had 'worked for Chicherin'.

Any association with Georgy Vasilyevich Chicherin was dangerous on a number of counts. He had been a member of the Russian diplomatic service in the time of the Tsar, but he found himself increasingly at odds with the system and its masters. In 1904, taking advantage of an inheritance, he left the diplomatic service to become a professional revolutionary and was active in the revolution of 1905. At that time he was a member of the Socialist Revolutionaries but, forced into exile, his thinking developed and he espoused Marxism. In 1907, whilst Heinrich's gun-running conspiracy was falling apart, Chicherin was helping to organise the RSDRP's Fifth Congress in London.[9] After the London Congress, he lived in Germany and then in France, where he collaborated with German and French socialists and worked on behalf of Russian political prisoners. During 1914, as the Germans were advancing into France, Chicherin sought refuge in London. Here he continued to work for Russian political prisoners and exiles, and his efforts inevitably brought him into contact with British socialists, particularly the BSP and within that party the internationalists and the pacifists, precisely the group that Heinrich Fischer aligned himself with. In the trade unions, Chicherin's work was supported strongly by the ASE, Heinrich's union. As the war unfolded, Chicherin took up the issue of the 30,000 or so Russian-Jewish immigrants who were threatened with call-up into the armed forces, and this crisis became more acute when Russia withdrew from the hostilities. Chicherin's 'pacifist propaganda' got him arrested and interned in August 1917, but when British socialist and trade-union agitation for his release was joined by strong diplomatic pressure from Leon Trotsky, the Soviet Union's Commissar for Foreign Affairs, Chicherin was freed and back in Moscow in January 1918.[10]

Chicherin did not formally become a Bolshevik until his return to Russia, but he was immediately appointed to be Trotsky's deputy. Within eight weeks of Chicherin's arrival in his native land, Trotsky was appointed People's Commissar for Military and Naval Affairs, with responsibility for founding a Red Army, and Chicherin was named as his successor in the foreign affairs role. He was central in the negotiation of Soviet diplomatic recognition and trade deals until his retirement in 1930, when he was succeeded, by his deputy Maksim Litvinov. Chicherin died in 1936 and, like Heinrich Fischer, he may well have been lucky to die when he did. With his record, he would have been marked out as a likely enemy of the people. He had also crossed swords with Stalin himself in a series of foreign affairs and national self-determination articles published in 1921 under the title *In Opposition to Comrade Stalin's Theses*. Stalin spoke out against Chicherin at the party congress later that year.[11] To have had dealings with Chicherin, as the Fishers did both before and after their arrival in Moscow, was not a comfortable note to have on an NKVD record in 1938. Equally incriminating were the memoranda stating that Fisher's wife had once lived in an area controlled by the Whites and that his wife's brother was a Trotskyist.

The Great Purge touched most aspects of Soviet life in the late 1930s. Sergei Kapitsa has a poignant memory from his schooldays back in Russia:

I went to a school ... in the centre of Moscow, where children from rather high government families studied. It was terribly hit during the '37 and '38 purges. I can only say that the director of this school, he did a very noble and, I think, a very brave thing in those days and did everything in his power to somehow let these poor boys and girls from the families that were hit by the purges feel they were still decent citizens and could carry on. I think that was really one of the remarkable facts of that life.[12]

When she looked back to the time when she was nine or ten, Evelyn remembered the plight of one of her grandmother Lyubov's friends:

This Alice, she was the wife of one of the Old Bolsheviks and her husband was arrested ... and shot. Her son was arrested ... and shot. And she was not arrested. She worked at the Marx Engels Lenin Stalin Institute. Yes, they had such a place with that name. Well, probably she considered her family misfortunes quite apart from the government and socialism. She just believed in communist ideas very sincerely. I thought that ... I still think ... that she was a wonderful personality. You see, these people, they were idealists. I wonder how they managed to ... go on. Probably they didn't notice anything around them. I don't know. I can't understand it.[13]

Whilst the people at the bottom coped in whatever way they could, at the top Stalin was consolidating his power, but the obsession that continued to gnaw at him was that he had allowed Trotsky to escape. First Trotsky had been sent into internal exile and then into exile overseas before Stalin was strong enough to arrest, convict and execute him. Trotsky was in Turkey between 1929 and 1933, in France until 1935 and then in Norway for a year until 1936. Although the dates do not match precisely with the declassified records, Willie was active in Norway and France in the 1930s when the NKVD was trying to assassinate Trotsky, codenamed STARIK or 'Old Man'.* Success in the task to eliminate Trotsky had to wait until 1940, when Trotsky felt safe in Mexico and when Willie was out of the service. Nevertheless, the hunt for Trotsky was the prime goal for the NKVD and a driving force behind its management changes in the 1930s.

---

* Andrew and Mitrokhin also mention that Willie served in Turkey in the 1930s, but none of the declassified records, or other evidence, confirms this.

The Great Purge was in place in early 1936. NKVD chiefs were secretly briefed on the discovery of a vast plot to assassinate Stalin and the Politburo and seize power. Incredulous that such a plot could have been hatched without even the merest hint from their vast network of informers, they knuckled down to the task in hand. Stalin, the 'Big Boss', was in overall control of the investigation, with the support of his Secretary of the Central Committee, Nikolai Yezhov.[14] Genrikh Yagoda let his men loose, but despite the arrest of Zinoviev and Kamenev and their fourteen co-defendants, his efforts did not meet Stalin's requirements. He was dismissed in the autumn of 1936 and subjected to his own NKVD's interrogation techniques, Yagoda not only confessed that he himself had planned to kill Stalin and the entire Politburo, but also that he had been in the pay of the German secret service.[15] His successor as head of the NKVD, Yezhov, presided over the arrests, trials and executions of the Red Army elite and, on 15 March 1938, of Yagoda.

Yagoda's real crime was that he had not pursued Trotsky with the vigour that Stalin required and Yezhov atoned for this by decimating the NKVD. Particularly, the INO and its polyglot personnel were laid waste. Like Stalin, Yezhov was a xenophobe and not only mistrusted foreigners but also those who had anything to do with them. Throughout 1937 and 1938 Orlov's team, the European illegals, were picked off one by one. Theodore Maly, the illegal NKVD *rezident* in London from April 1936 until June 1937, was initially recalled to Moscow to discuss his UK work permit policy. As a non-Russian and former priest he knew that he was particularly vulnerable. '[He] decided to go there because [then] nobody can say: "That priest might have been a real spy after all."'[16] Maly was fully aware of the risk he took. As he said to a friend, 'If I don't go back, it will be taken as proof that I'm an enemy and everyone will say, "What else do you expect of an ex-priest?" I am going back to prove that I'm not guilty of anything and that death does not scare me.'[17] He was detained in Moscow, then arrested, charged, convicted of Trotskyism and shot in 1938. Maly's vulnerability was made worse by his association with Ignaty Reiss, another illegal operating in western Europe, who had allegedly siphoned a proportion of his operational funding into a private bank account before defecting. Reiss had been tracked down by two NKVD assassins posing as businessmen and shot on a deserted roadside just outside Lausanne on 4 September 1937.[18]

Dmitry Bystrolyotov, an illegal who had operated throughout Europe in the 1930s, survived, but at great personal cost. It is likely that he was the spy in Willie Fisher's story who, travelling on a Hungarian passport, feigned alcoholic oblivion to avoid meeting the Hungarian nobleman. In 1937 he was lionised by Yezhov and sent to Germany to contact a Soviet agent close to Hitler's high command, but within months he was brought back to Moscow. Suspended and in a desk job, he was arrested in September 1938. As interrogation turned to torture, he suffered a fractured skull, broken ribs and a punctured lungs so to escape death, but knowing that his tactic was not guaranteed to save his life, he signed the confession dictated to him. He admitted to spying for foreign governments and was lucky to avoid execution, being sentenced to twenty years in prison. He served sixteen years and, after rehabilitation in 1956, worked as a translator. His wife, however, did not live to see this. As the wife of an enemy of the people, she was sent to a labour camp and committed suicide before the war began in 1941. Bystrolyotov's mother poisoned herself.[19]

The Great Terror was planned but its execution was chaotic. At the local Party and NKVD levels, simple disagreements in practical everyday politics led to denunciations, arrests, jail sentences, exile into the *gulag* and executions.[20] At the Lubyanka, Yezhov began by purging his counter-intelligence cadres in 1937 and his Foreign Department in 1938.[21] The outcomes were predictable, and only gradually did it dawn on the Council of People's Commissars, the Sovnarkom, which had nominal oversight of the sentences, that the decimation of the counter-intelligence service was leading to a drastic loss of manpower and expertise. The service was virtually devoid of experienced investigators. Some gaps were hurriedly filled with untrained soldiers, who were particularly brutal in their interrogations – 'the hammer warriors', Willie and Rudolf called them.[22] When Yezhov started on the Foreign Department, the effect was equally catastrophic. Department heads and their deputies were paralysed with fear. The chaos was such that for a period lasting more than four months in 1938, no foreign intelligence reports at all were forwarded to Stalin.[23] With the collapse of the service a very real possibility, policy changes emerged. This was particularly the case when Lavrenty Beria succeeded Yezhov as head of the NKVD on 24 November 1938. In early 1938 Beria had control of the Party and the NKVD in Georgia, and had been elected to the Supreme Soviet

Presidium and the Foreign Affairs Commission in Moscow.[24] Yezhov saw Beria as a rival and put in motion a plan to eliminate him. With wind of the plot, Beria headed to Moscow and a meeting with Stalin. By this time, Stalin may have seen the need to dispense with Yezhov and activated *his* plan by installing Beria as first deputy chairman of the NKVD, and Yezhov's assistant.[25] Unlike his immediate predecessors, Beria had a solid power base, broad party experience and a record of secret police service, and he made his mark quickly on the NKVD, even running agents himself.[26] He expressed his concerns to his Presidium colleague and Secretary of the Ukrainian Communist Party, Nikita Khrushchev: 'What's going on here? We're arresting people right and left, even secretaries of regional committees. This whole business has gone much too far. We've got to stop it before it's too late.'[27]

Yezhov could see that his time was over and within months submitted his resignation, but Beria had already sealed Yezhov's fate. In October 1938 he manoeuvred two NKVD regional directors to write to Stalin inferring that Yezhov was on the verge of instigating arrests of the Soviet leadership itself.[28] Yezhov retained a minor responsibility as Commissar of Water Transport until March 1939, but he was arrested and detained prior to execution in 1940.

Whilst the power struggle continued to play itself out, the NKVD improvised to survive, and at the middle and lower levels of the organisation, ambitious officers took advantage of their opportunities and played the system. Gradually, imprisonments or dismissals became more likely than executions. The sacking rather than the execution of Willie Fisher, who was extremely vulnerable, was one result. ('He was lucky it was Russia,' said Kirill Khenkhin. 'Russia was inefficient. If it had been Germany, he *would* have been shot.') Even the fact that Rudolf Abel escaped the firing squad after his brother's conviction and execution may have been due to Beria's appointment and the beginnings of the policy change. Arnold Deutsch even escaped the indignity of dismissal. In a memorandum dated 11 October 1938, Zelman Passov, the NKVD head of Foreign Intelligence for only a few weeks until he too was purged, suggested to Beria how Deutsch's case might be managed:

At the end of 1937, the eminent recruiter of the illegal apparatus, the temporary employee Comrade Lang, Stefan Georgievich [Deutsch], was summoned back to the Soviet Union. His recall was connected with the treachery of RAIMOND [Ignace Reiss], who knew where he worked. For eleven months he has been without work being maintained at our expense. Bearing in mind his work abroad cannot be decided now, I request your agreement to finding work for Comrade Lang outside our organisation.

Beria concurred, replying, 'Arrange temporary work for him outside the NKVD.'[29] Another of Orlov's protégés, Aleksandr Korotkov, even challenged his dismissal from the service. He appealed against the decision in a letter and his discharge was rescinded.[30]

The staff losses and rapid promotions also impinged on Willie Fisher's and Rudolf Abel's futures. Yakov Serebryansky, who headed the Administration for Special Tasks unit of illegals, the unit responsible for assassinations on foreign soil, was recalled to Moscow in November 1938, arrested and sentenced to death. His successor as head of Special Tasks was to be Pavel Sudoplatov, an experienced intelligence officer who had earned Yezhov's and Stalin's approval by murdering the head of the anti-Soviet Ukrainian Nationalist Organisation, Yevhen Konovalets, in May 1938. Sudoplatov was not immune from convulsions in the NKVD and was himself suspended from operational duties for a short whilst in late 1938, but it was he who was finally given the task of hunting down and killing Trotsky. His success in this venture earned Stalin's and Beria's gratitude, and gave him scope to head a unit which took the NKVD into the next stage of its development.

Willie and Rudolf did not see this as they were out in the cold struggling to earn their livings. Rudolf had found work as a security guard for a whilst, but was eventually fired from that job. Willie was devastated by his dismissal. The loss of income hit him harder than the loss of status and he was aghast that the party of which he was a member and which he had served so diligently could treat him like this. With his father and brother dead and his relationship with his mother fractured, he had forged an emotional bond with the party. Evelyn did not hear him talk about his dismissal at home, but she remembered that he was morose and distant.[31] He worked first as a freelance translator with the Patent Licensing Bureau of the USSR Chamber of Commerce and spent hours wrestling with a translation of the patent of a new mechanical sieve. Pyotr Kapitsa had learned of Willie's predicament and, as a director of the Chamber of Commerce, went out of his way to help him at a difficult time. In fact Willie picked up bits of freelance work, translating patents from English into Russian, for the bureau for the next ten years.[32] But life for an officer dismissed from the NKVD was not easy and Willie remained unemployed, until he finally made contact with Andrei Andreev, a member of the Politburo.[33]

Andreev had been a Bolshevik since 1914 and, in his responsibility for Anglo-Soviet trade union affairs in the 1920s, would have known Heinrich. He may even have known of him and been in contact with him before the Fishers arrived in Moscow, but he would have had dealings with Heinrich once the old man was working for the Comintern. It is also likely that Willie had been an interpreter and translator for meetings with British trade union delegations in the 1920s.[34] Andreev was an archetypal party man who had supported Stalin from the early 1920s.[35] It is entirely possible that the old political fox Heinrich Fischer had told his son to approach Andreev were he ever to find himself in trouble. The approach paid off. 'Why didn't you ask me before? Where would you like to work?' smiled Andreev. Willie chose a Moscow aircraft factory and, although he recalled the personnel manager as the most miserable boss he ever had, he enjoyed the work and was happy in his time there, staying until the autumn of 1941.[36]

10

SPECIAL TASKS

Although he had not been given the status of a reservist, Willie Fisher was recalled to the service and reinstated as a lieutenant in the NKVD in September 1941. His reassessment report checked back over the reasons for his dismissal. The vague charge that he had been writing to people in Germany in the 1920s actually concerned official correspondence with the Soviet ambassador in Berlin that he had translated. The two suspicious English visitors to his apartment were now revealed as CPGB members who were in Moscow for a conference. Conceivably, they had been with a delegation overseen by Andrei Andreev. Best of all, Willie's brother-in-law Ivan, who had been serving an eight-year jail sentence for the crime of being 'an enemy of the people', had been released early, his alleged dalliance with Trotskyism expunged from the record. (This brought huge relief to Ellie's family, who knew that their association with Ivan had kept them in danger during the purges.) Willie's links to the deceased but discredited Georgy Chicherin were not referred to in the reassessment report. As Willie would have known, he had been watched and informed on during his time outside the organs and the report noted that his current place of work was 'a technical plant'. Nothing compromising had been found by informers and his good character was confirmed.[1]

The NKVD that he rejoined had undergone significant changes. Lavrenty Beria was firmly installed as its chief and had brought in a number of his Georgian henchmen to consolidate his position, to help him repair the damage wreaked by the purge that had become known as the *Yezhovschina*, and to modernise and formalise its system of control.[2] In fact, such was the task that the counter-intelligence, espionage and political security roles of the NKVD were separated into a new administration, the *Narodnyi Kommissariat Gosudarstvennoi Bezopasnosti* ('People's Commissariat of State Security'), the NKGB, which was headed by Beria's senior and trusted lieutenant Vsevolod Merkulov.[3] It was with this commissariat that Willie would soon become associated, as well as its Fourth Directorate, Special Tasks, now headed by Pavel Sudoplatov.[4]

Pavel Anatolyevich Sudoplatov was four years younger than Willie, but he had risen quickly and steadily in the Soviet system from the age of twelve, beginning as a signaller in the Red Army during the civil war. Before he was fourteen, he was working as a telephone operator and cipher clerk for the Cheka in the Ukraine.[5] He married Emma Kaganova, a fellow Chekist, when he was twenty-one and running informers and safe houses in his native Ukraine. In 1934 he was selected to be an OGPU illegal and put through the intensive training for his new role, so both in this and in communications he had career experience similar Willie's. Something else they had in common was working with Orlov, for Sudoplatov served briefly with SCHWED in Spain, but Sudoplatov's most important role in the mid-1930s was to infiltrate the anti-Soviet Ukrainian nationalist movement. He gained the confidence of its leader, Yevhen Konovalets, and received orders from Stalin personally to kill him.[6] Sudoplatov's plan, to give Konovalets a box of his favourite chocolates booby-trapped with a bomb on a thirty-second time switch, worked as intended. The murderer returned to Moscow in triumph and was parked in a desk job at the Lubyanka for only few months when, at four o'clock on a November morning in 1938, he was suddenly ordered to see Beria in the company of Merkulov. Nikolai Yezhov was still in his post and the purge was continuing, but at this point Beria had effective control of the NKVD. Sudoplatov was informed that he had been appointed acting director of the NKGB Foreign Department with immediate effect and was instructed to begin work at once, reporting directly to Beria himself on urgent matters.[7] He went directly to the office of his predecessor, Zelman Passov, the man who had been his chief until barely minutes before, and began to go through the contents of the safe:

Another document was a recommendation to the Central Committee and the Presidium of the Supreme Soviet that the Order of the Red Banner be awarded to me, Pavel Anatolievich Sudoplatov, for fulfilling an important government assignment abroad in May 1938. It had been signed by Yezhov. There was also an unsigned document to make me assistant director of the Foreign Department. I took these documents to Merkulov, Beria's deputy, who smiled and, to my great surprise, tore them up before my eyes and threw them into a wastebasket to be destroyed. I remained silent but felt cheated out of the commendation I was to receive for risking my life and succeeding in a dangerous task. I did not understand at that moment how lucky I was to lose a medal and a promotion.[8]

Sudoplatov was acting director of the Foreign Department for only three weeks before he himself was suspended and investigated for Trotskyite activity.[9] Like Willie he feared arrest and imprisonment, but also like Willie he was spared as Beria took over from the doomed Yezhov and the pace of the purge slowed. Unlike Willie, however, he was not sacked but simply kicked his heels behind his desk until March 1939, when he was summoned to Beria's office and thence, with Beria by car from the Lubyanka, to the Kremlin and an audience with Stalin. There, his success in the elimination of Konovalets remembered once more, Sudoplatov was formally appointed a deputy head of the NKGB Foreign Intelligence Department under the rising Beria protégé Vladimir Dekanozov and given the task of assassinating Trotsky. He was to report directly to Beria, by word of mouth and in handwriting only, not by typescript.[10]

By 1939 Trotsky was in exile in Mexico, and Sudoplatov needed Spanish speakers to achieve his goal. He turned to Leonid Aleksandrovich Eitingon, a Chekist he had known since 1933 and had met again in Spain, where, as Colonel Kotov, he had run Orlov's guerrilla training camps and operations behind enemy lines during the civil war. Eitingon had been born Naum Isaakovich Eitingon in 1899 and was a Socialist Revolutionary during the Revolution, joining the Red Army in 1918, the Cheka in 1919 and the Bolshevik Party in 1920.[11] He was an experienced illegal and had worked in China. He had served as Yakov Serebryansky's deputy in Special Tasks in 1930 and, although the younger Sudoplatov outranked him, he was untroubled, for career and promotion were of no interest to him. Eitingon had flair, panache and a sense of humour and the dour Sudoplatov liked him, as did most of his comrades; however, Emma Sudoplatov did not, as he was a womaniser. He had had three marriages and any number of mistresses, one of whom was Caridad Mercader del Rio.[12] A Spanish aristocrat, Caridad had become an anarchist, but was converted to communism by Eitingon during the civil war and then recruited as a Soviet agent along with her son, Ramón. Sudoplatov and Eitingon moved quickly. Eitingon and the Mercader group entered Mexico via the United States in the summer of 1939. Ramón posed as a Spanish-American Trotskyist and early in 1940 he befriended Trotsky's protectors. Eitingon's first plan was for an armed gang of twenty or so assassins, disguised as Mexican police officers and soldiers, to gain access to Trotsky's villa and this was achieved just after dawn on 24 May. They bombed and concentrated their gunfire on Trotsky's bedroom, but their quarry and his wife survived. In Moscow, Sudoplatov rued the fact that Eitingon had not led the armed assault himself, but all was not lost as Ramón remained unsuspected and visited the Trotsky home regularly. Three months after the armed attack, on 20 August 1940, whilst Eitingon and Caridad waited nearby in a getaway car, Ramón visited Trotsky and stabbed the old man in the skull with an ice pick whilst he sat reading one of the young man's articles. Ramón had hoped simply to walk from the villa to the waiting car, but Trotsky's scream alerted his entourage and Ramón was overpowered and arrested. (Given a life sentence for murder, he served twenty years in prison and was privately honoured by Khrushchev in Moscow before retiring to Cuba.) After going into hiding in the Caribbean and then travelling via the United States and China, Caridad and Eitingon arrived in Moscow shortly before the war started in 1941. Eitingon promised Caridad that he would marry her, but although she was honoured with the Order of Lenin, the promise of marriage was never kept. She was refused an exit visa from the Soviet Union and lived alone and unhappily in Moscow, forever tormented at her own part in the fate of her son.[13] Meanwhile, Sudoplatov, Eitingon and the NKVD, under Beria's guardianship, had achieved what Stalin had most wanted since the death of Lenin, an assassination which the NKVD under Yagoda and Yezhov had been unable to deliver. They had eliminated Trotsky and glorified the NKVD, thus giving the organs a new opportunity to evolve as Beria wished and keeping the heroes safe whilst Stalin remained in power.

Trotsky's death removed a major item from the NKVD's agenda, but there was still much to be done. Vyacheslav Molotov's non-aggression pact with the Nazis on 23 August 1939 included secret protocols detailing the division of the Baltic states and western Poland between the Soviet Union and Germany and this in particular demanded urgent foreign intelligence activity. Foreign intelligence was particularly short staffed, and senior officers began to track back to locate former department members who had been dismissed, or who were in jail or in the *gulag*. Willie Fisher's former senior officer in London, Arnold Deutsch, who was the acting illegal *rezident* in 1935, was visited by an officer in March 1939 and asked to provide notes on his network and the political structure in the United Kingdom. When this work was complete, Deutsch sought a meeting with Pavel Fitin, Beria's head of Foreign Intelligence, with a view to picking up his foreign intelligence career in the changed circumstances. Fitin was sympathetic, and Deutsch was assigned to be the new illegal *rezident* in the United States, but the war in the Far East intervened to hold up his departure (he was due to travel by sea from India, but was marooned in Bombay and had to return to Moscow). When he did finally set sail, fate intervened: his ship was torpedoed in the Atlantic and Deutsch perished.[14]

When Hitler invaded the Soviet Union, in Operation Barbarossa on 22 June 1941, not only was the nation unprepared, but its next expectation was that the Nazis would seek to secure territory and resources as a first objective. In fact, the Nazis' objective was to decimate the Soviet armies, and this they achieved. The work of Sudoplatov and his Administration for Special Tasks was to prove crucial as the Soviets defended their land and developed a strategy to fight back. Sudoplatov himself was given the top-secret task of seeking peace with Hitler, with the Bulgarian ambassador to Moscow as a go-between, but the plan came to nothing.[15] Meanwhile, the policy to consolidate the cadre of erstwhilst foreign intelligence officers continued. The records, prisons and the *gulag* were trawled, and victims of the purge, whose skills were needed, were located, released and recalled to the service.[16] Serebryansky, Sudoplatov's predecessor as director of the Administration for Special Tasks, although sentenced to death in 1938 during the Great Purge, allegedly for spying for the British and the French (and no doubt for his association with the defector Aleksandr Orlov), was still in prison awaiting execution in July 1941.[17] Sudoplatov had him released.

Serebryansky had a long record as a revolutionary, spy and assassin. Like Eitingon, he was originally a Socialist Revolutionary, but he was older than Eitingon and had led assassination squads in the pre-revolutionary period. At this time he had earned his living as a theatre lighting director, but had actually begun his working life as a pharmacist.[18] By the late 1920s, Serebryansky had risen to be a senior Chekist active in foreign intelligence. Operating in parallel with legal and illegal *rezidenturas* his 'Yasha Group' had networks of local national communists and Comintern functionaries in Scandinavia, Germany and France[19] but its 'speciality' was assassination. Its leader went back to his original profession and improvised with drugs and chemicals to devise untraceable poisonings,[20] as well as organising shootings, bombings and 'accidents'.[21] In 1936 Serebryansky was based in Paris training saboteurs who could operate against Trotskyists and other non-Stalinist communists outside Spain, complementing Orlov's work in the Spanish Civil War.[22]

Willie Fisher's return to the service in September 1941 was part of the same policy. There was a desperate shortage of trained radio operators and Willie was pulled back into the NKVD department for training undercover radio technicians. However, events were moving at speed and he soon found himself called upon by other departments, including the Administration for Special Tasks, when his skills and experience were needed. Also in 1941, but later in the year, Rudolf Abel was called back into the service, also into training and Special Tasks. Sudoplatov's empire was expanding. Eitingon was his deputy, Serebryansky became a section head and Willie was promoted to captain and head of the Special Tasks radio communications section.[23]

Special Tasks became the principal unit responsible for intelligence operations against Germany and its satellites, organising guerrilla warfare, establishing illegal networks in the German-occupied territories, running secret operations in the Soviet Union to deceive the enemy, and planting disinformation rumours.[24]

The Soviet administration, its families and Chekist families were evacuated east, to Kuibyshev. Ellie, her mother, Evelyn, now twelve, and her teenaged cousin Lidiya travelled and were billeted together. (In 1942 Lidiya joined the armed forces and served as a radio operator in the Red Navy.) In Kuibyshev, Lyubov chose to stay with the surviving elderly members of the Old Bolsheviks' Society. The evacuations were essential, for in October and November of 1941 the Germans were close to the centre of Moscow. The day of the anniversary of the revolution parade in Red Square was particularly tense. Sudoplatov had a position close to Lenin's tomb and took Willie and a junior field radio operator with him. Such was the danger, their job was to remain constantly in touch with headquarters and the front line and to report urgent news to Merkulov and Beria on the rostrum.[25] Rudolf occasionally stayed with Willie at the Fishers' apartment when they took on patrol and communications duties in the Moscow streets at night and then headed to the training school at dawn to teach their new radio recruits by day.

One young recruit was Kirill Khenkin. Although born in Russia, Kirill had spent part of his youth in the United States and in France. In Paris in the 1930s and barely out of his teens, he had volunteered to fight in Spain with the International Brigade.[26] One of Orlov's own agents had learned of this and, aware of Kirill's knowledge of Western culture and his linguistic skills, had changed the young man's mind about fighting as a soldier. He arranged for him to meet Orlov himself, to be considered for intelligence work. Orlov did not find Kirill suitable as an agent or an illegal, but had him assigned to work with a guerrilla unit. After Spain, Kirill made his way back to Moscow and, when the Great Patriotic War started, volunteered once more for intelligence work. His skills and experience were in demand again, and he was one of thousands of immigrants, émigrés, foreign nationals and specialists whose expertise was needed. A colleague of Serebryansky as a section head was Mikhail Maklyarsky, who before the war had been a dilettante in the world of Soviet arts and entertainment. Maklyarsky recognised that Kirill's surname was the same as that of a family of actors and entertainers, and discovered that Kirill was the nephew of Vladimir Khenkin, a popular comedian and a 'People's Artist of the Republic'.[27]

At the time of the German advance on Moscow, Kirill was a member of the Special Purpose Motorised Infantry Brigade, but with Maklyarsky excited by his family background and impressed by his excellent English and French, the young man was now earmarked for illegal work and required to take classes in radio operation at the training school. It was here that he met Willie and Rudolf. 'They were introduced to us recruits together,' said Kirill, 'Comrades Abel and

Fisher. They were always together, and I'm not sure that all the senior officers could tell who was who. They were Abelfisher. Fisherabel. Or people said, "Look, the Abels are coming." It was a sort of joke.'[28] Then, as Kirill's training progressed, he found himself removed from his dormitory and billeted with Willie Fisher. With Ellie and Evelyn evacuated, the Fishers' apartment was home to Willie himself and, for a whilst, a young German veteran from the International Brigade in Spain. When Kirill arrived Willie greeted him in English ('To speak in English was a psychological haven for Willie') and there began a friendship that was to last until Willie's death in 1971.

The accommodation arrangement was partly to release Kirill's bed in the brigade dormitory, but also so that Willie could tutor his charge in the technique of radio operating. Kirill was a better pupil than Kitty Harris had been but he was still not a radio natural. Perhaps it was because Willie's relationships with men were easier, perhaps the circumstances of war, but Willie was less agitated with Kirill's deficiencies with radio than he had been with Kitty's. Kirill's initial task was to assemble the radio receiver and transmitter. On the first morning Willie gave Kirill the parts, the diagram and the instructions, and then left for the day. That evening when Willie returned, Kirill had still not managed to construct a set that would work. Willie shrugged and made it himself. Kirill spent the next days transmitting and receiving messages from the training school and other students dotted about Moscow in similar apartments and training set-ups. The evenings were also spent in tutorial, on operational techniques as an illegal.[29] The tutorials were as often as not in the form of stories, some of which Kirill was to come across again more than thirty years later when he settled in the West and read Orlov's *A Handbook of Intelligence and Guerrilla Warfare*.

The two men divided their rations, mainly meat, rice, bread, tea and sugar. Willie liked to do the cooking and Kirill deferred to him as the cook, whilst he looked after the stove and the gas meter. Kirill suspected that the arrangement was as much to do with the cook getting a larger share of the meal as he tasted and tested the contents of the pan, as it was for Willie to demonstrate his skills. Many of their conversations took place over the stove. Rudolf often visited and then their conversations were in Russian. These conversations, too, were tutorials in espionage technique and tradecraft, but Willie and Rudolf would often talk about their superior officers and about how to survive in the murderous Soviet world. They liked Serebryansky, who would occasionally get them a meal in the generals' refectory,[30] and Eitingon, particularly his sense of humour and his informality, but they were less enamoured of Sudoplatov who was younger than they were and ambitious.[31] When they could get it, the three of them drank vodka and talked on until dawn. The Fishers' apartment was a domestic sanctuary and from it they ventured out for their missions each day, and for longer periods as the war went on. Kirill was being trained as an illegal and became something of a protégé of Maklyarsky, who had him taking messages to and from safe houses. Rudolf and Willie continued training the new cohorts of recruits as they arrived, but were increasingly used in the field.

Techniques that the NKVD had employed from the beginning – resettling, infiltrating and undermining ethnic and national groups to consolidate the Soviet Union and Stalin's personal political control – were now used in the struggle against the German invader. The Germans were well aware that in the communities of White Russians, Ukrainians and others in western Europe, and in the areas of the Soviet Union that the Third Reich now controlled, there would be many only too pleased to work for them. The Soviets were prepared for this and had sleeping agents ready to begin work when required. The most successful of these was Aleksandr Demyanov, who had impeccable credentials as a White Russian. Finding him destitute in Leningrad in 1929, the NKVD had recruited him initially to inform on White terrorists, but later moved him to Moscow, where, controlled by Maklyarsky, he worked as an electrical engineer at the Moscow Central Cinema Studio. Here he mixed with the Russian cultural elite and cultivated the company of foreign visitors and diplomats.[32] Maklyarsky sent him to the Novodevichy Monastery to make the acquaintance of an elderly aristocrat, who had claimed sanctuary there. Demyanov developed the relationship and introduced other 'sympathisers' to what was, apart from the ageing aristocrat, a bogus group of anti-Soviet White Russians. The objective was to attract the attention of Western agents and, shortly before the war started, the Germans bit and began their attempt to recruit Demyanov as an agent of the Abwehr, their military intelligence service. He demurred, and when war broke out joined a cavalry unit in the Red Army.

At this point, Operation Monastery was born. Together with the GRU (*Glavnoe Razvedyvatel'noe Upravlenie*, 'Main Intelligence

Directorate'), the Soviet military intelligence service, the NKVD created 'Throne', an imaginary underground organisation of German sympathisers and a puppet government in waiting for when the Germans were victorious, with Demyanov a key member. In December 1941 he crossed the German line as an envoy from 'Throne', but the Abwehr were not inclined to enter into any agreement with the organisation. However, they were interested in Demyanov.[33] They checked their knowledge of him going back years and, having assessed as reliable, they trained him and sent him back into Soviet enemy territory as one of their own agents. Demyanov, known as Max to the Abwehr and as Aleksandr, code name HEINE, to the NKVD, had been in at the beginning of Operation Monastery and remained at the centre of the deception games it played.[34]

Aleksandr's cover was as a communications officer in the Red Army High Command and by the middle of 1942, barely a year after his return to the service, Willie Fisher was running the radio control of Operation Monastery.[35] The operation worked at a number of levels. Abwehr agents sent into Soviet territory to contact Max (Aleksandr) and his ring, known as Flamingo,[36] were either turned into double agents, imprisoned or, on occasions, allowed to return to their German bases, unaware of the deception. Intelligence from Max, coming from the Novodevichy Monastery, where the elderly Russian aristocrat continued to assume that he was at the centre of a German ring, predicted operations. He implied that planned minor offensives were to be major battles and that estimates of troops and armour in particular locations were lower than the numbers that would actually be involved. In the massive battles at Stalingrad and Kursk, Max and Operation Monastery were crucial. Max told the Abwehr that diversionary attacks were in fact major onslaughts. Even Marshal Zhukov was unaware of these deceptions and suffered heavy losses when, through Max, the Germans learned of his attack on their lines near Rzhev whilst the real attack was to the south-west at Stalingrad. Although Stalin mistrusted official intelligence reports from London, it was clear that British intelligence knew of Max's existence through intercepted German radio messages decoded at Bletchley Park. They alerted Moscow to a German source close to Red Army High Command. The Soviet agents in London, Blunt, Philby and particularly Cairncross, also briefed their Soviet masters. Everything fitted and the Soviets knew that their deception was secure.[37]

Throughout 1942 and into 1943 life in the Fisher *ménage* carried on in much the same way: Willie moved between Moscow and the war zones, sending and co-ordinating radio messages for Operation Monastery as required; Rudolf visited regularly and Kirill continued his training as an illegal. However, it gradually became clear to both Willie and Rudolf that the younger man was not cut out to be a Chekist, or even an agent. At the same time it was dawning on Kirill that if he were a spy for the Soviet Union, he would never be free and would always have to respond to orders from Moscow. He did not know whether the problem was caused by feelings that had been dormant from his time in Spain which were now nearing the surface, or whether it was an awareness that his time in the West had given him a culture and an aestheticism that were incompatible with the demands of the organs, but the result was that he was gloomy. In conversation, Willie would drop comments about the tedium of the work, and he also frightened Kirill by reminding him of the sackings, the imprisonments, the torture and the killings. Once, he was quite blunt, using a slang English expression from the days of the Empire, 'This isn't a job for a white man.' But also in conversation, he implied a course of action that Kirill might take: one couldn't simply 'leave' the NKVD; one had to be found 'unsuitable'. Willie was not explicit, but from his remarks Kirill decided to present himself as being overzealous. He came up with eccentric ideas which he passed on to his superiors, often telephoning directly on their office extensions. He devised complicated plans and wrote them up as ostentatious documents, becoming so enthusiastic about his communism that he began to irritate his officers to such an extent that he was indeed found 'unsuitable'. He was moved away from the organs to regular military service, and away from the Fishers' apartment, but he stayed in touch, visited regularly and met the rest of the family on their return from Kuibyshev.[38]

Evelyn was now into her teens and alert to the realities of both the war and the regime. When she had journeyed to Kuibyshev as the war started, she had seen coaches of refugees and wounded civilians at railway halts, and away from her sheltered home experienced another side of Soviet life: 'We were well fed, but the refugees were starving, dying. My mother collected food for them. It was stopped. A guard stopped her. He said, "We will not accept this petit-bourgeois philosophy." That was the only time I saw corpses.'[39] After their return they were safe in Moscow, but Lyubov was now very ill:

Hampstead Road, Benwell, in the late 1990s. The Fischers' ground-floor flat, where police found Mauser cartridge clips, is to the right. (David Saunders)

Cullercoats Bay, looking towards Brown's Point, or Marconi Point, site of the 1906 radio mast. (Ken Slater)

Fisher family photograph, c. 1917. Willie, standing left, is wearing his school cap. (Fisher family album)

Evelyn, Ellie and
Willie in Norway,
c. 1933.
(Photo courtesy of
Nina Westgaard)

Willie with his
Soviet service
radio. He is
reading the
American *Radio
News*.

Rivermead Court, where the Fishers moved in 1936.

Rudolf Abel.

Alfred Nagel after his arrest.

Pavel Sudoplatov.

Leonid Eitingon.

Aleksandr Orlov.

James B. Donovan.
(Donovan–Amorosi
family album)

Left to right: Valentina Martens, Aleksandra Abel, Willie Martens,
Rudolf Abel, Ellie and Willie Fisher. Photograph taken during Willie's
home leave, summer 1955. (Fisher family album)

Willie Fisher at the time of his trial in New York, 1957. (World Wide Photos)

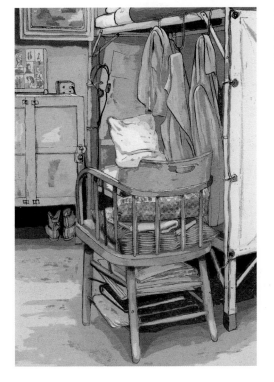

Corner of a Prison Cell by Willie Fisher, c. 1959. (Fisher collection)

Glienicke Bridge: the site of the Abel–Powers exchange, 10 February 1962.

Willie Fisher's tombstone in the Donskoi cemetery, Moscow. Also commemorated are Ellie, Heinrich and Lyubov (although Lyubov died in 1944, not 1945 as inscribed), and Ellie's mother and sister.

During the war the Old Bolsheviks who were evacuated had special ration vouchers. They could go to a restaurant and eat there, or take the food home, or take money instead of food. But they decided they would give these vouchers to the orphans and they had just the ordinary ration cards. This was probably why she fell ill ... she had tuberculosis ... she was undernourished. But right to the end she was interested in politics and the war. She was very concerned about the second front. She thought it was very important. She used to ask me every day, 'Any news? Any news?' And I finally told her, 'The British and the Americans have landed in France. There is a second front.' She was delighted. I remember she had black eyes and they sparkled. And on the next day she died.[40]

Willie was not at home when his mother died and he did not attend her funeral, determined that there was to be no reconciliation between them before her death. As Evelyn commented, 'He knew that she was ill and would soon die when she came back from Kuibyshev, and he chose not to be in Moscow. He volunteered for any work that would take him out of Moscow.'

After Stalingrad and Kursk, and as the Red Army continued to advance, the deception games became more sophisticated still, and there were more opportunities for Willie to be on missions away from Moscow. With military counter-intelligence, the NKVD developed *Smert' Shpionam* (SMERSH), 'Death to Spies', or 'Special Methods of Exposing Spies', headed by Viktor Abakumov, who reported directly to Stalin.[41] At the same time as Soviet territory was being liberated, SMERSH hunted down collaborators and anti-Soviet elements to kill them, imprison them, send them into forced labour in the *gulag* or, better still, to turn them into informers and double agents. A key part of its strategy was to identify 'spies' and 'spy rings' and turn them to work for the Soviet cause without them being aware of it. A version of this strategy was employed in Operation Berezino, a development from Operation Monastery rather than a SMERSH project, in which Willie was centrally involved once more.

As the German army retreated through the flat, forested and swampy terrain of Byelorussia, some units became isolated, but still had the capacity to slow the Russian advance. During a two-week battle near the River Berezino in July, 1,800 German soldiers had fought but barely 200 had survived.[42] A Lieutenant Colonel Heinrich

Scherhorn had been captured in this action, questioned and then taken to Moscow and the Lubyanka, where he was interrogated personally by Pavel Sudoplatov, who decided to hatch a plan. During interrogation, Scherhorn showed that he was deeply pessimistic about a German victory and the NKVD saw how they could exploit him and the situation. He was driven back to a secret destination near the Berezino, where, in a small hut, he was briefed by Leonid Eitingon, who was put in charge of the operation, Mikhail Maklyarsky and Yakov Serebryansky on what they intended to do.[43] Their plan was to make out that hundreds of Germans had survived the July battle and had been joined by stragglers from other units. Scherhorn laughed at this plan and did not believe that the German General Staff would accept that a group of this size could remain safe from partisan guerrilla activity, let alone obtain adequate rations, but he was wrong.[44] Eitingon, Maklyarsky and another senior NKVD officer and veteran Chekist, Colonel Georgy Mordivinov, stayed in the Berezino area,[45] where they identified suitable geographical locations that could reasonably be said to be hiding a group of German soldiers. When this was done, Flamingo contacted the German High Command on 19 August 1944:

> Aleksandr returned to Moscow. His unit is stationed in Berisino at this time. He informed us that there is a large German unit hidden in the forests of Beresino, which is unwilling to surrender to the Bolsheviks. Aleksandr was informed about this by a captured German corporal who told him that the leader of the group was Lieutenant Colonel Heinrich Scherhorn. The unit intends to work its way through to the German front, but this intended march is complicated by the presence of fifty wounded soldiers as well as insufficient supplies and ammunition.
>
> The corporal did not give any information about the hiding group. Aleksandr asked whether you are interested in the matter. If you are, he will have the opportunity to get in touch with Scherhorn's group through his agents in Beresino. Aleksandr had to leave Moscow on August 8. Presto 1 [leader of the intelligence group].[46]

At first the German High Command did indeed suspect a trick. They were surprised that a corporal had so much information and could not square the references to the leader of the 'unit' or 'group' as Lieutenant Colonel Heinrich Scherhorn, who they had in the records as a battalion commander. Nevertheless, a week later, they sent a message to the Flamingo group wanting to know exactly where this 'Scherhorn unit' was located; once this was established, they would parachute in radio operators to take over the communications. Flamingo replied, asking for more money for Aleksandr so that he could continue his work without raising suspicions in the Red Army. The Germans did not respond to this request but then Flamingo was in contact again, with specific information and requests. Aleksandr had identified the area where the troops were located and gave a precise dropping zone, 20 miles north-west of Berezino town, where the radio operators would be safe. The hidden troops would fire a short sequence of red-and-white flares to identify themselves and make contact. The Flamingo message also gave a list of the food, medical supplies, ammunition and money that the German soldiers needed. The German High Command was convinced, and less than a month after the first Flamingo message three men and supplies were parachuted to Scherhorn's unit.[47] One of the parachutists was severely wounded, but the two able-bodied men were both Russians who were working for the Germans: Sadovnikov, an agent, and Dedkov, his radio operator. As well as Scherhorn himself, the Special Tasks unit had a group of ten Germans who had been turned and were working for them, and this team convinced Sadovnikov and Dedkov that there were indeed two thousand trapped troops.[48] Covert Special Tasks soldiers purloined the supplies, and then interrogated and incarcerated the two men, but not before they had contacted their German commanders to confirm their own safety and of the existence of Scherhorn's small army.[49]

It might be supposed that this was the end of the affair. In barely a month, Special Tasks had fooled the enemy, captured two traitors and purloined supplies, but they were able to exploit the situation even further. Willie Fisher now joined Eitingon, Maklyarsky, Mordvinov and Serebryansky as the senior radio operator in the field. The next message that Eitingon and Maklyarsky composed for relay to the German High Command, via Aleksandr, was set out as a full communication from Scherhorn himself. 'Scherhorn' reported the safe arrival of the supplies and informed his superiors that the unit of survivors and stragglers now consisted of 2,500 men under his command. He asked for further supplies of small arms, ammunition, drugs and dressings. He also reported that Sadovnikov and Dedkov had arrived safely but that all their equipment had been lost. Radio operators and equipment were desperately needed for Scherhorn to maintain contact with his phantom scattered command, which was isolated, the main German force now being 300 miles to the west.

Throughout October and November, the Germans dropped tons of food, arms, cash, medical supplies and radio equipment. All the drops were monitored and collected by the Soviets, and the intelligence agents and small SS units parachuted in by the Germans were captured.[50] The first of these SS units was engaged by Soviet troops, and their radio confiscated. The second SS unit reported that the first group was safe, but that their radio equipment had been damaged. They also said that they had not encountered any Soviet troops. These reports, which were prepared by Eitingon and transmitted by Willie, added credence to Scherhorn's independent reports. As the autumn wore on, the Germans sent in a doctor and an airman to supervise the preparation of a landing strip so that the wounded could be flown out. Willie's radio messages back to German HQ reported that the doctor had been hurt as he landed, and that the runway remained incomplete because the soldiers could only work at night and had inadequate tools and machinery. An independent message, purportedly from the second SS group, confirmed that Scherhorn was alive and well and that he did indeed command 2,500 German troops trapped behind enemy lines. One of the SS radio operators was dropped wearing a Red Army uniform and the NKVD watchers allowed him to find his way to Scherhorn, who briefed the man on the numbers and location of the imaginary troops; the radio operator then left, only to be captured later. Scherhorn was well aware that there were NKVD soldiers hidden in and around the hut with machine-guns trained on him and his visitor.[51] What Scherhorn did not know was whether the SS man was genuine, or whether he was being tested by a Soviet German. But the Soviets achieved their aim. After receiving the message from their radio operator, who had been briefed personally by Scherhorn, the Germans were convinced that the hidden army existed and needed help desperately, so they redoubled their efforts to aid the beleaguered soldiers. The continuing worry of the German High Command was that they were being tricked into forwarding supplies that were just being stolen by the Soviets, but the Germans too needed to keep testing their own agents. If they had been turned, there was still an option of using them as double agents.

The operation continued. As the winter of 1944 closed in, the

German High Command radioed orders to Scherhorn that he should create two smaller groups of his best men to break out and locate the safest route for the force to retreat to the German lines. Now, Willie's team was sending radio messages each day to German HQ, and supplies were still coming in including, on one occasion, a box of Iron Crosses for Scherhorn to present to his bravest soldiers. They were unpacked by Mordvinov, who, never missing an opportunity for a joke, called his men together and presented the medals: 'We're doing very well, gentlemen,' he said gravely, 'for our work is being honoured by the German High Command. Now turn round and pin these medals to your arses.'[52]

As 1945 began, the Allied advance into Germany from the east and the west was giving Hitler an increasing number of crises, but Scherhorn's plight remained high on his agenda. In March General Otto Skorzeny, whose elite airborne SS unit had been used to find and free Benito Mussolini when he had been imprisoned by the Italian government in 1943, was brought in by Hitler to locate, supply and free Scherhorn and his men. At the same time, Hitler promoted Scherhorn to full colonel and awarded him one of Germany's highest honours, the Knight's Cross.[53] It was all in vain for within weeks the war was over. Records show that during Operation Berezino the Germans flew thirty-nine missions to help the fictitious army, dropping a total of twenty-five agents and intelligence officers[54] (all of them captured), thirteen battlefield radio stations, 255 pieces of artillery and smaller arms, ammunition, uniforms, medical supplies and nearly two million roubles in cash.[55] Scherhorn remained a prisoner of war and was repatriated in 1949. Willie ended the war as one of the NKVD's heroes, although not all the details of his exploits in Operations Monastery and Berezino have been revealed. Sudoplatov later described Operation Berezino as the most successful radio deception game of the war, with Willie Fisher as its chief radio officer.[56]

During the hostilities, and as they came to an end, Willie had other roles and made the acquaintance of other figures in the military, intelligence and political worlds. Throughout 1944 and 1945, as the Red Army moved west and the war was coming to an end, Stalin was making plans to exploit the peace in his new sphere of influence in eastern Europe. The Russian-, German- and English-speaking Willie Fisher was useful at this time and, as he was keen to be away from

Moscow as much as possible, it is not surprising that he was sent on a mission to Chernovtsy in the Bukovina region in southern Ukraine.* He was accompanying another officer, Captain Adamovich, to give a final briefing to four newly recruited agents who would take on the guise of anti-Soviet emigrants (ethnic Poles, Ukrainians and Germans) and begin to operate out of Warsaw, Krakow, Danzig and Berlin. Adamovich left Moscow for the Ukraine first, carrying a pack of photographs of NKVD undercover officers in the four cities, whom the new agents would need to recognise as contacts. The captain checked in at the office of the head of the Ukrainian NKVD, Ivan Serov, a man who had been instrumental in some of the Soviet Union's most brutal crimes during the late 1930s and early 1940s, including the massacre of the Polish army officers in Katyn Forest and the mass deportations of people from the Baltic states. Adamovich made arrangements for the radio training programme for the new agents that would be provided by Willie, but after leaving Serov's office he just disappeared.

There then unfolded an episode that taught both Willie Fisher and Pavel Sudoplatov some harsh lessons. When he realised that Adamovich was missing, Willie informed Serov, at which point Serov flew into a rage and reported the matter to Nikita Khrushchev, first secretary of the Ukrainian Communist Party. Chagrined, but in no doubt that he had done the right thing, Willie waited in Chernovtsy, little knowing that his inexperience of Soviet politics at this level would reverberate. He had omitted to inform Sudoplatov in Moscow, and the first Sudoplatov knew of the problem was a summons to Laventry Beria's office to take a phone call from Khrushchev in which he was threatened with dismissal. Beria followed this up with an order to Sudoplatov to find Adamovich and bring him to Moscow immediately, threatening Sudoplatov with arrest if he did not comply. Beria then began a search for Adamovich himself.*

The hapless captain was found two days later, at his Moscow home,

---

* Sudoplatov, in his book *Special Tasks*, says that he sent Willie there at the time of the Molotov–Ribbentrop Pact in 1939, before the German invasion of June 1941, and Sudoplatov was not his boss until the autumn of 1941. Moreover, Evelyn Fisher says that whilst her father did not travel anywhere between December 1938 and September 1941, he did go to Bukovina towards the end of the war. So, given that all the main persons in this story – Krushchev, Serov and Sudoplatov himself – were in the jobs he describes in 1944–5, and that Willie was able to undertake the mission at that time, these events described by Sudoplatov as from the period 1939–41 are transposed to the period 1944–5.

in bed. Luckily it was Sudoplatov who located the absentee, simply by phoning Adamovich's wife. Adamovich's explanation was that he had got into a drunken brawl in Chernovtsy and, badly beaten and concussed, he had found his way to the railway station and boarded a train for Moscow. During the fight he had lost the photographs. These had been found by a Ukrainian NKVD unit, which then worked on the assumption that German agents had abducted Adamovich. With Serov and Khrushchev aware of the shambles, Beria was furious and cursed Sudoplatov, but, despite the humiliation that he had endured, Sudoplatov saw that Willie had learned from the experience. Willie was now far more aware of the 'bureaucratic intrigues' at Lubyanka and Politburo level, and the footwork needed to negotiate them. Sudoplatov liked Willie, trusted him and respected him. Sudoplatov was also wiser after the event and worked hard at repairing the relationship with Beria.

The Fisher family retained more domestic memories of the episode, though. As the mission collapsed around him, Willie was required to get out of the Ukraine via Romania and was carrying with him some onions, which he had bought in Chernovtsy. He laid low in Romania for a whilst, but had time and money to buy some soap and sweets as gifts for the family. When he finally arrived back in Moscow, he was outraged that he was required to pay duty on the onions, which he had actually bought in the Soviet Union.

For Willie and his comrades, apart from the adventure, other wartime memories included the friendships they made. Kirill Khenkin's friendship and admiration for Willie endured as he remembered how Willie had shown him how to operate and how to survive. Willie did the same for another young Chekist, who was also to pay tribute to him many years later. This was Konon Molody, codenamed BEN, who eventually became known in the West as the Soviet illegal Gordon Lonsdale, who ran the Portland spy ring and was arrested in London in January 1961. In 1943 Molody was a partisan and radio operator in Byelorussia, with cover as a poor itinerant worker in sympathy with the Germans. He was operating with *Volksdeutsch* documents near Minsk and it was here, he says, that he first met Willie, whom he knew as ALEC, also operating behind enemy lines. Molody had a job in an office 'recruiting slave labour for Germany' whilst he kept up regular contact work and radio communications. One day in September 1943 he was picked up by the Germans, allegedly because his documents were not in order, and detained in a command post. Here, he says, he was approached

> by an officer of the Abwehr, who, after a brief interview, selected me as a potential German agent for use behind the lines of the Red Army. He told me that my first assignment would be to a German intelligence training establishment, but that I would first have to pass a medical test. To my astonishment ... I was rejected as unfit and turned loose...
>
> It was only considerably later that I discovered the full explanation of this extraordinary incident. The Abwehr officer ... was in fact a Russian intelligence officer who had penetrated the Abwehr. His code name was ALEC. His job in the German Intelligence Service was to recruit agents for use against the Red Army. He used to find his human material amongst Russian prisoners of war, slave labourers, and from the command posts. When my friends in Minsk learned of my detention, and my resulting precarious situation, they had immediately informed headquarters, and headquarters had in turn instructed ALEC to do all possible to get me out. This was my first introduction to one of the most remarkable men I have ever met in my life, who is indeed one of the most astute intelligence officers of all time. My association with him was to be long and fruitful, and range over many countries.
>
> Since ALEC and I were already known to each other, headquarters decided to team us up. My main duty was to act as ALEC's radio operator transmitting his information back to the centre. The intelligence he obtained included a considerable amount of information about future German military operations ...
>
> But perhaps the bulk of ALEC's information concerned German intelligence operations against the Soviet Union. He was able to give, on almost all occasions, advance notice of German agents to be dropped behind, or infiltrated through, our lines.[58]

Molody's view of Willie coincides with Kirill's. Again, Willie was in his element teaching, training and being a mentor to an intelligent younger man. These men survived the Great Patriotic War and, like the Soviet Union itself, they were exhausted but triumphant. For Willie, Operations Monastery and Berezino were perhaps his greatest triumphs, but they would not be what was to make him famous.

11

TRAINING FOR A NEW ASSIGNMENT

In Red Square on 9 May 1945 the Soviet Union that celebrated its victory over Nazi Germany was a devastated country. Millions of its citizens had been killed in the war and the purges which had preceded it. Mines, industries, roads, railways, towns, villages, homes, farms, livestock had been obliterated; the losses were incalculable, but ran into billions of dollars. The NKVD, however, did not break stride as it adapted to its work in a new national and international situation.

Willie's war record had been impressive and he was honoured with the Red Star and the Order of the Red Banner. He had been cool under fire and in the deceptions of Operation Monastery and Operation Berezino he had convinced both Germans and Russians that he was German. In the Special Tasks missions, particularly those in which Pavel Sudoplatov felt himself to be in competition with Viktor Abakumov's SMERSH to hunt down traitors and double agents, Willie had had no trouble in convincing Russians that he was Russian, even though his pronunciation was still not perfect. And of course, he remained Soviet through and through. He was therefore selected for very important work.

Rudolf Abel, however, was to take no part in these post-war tasks. Like Willie, he had operated behind enemy lines during the Great Patriotic War, although predominantly on the Caucasus Front. He too had been honoured with the Red Star and the Order of the Red Banner for exceptional courage, self-denial and valour during combat, but his career was coming to an end. An internal report dated 16 April

1945 did 'not find him totally positive'. He was, it said, 'trusted, but not fully'.[1] He was now a colonel, but at forty-six he was seen as 'too old'. On 27 September 1946 he was dismissed from the service once more, this time for good. He remained a close friend of the Fishers and was a frequent visitor to their apartment and dacha, but his career was over and in the Lubyanka he was still remembered as the brother of Waldemar, whose execution for alleged treason had occurred barely eight years before.[2]

The post-war Soviet Union had come of age. Stalin was unassailable; the power he had achieved through assassination, mass incarceration, forced labour, deportations and genocide was now coupled with his reputation of victorious war leader. Beria had met the targets demanded of his NKVD and his power base had also been consolidated. Stalin's Soviet Empire and its sphere of influence had expanded. His Soviet Union was now a 'Great Power' but there was still much to be done. He knew, not least from the Cambridge spy ring, that his allies in the war against Nazi Germany had kept intelligence from him. The Americans had won the race to create the world's first atomic bomb and had used it in Japan, and Stalin wanted the bomb. Although the Soviet Union had helped to create the United Nations, much of its support was rhetoric as it consolidated its control over the nations of eastern Europe. As the Second World War ended a new war, the Cold War, began.

The Cold War was to be a geopolitical war waged to a great extent by intelligence services. Willie was an ideal soldier for such a war, so much so that there was competition for his services as the organs went through a period of post-war reorganisation. The Soviets were aware of the establishment of the Central Intelligence Agency (CIA) in the United States in 1947 to co-ordinate the work of the American intelligence and security authorities. The Foreign Minister, Vyacheslav Molotov, argued that the Soviet Union needed to respond, and he proposed linking the foreign intelligence administrations of military intelligence, the GRU, and the new Ministry of State Security (*Ministerstvo Gosudarstvennoi Bezopasnosti*, the MGB), which was the immediate post-war mutation of the organs. Stalin was sympathetic to Molotov's argument, which not only covered the Americans' move, but also constrained the increasingly powerful Beria, whose henchman, Abakumov, was in charge of the MGB. The new body was the Committee of Information (*Komitet Informatsii* or KI), and

Molotov himself was put in charge, pulling foreign intelligence closer to the Foreign Ministry than at any time in the history of the Soviet Union.[3]

Sudoplatov and Leonid Eitingon were particularly affected by the changes because their small empire was being broken up. In the summer of 1946 they were summoned to see Abakumov. When they arrived, he said, 'Almost two years ago I made up my mind not to work with you two, but when I proposed relieving you from your duties, Comrade Stalin said that we should manage to get along with each other. So we'll work together.'[4] Almost immediately they were embroiled in the inevitable commission set up to investigate the record of Abakumov's predecessor, their wartime boss as head of the NKGB/MGB, Vsevelod Merkulov. Sudoplatov was incensed to find that his own record was called into question, but he reacted quickly by retiring his senior officers, like Yakov Serebryansky, who had been purged in the late 1930s and whom he had had released from jail for wartime service. This policy may have reached down to Rudolf's level, and it may have been this that had precipitated his retirement.

A few months later, Sudoplatov and Eitingon were safe again. They had lost the wartime Special Tasks brief but were appointed head and deputy head respectively of Diversions and Intelligence, a bureau within the MGB that would be brought into action should the Cold War erupt into armed hostilities. The internal reorganisation of security and intelligence continued, with staff being moved from section to section. Willie was safe, although perhaps more from Andrei Andreev's than from Sudoplatov's patronage, and because of his particular skills and experience. Sudoplatov still regarded Willie as a protégé, but although he was still powerful enough to advise on Willie's next mission, the decision was not entirely his.

At the Lubyanka another boss was now in place who had also followed Willie's career with interest. Aleksandr Mikhailovich Korotkov was head of the MGB Illegals Department at the end of the war and he became head of the KI Illegals Directorate in 1947, when the MGB and GRU illegals managements were pulled together.[5] Korotkov's experience in the organs went back a long way. He was the son of a successful banker, but in the wake of the revolution the family had been victimised by the Bolsheviks.[6] Divining the future, Korotkov looked for a menial job so as to obtain the credentials of a worker, and he found work as a lift operator. 'He had a job at the

Lubyanka. He was the elevator boy,' remembered Kirill Khenkin, somewhat contemptuously. However, for advancement in the Soviet Union, Korotkov had found a perfect position. In the elevator, he learned very quickly just what was going on at the Lubyanka, and he rubbed shoulders with officers at every level. He started to train himself to be an intelligence officer and began to learn German. As a keen sportsman he trained at the NKVD Dinamo sports club and it was not long before he was noticed by Genrikh Yagoda's personal secretary, Veniamin Gerson, who suggested that he be recruited into the Foreign Department.[7] Now an officer, he was appointed assistant to Aleksandr Orlov when Orlov was the NKVD *rezident* in Paris in 1933 and he earned the approval of his superiors by supervising the killing of Trotskyites and White Russians. Orlov's defection and the purging of Yagoda and Gerson were major setbacks for Korotkov. He was mistrusted, but not directly affected until 1939 when he was dismissed. His appeal was successful, no doubt another of Beria's decisions to hold on to or reappoint experienced staff.

Like Willie Fisher, Korotkov had a good war. In 1940, shortly after his dismissal was rescinded, he was sent on a mission to Germany to re-establish contact with the *Rote Kapelle*, the Red Orchestra, the Soviet Union's most important espionage network in western Europe. One of the Red Orchestra's contributions to Soviet intelligence during the war was to learn that the Germans had a source in the upper echelons of the Red Army, proving to the Soviets that Operation Monastery and Operation Berezino were secure. For much of the Second World War Korotkov controlled the Red Orchestra, and promotion to chief of the KI Illegals Directorate was his reward. Korotkov was passionately committed to the role of illegals, but the cadre of reliable Moscow-based cosmopolitan communists was limited and dwindling. Willie was the ideal candidate and from late 1946 he began the lengthy and rigorous training to equip him for life and work as a spy in a Western country, operating outside the diplomatic system.

His second British passport, the passport he had used during his mission in the 1930s, had expired in the summer of 1941 and now there was no possibility of renewal. A further mission to the United Kingdom also seemed unlikely as the revived work of the Cambridge Five was being well managed by the legal *rezident* based at the Soviet embassy in London. Korotkov's first plan was to set Willie up as head of the illegal networks throughout western Europe, but Sudoplatov vetoed it. In his job as Head of Special Bureau Number One for Diversions and Intelligence, Sudoplatov was responsible for policy on penetrating coastal installations in Norway and France, and he felt that Willie would be better employed in updating the illegal radio networks in western Europe, not running agent networks.[8] Sudoplatov was also jealous of Korotkov's enhanced power and objected strongly to any officer both running agent networks and managing radio operators. The risk of discovery and exposure was too great, he argued.

Willie's training included extensive political briefings on new party thinking and the changed situation in the West. He pursued his interest in physics, particularly atomic physics, was updated on the latest techniques and technological advances in espionage tradecraft, and instructed on new approaches in spotting, recruiting and handling agents.[9] The Centre recognised that the old way of tapping into an existing pool of fervent, or at least compliant, local communists or Soviet sympathisers needed elaborating to work in the post-war West. One of the lessons of Operation Berezino and SMERSH was that the turning of agents and activists from the other side, or recruiting agents who thought they were working against the Soviet Union, were techniques likely to bring results. Willie had reservations about this new approach. He had seen how communism had developed in the West and in his soul kept to the politics of the Old Bolsheviks and the original Comintern, maintaining his father's ideas, but he had also learned his father's cunning, so he kept quiet and dutifully followed the new policies.[10]

Still, Willie's precise deployment continued to be debated. Endeavouring to outflank Korotkov, Sudoplatov again suggested that Willie be used to reconnoitre the state of Soviet espionage networks in France and Norway but also that he should do the same job in North America. This, together with gathering intelligence on military bases and stores, would enable the Soviets to estimate how quickly the Americans could get reinforcements into their European bases if tension increased, say over Berlin. It was Eitingon who broke the logjam[11] with the suggestion that Willie should simply be sent to the United States, given that his native language was English and that a mission for him in the United Kingdom was neither wise nor necessary. He would be the ideal illegal for the task. He could pick up and reorganise the existing network that had been forwarding atomic secrets since the early part of the decade, and could put a new radio communications system into place. His family was small, secure and close and at home in Moscow they would be the perfect insurance policy against defection. Importantly, too, Eitingon read the politics and saw that his friend and comrade Sudoplatov was vulnerable and needed to be helped off the hook. He reasoned that, as Korotkov was the more powerful in this situation, Sudoplatov could only block the decision; the longer he held out, the more vulnerable his position would become.

As the consummate champion of the illegals policy, Korotkov had acquired in Willie a prototype Chekist. With a staff of eighty-six, Korotkov prepared his recruits for work in the cultures in which they would operate.[12] Willie was comprehensively briefed on American history, geography, economics and culture. Informally, he also absorbed knowledge of the American way of life from Willie Martens, another Chekist, who was younger than Willie Fisher and because of this, rather than because of any discrepancy in their physical stature, was known as 'Willie the Small'. Willie Martens also knew Rudolf well and, as a variation on the 'AbelFisher double act', the three Chekists were sometimes referred to as the Three Musketeers.[13]

Willie Martens and Willie Fisher also had other things in common. Both were the sons of Russo-Germans; indeed, their fathers had known each other and had known Lenin in St Petersburg in the 1890s. Both Heinrich Fischer and Ludwig Martens had taken refuge in England after internal exile in Russia, but Martens had attracted the suspicions of the London police and had sought a new refuge in the United States. Here he became active in business and, when the US government declined to recognise the Soviet Union after the revolution, he became an unofficial and non-accredited Soviet ambassador.[14] His role was short-lived and he was deported to the Soviet Union in 1920, with his wife and son, Willie, who had been brought up in the United States. Like the Fischers, the Martens were Old Bolsheviks and were presented with a dacha, not far from the Fischers' dacha, in the 1930s. The two boys had known each other for years, and Willie Martens had told Willie Fisher a great deal about life and politics in the United States.

Willie Fisher's formal training continued and in 1948 he was given the identity of a man who had been born in Lithuania in 1895, named Andrei Yurgesovich Kayotis.[15] As a young man, Kayotis had travelled to the United States, sought US citizenship and eventually settled in Detroit, Michigan. In the autumn of 1947 Kayotis, aged fifty-two and unmarried, returned to Europe to visit relatives.[16] When he stopped in Denmark to obtain travel documents for the Soviet Union which would allow him to enter Lithuania, now a Soviet socialist republic, the Soviet embassy in Copenhagen retained his passport for his return. In Lithuania he became unwell and was admitted to hospital, where he died. The identity of Andrew Kayotis was perfect for Willie, and Kayotis's American passport was taken to Moscow where it acquired Willie's photograph. Everything was now set for Willie's mission to the United States. He was given a new code name, ARACH,[17] and before his posting he swore the illegals' oath:

> Deeply valuing the trust placed upon me by the Party and the fatherland, and imbued with a sense of intense gratitude for the decision to send me to the sharp edge of the struggle for the interest of my people ... as a worthy son of the homeland, I would rather perish than betray the secrets entrusted to me or put into the hand of the adversary materials which could cause harm to the interests of the State. With every heartbeat, with every day that passes, I swear to serve the Party, the homeland, and the Soviet people.[18]

Willie was called in for a final briefing from Molotov himself in October 1948.[19] A day or so later he left Moscow from the Leningrad station, with Victor Abakumov watching from the shadows, ensuring personally that the departure went smoothly.[20] From Leningrad, Willie journeyed to Warsaw, where he left his Soviet passport and, as the US citizen Andrew Kayotis, he travelled on through Czechoslovakia, Switzerland and France. On 6 November he boarded the SS *Scythia* at Le Havre and sailed for Canada.

The *Scythia* docked in Quebec on 14 November 1948 and from here ARACH crossed the border into New York State on 17 November.[21] He travelled to New York City, where on 26 November he met the famous MGB/KI illegal Iosif Romualdovich Grigulevich, codenamed MAKS or ARTUR. (Grigulevich had been part of the Sudoplatov–Eitingon operation to eliminate Trotsky in Mexico eight years earlier.)[22] Willie handed Grigulevich the Kayotis passport and travel documents, thus utterly dispensing with his Kayotis identity, and in return received a pack with documents to support his new legend. Willie Fisher was now Emil Goldfus.

In fact, he had learned Emil's history during his Moscow training, as the organs had obtained Emil's birth certificate more than ten years previously. From its early days, the service was master of a ruse to obtain and use documents of deceased people, a technique regularly exploited by criminals and confidence tricksters. The real Emil Goldfus had been born of German parents in New York City on 2 August 1902, but had died in infancy little more than a year later, on 9 October 1903.[23] The NKVD had acquired his birth certificate during the Spanish Civil War, when it held identity and travel documents of International Brigade members.[24] Someone had trawled the records to find details of infant births and deaths in New York, acquired Emil's birth certificate and carried out detailed research on the Goldfus family. The parents were deceased and no other relatives discovered; Emil of course had never started school, so the chances of an imposter ever being discovered were remote.

The pack that Grigulevich gave Willie included Emil's birth certificate, a bogus draft card and a forged tax return. He also received $1,000 in cash. Emil's legend was carefully constructed, and there were aspects of it that could be proved if Willie was tested. As the legend went, Emil's parents were German, his father a house painter. He had spent his childhood in New York, left school at sixteen and went to work in Detroit. This meant that part of the Andrew Kayotis legend could simply transfer to Emil Goldfus. Emil had then spent time in Grand Rapids, Michigan, and Chicago, before returning to New York just a year before, in 1947.[25] He was not to seek employment but should present himself as semi-retired and self-employed. Willie Fisher then took his leave of Grigulevich and immersed himself in the hurly-burly of life in the United States of America, the Main Adversary.

12

FIRST US MISSIONS

'I could never work out what the hell he was doing there,' was Kirill Khenkin's considered assessment of Willie's thirteen years in the United States.[1] In the early 1990s a senior Soviet intelligence officer was contemptuously dismissive of Willie's work there: 'He was simply living in New York, doing nothing of importance and painting his pictures.'[2] Khenkin's observation was perhaps one of frustration for on his return from the United States, Willie was much more circumspect in comments he made about his work than he had been in the heat of the Great Patriotic War when he, Rudolf and Kirill faced death or capture. For his part, the Soviet officer was throwing Western intelligence off the scent, for it is hardly likely that the Soviets would have kept Willie in the United States for all those years 'doing nothing of importance'. In the United Kingdom and the United States, the NKVD and the NKGB had been successful in the 1930s and 1940s in infiltrating government departments and the scientific and technical communities which were working on the atomic bomb. By the time Willie arrived in the United States, the new MGB/KI was under pressure. The wartime alliance had collapsed, and debriefings and confessions by Soviet defectors had weakened the networks and overburdened the legal and illegal *rezidents*. At the Centre, knowledge of the United States was limited, and officers who served there were rarely trusted and often recalled. 'We were leery of sending our people out of the Soviet Union for fear of defections. Most of our officers worked in Moscow, with the result that the few men posted in foreign countries had a workload so crushing that many of them cracked under the pressure.'[3] Aleksandr Korotkov's and Pavel Sudoplatov's experience was predominantly in the Soviet Union itself, and to an extent in eastern and western Europe. Eitingon did know the United States, and his suggestion that Willie should be the new illegal *rezident* there (in effect, giving Willie the job that was originally destined for his former case officer, Arnold Deutsch) did open the opportunity for a new start. 'I stressed that he should not trust old sources of information,' said Sudoplatov. 'He should make new confidential contacts and then check people who were used by us in the 1930s and 1940s, but in every case it should be entirely his decision to contact them, meaning that they should not be told by us that he would appear in the West.'[4]

It is still not possible to know precisely what Willie was doing in America. The specific records remain classified, but there are some useful clues and from these Willie's work can be divided into two phases, or three, if the years he spent in prison are kept separate. The first phase, from his arrival in 1948 until the autumn of 1952, was short and had some successes. The second phase, from late 1952 until the autumn of 1957, was fragmented and much less successful. The third phase, trial and imprisonment, became an unexpected bonus for the Soviet Union, and even perhaps for Willie himself.

Willie did not stay in New York after he met Iosif Grigulevich, but travelled across America. Travelling quickly and unnoticed within the USA would be regularly required of him in the future. He was therefore acclimatising himself to American culture and systems, whilst at the same time undertaking missions. His first tasks were on the west coast. The civil war in China was reaching its climax, and the United States was supporting Chiang Kai-shek's nationalists against Mao Zedong's advancing communist forces. Willie was required to monitor cargoes of military supplies destined for the nationalists and emanating from strategic sites at Long Beach, California. There was even a plan to sabotage these shipments with explosive devices planted by agents recruited from within the Chinese-American community, but it was never approved.[5]

Whilst on the west coast, Willie travelled into Mexico, which was an important country in Soviet intelligence history and tactics, for it had been Trotsky's last hiding place and where the NKVD had killed him. A drug store in Santa Fe, New Mexico, had served as a base camp for the assassination team, and the same drug store remained an NKVD safe house and clearing centre for atomic secrets gathered from the Los Alamos National Laboratory from 1942. For a year it was run by Willie Fisher's former pupil, Kitty Harris, who took documents and reports to the *resident* in Mexico City for communication to Moscow.[6] Contact with a legal *resident* was easier and safer in Mexico than in New York or Washington, DC. Moreover, Mexico City was a good meeting place for agents and officers and a way into South America; it also offered an escape route should it ever be required, and a link to a planned associated network in Brazil, Argentina and Paraguay, which Willie would also be required to manage. The system was in place when the Korean War began eighteen months later. Soviet personnel with bomb-making skills were infiltrated into the United States, where they remained for two months, but again the plan was not put into operation. The men were stood down and travelled back to Moscow via Mexico, Buenos Aires and Vienna. Willie was also looking near the Mexican border for radio transmission sites and sites for storing weapons and explosives, should these ever be needed.[7]

Willie's travels continued into 1949 and he undertook a mission on the east coast of the United States. Here he made contact with Kurt Wissel, a German-American who had worked for the cause in Europe in the 1920s and 1930s. Wissel had been an associate of the German communist Ernst Wollweber. They had been active at the top of an illegal NKVD network in the Baltic at the time of the Spanish Civil War, probably run by Yakov Serebryansky, which targeted ships supplying the Spanish Nationalists.[8] It is likely that Willie had known Wissel and Wollweber during his time in Norway. Before the war, the explosives expert Wissel had emigrated to the United States, whilst Wollweber had found refuge in the Soviet Union. Here he had been a member of the group recruiting German prisoners of war to work for the Soviets. After the war Wollweber had returned to what was now East Germany, where he became Minister of State Security under Walter Ulbricht, although he later fell out with Ulbricht and, accused of 'anti-Party behaviour', was dismissed from the government.[9] Wissel's post-war career, meanwhile, had seen him become a senior engineer for a shipbuilding company in Virginia. He had contacts with the German community on the east coast, and the framework of a cell of sympathisers available to be called upon if orders for sabotage operations were received, together with a network of safe houses near the ports. The safe houses, the radio sites, the sleeping networks, the active networks, and the routes for saboteurs and terrorists were to be in place should the Cold War become the Third World War, with the United States and the Soviet Union in direct armed conflict with each other. The Soviet intelligence chiefs called this eventuality the Special Period.[10]

Willie's journey and his first missions lasted some six months. Then, in the summer of 1949, he made contact with Yury Sokolov, the Soviet legal *rezident*, who was with the Soviet mission to the United Nations in New York.[11] The briefing took place in Bear Mountain State Park, in the Hudson valley, about 50 miles north of New York City. The two men took one of the park's hiking trails and, as they walked in the open, Sokolov outlined the situation in New York and supplied Willie with more funds in cash. 'Big Yury', as Sokolov was known to his KGB comrades, was impressed with Willie's confidence and his facility in English, which he had no hesitation in demonstrating when asking a passing park warden the right time. 'You'd better not do it and show your accent,' Willie had said.[12] Willie was also picking up the new task of taking over the running of the VOLUNTEERS network and was about to meet two people who were not only committed communists and reliable agents, but who would become lifelong friends, Morris and Lona Cohen.

Willie Fisher and Morris Cohen had a great deal in common. Harry Cohen, Morris's father, was born in the Ukraine. Like Heinrich Fischer, Harry Cohen was a member of the RSDRP. He had joined the demonstrations against the Tsar after the 1905 revolution, but fled to the United States later that year when the pogroms showed no sign of abating. In New York the nineteen-year-old Harry met and married Sonya, a Lithuanian and, like Harry, a Leninist. They had two sons, Abner and Moishe (Morris), who was born in July 1910. A member of the extended family remarked that, 'Moishe got communism as his mother's milk. The real question isn't why Moishe became a communist. The real question is why Abner did not.'[13] Morris's first love was sport, and although a promising football career was cut short by a knee injury, he kept in touch with the sport by becoming a team coach and press officer at his universities in Mississippi and Illinois. In 1935 he joined the Communist Party of the USA and was expelled from the University of Illinois for his political activity. Back home in New York, he picked up his graduate studies in journalism, coached football at his old high school and organised for the Communist Party. He volunteered to fight with the International Brigade's Abraham Lincoln Battalion in Spain in February 1937 and set sail for France in July, just a week after meeting Lona Petka, a young New York comrade.[14]

Morris had only been in Spain a few weeks when he was wounded at the Battle of Fuentes del Ebro. In hospital with damaged legs, he made a name for himself as the most dedicated communist in the ward. It was in hospital that he was talent-spotted for espionage training and later Aleksandr Orlov personally selected him for the secret spy school near Barcelona.[15] He did well, and was asked if he would work for the Soviets when he returned to the United States. He agreed, and this was his entry into the NKVD.[16] Back in America at the beginning of 1939, Morris got a job as a security man for the Soviet Union's stand at New York World's Fair. Only a few weeks later his Soviet case officer, Semyon Semyonov, contacted him and his secret work began.[17]

Whilst Morris had been in Spain, Lona, a second-generation Polish-American and a Communist Party member, had continued to live in New York. She worked as a nanny to the Winston family, a wealthy dynasty whose prosperity came from bed-linen manufacture, where her principal role was as governess to Alan, the Winstons' ten-year-old. Her spare time was spent working for the party and walking out with Morris, whom she married on 13 July 1941. It was only after their marriage that Morris told Lona that, as well as being an American communist and trades union activist, he was working for the Soviet intelligence service. Initially she was angry, but she soon accepted his work and was recruited into the service herself.[18] They had various code names: together they were DACHNIKI, Morris was LUIS or VOLUNTEER and Lona was LESLI. In July 1942 Morris was drafted into the United States Army and Lona supported the war effort by working in an aircraft factory.[19] Morris was demobilised at the end of 1945, eligible for a small disability pension as well as for the benefits of the GI Bill.[20] He took a master's degree at Columbia University and settled down to be a history teacher in New York high schools.

Willie met Lona first. Their meeting place was the birdhouse in New York's Bronx Zoo. Willie actually tailed Lona to the meeting, on the New York subway, to be sure that no one else was following her. Lona suspected that she was being followed and used the 'dry cleaning' techniques she had been taught to shake off her pursuer – doubling back, going in and out of shops, changing subway cars and routes. Willie was waiting for her when she arrived at the zoo. A week later Willie met Morris at the same spot.

This was the beginning of Willie's mission in New York to take over the VOLUNTEERS group. The spy ring had been in cold storage since late 1945, when the defections in the West had shaken Soviet intelligence. In America in particular, the defection of agent Elizabeth Bentley was a disaster for Soviet intelligence. *Rezidents* and case officers were recalled to Moscow and the flow of atomic secrets from Los Alamos to Moscow was stopped. But the first phase of the VOLUNTEERS' work had been a triumph for the Soviet cause. At the beginning, before he joined up, Morris Cohen had his recruits acquiring details of machine-gun and radar technology to supply to the Soviets. Later, with Lona as courier whilst Morris was with the army overseas, atomic secrets flowed from Los Alamos to Moscow Centre, to the Kurchatov Institute and the Semipalatinsk testing site in Kazakhstan.

Now, in these heady times, Willie reactivated the VOLUNTEERS. In August 1949 the Soviet Union tested its first atomic bomb, a close copy of the Americans' first device and the result of highly secret material obtained by a number of Soviet agents, working independently of each other in the United States and the United Kingdom.[21] The news of the test was broken in the West a month later. Then, on 1 October, Mao Zedong claimed victory in the Chinese Civil War and declared the People's Republic of China. Chiang Kai-shek's defeated Nationalists sought refuge on the offshore island of Formosa. Willie's work was associated with both these triumphs, and he was rewarded with the Order of the Red Banner.[22]

He now began to establish himself as a New York resident, as well as the New York *rezident*. By early 1950, as Emil R. Goldfus, he was renting an apartment at 216 West 99th Street and setting himself up as a small-time businessman, semi-retired, working as a photographer and photofinisher, developing rolls of film and producing prints. He deposited his funds from the Centre in small sums of two or three hundred dollars or so in savings banks in various parts of the city.[23]

As this cover was marinating, he used another with the Cohens and their friends. With them professionally he was 'Milton', shortened to Milt, a name he also used in his social relationship with them. He was a guest at their New Year dinner in 1950 and again a few weeks later when they hosted a dinner party for friends.[24] With Morris and Lona, Willie found a surrogate family whose history and background resembled his own and whose modest domestic situation to an extent compensated for his absence from Ellie and Evelyn.

Back home in Moscow, his wife and daughter accepted the situation and got on with their lives. Ellie was still with the children's theatre orchestra and Evelyn had followed her university degree in languages with a job as an editor in the Foreign Languages Publishing House. Lidiya now worked as a shorthand typist and she along with other members of the family and friends, the Abels and the Martens, continued to visit the Vtoroi Lavrsky Lane apartment. In the summer they would meet at the dacha, where the women particularly tended the garden and exercised their black spaniel, Karina, and later her only puppy, Bambino. They wrote and received letters from Willie and made the best of things. 'That's the way it was,' said Evelyn.[25]

In New York, Willie's operational and social circle was widening. Not long after the social gatherings at the Cohens in early 1950, he was introduced to their young friend Alan Winston, who had remained in touch with Lona and Morris and assimilated their radical thinking if not their Communist Party membership. But it was not all plain sailing for Willie during 1949 and 1950. One of the VOLUNTEERS was a 24-year-old physicist, Theodore Alvin Hall, who was known to all as Ted. He was a gifted scholar and an outstanding young theoretical physicist when he began his studies at Harvard at the age of seventeen in 1942. Less than two years later, when he was still only eighteen, the brilliant young man was working on the Manhattan Project, the top-secret plan for the creation and use of a bomb from the uranium atom. Ted Hall's father, who was a little older than Morris Cohen, was a first generation American, the son of immigrants from western Russia. He was not a socialist, but his son Ted accepted the Marxist analysis of capitalist economics, and was drawn into the company of the Marxist thinkers and activists amongst his student friends at Harvard. He retained their friendship and, when he was working at Los Alamos, he decided that it would be dangerous for the world to have only one power in possession of the uranium bomb. On a fortnight's leave from Los Alamos in October 1944, he met up with his old Harvard friend and confidant Saville Sax in New York. The result of their conversation was that Ted Hall called in at the Soviet government's trading company, Amtorg, where, anxious to get rid of him quickly, an American employee simply gave him the name and number of Sergei Kurnakov, an American-based Russian who was an author and journalist on military matters. It turned out that Kurnakov was also a Soviet intelligence agent.[26] The result of this encounter was the subject of a cable from the official Soviet New York *rezidentura* to Moscow Centre on 12 November 1944:

> BEK visited Theodore HALL, nineteen-years-old, the son of a furrier. He is a graduate of HARVARD University. As a talented physicist he was taken on for government work ... At the present time H. is in charge of a group at CAMP-2 ... H. handed over to BEK a report about the CAMP and named the key personnel employed on ENORMOZ. He decided to do this on the advice of his colleague Saville SAX, a GYMNAST living in TYRE ... We consider it expedient to maintain liaison with H. through S.*[27]

Via Sax, and also on occasions via Lona Cohen, Hall was one of a number of American and British sources leaking atomic secrets to the Soviets during the mid-1940s. After the war, Hall followed a number of his senior colleagues to the University of Chicago and began work on a master's degree. He also fell in love with Joan Krakover, a seventeen-year-old undergraduate at the university. They were both active in radical politics and planned to marry, and prior to their marriage in June 1947 Ted felt it proper to tell Joan of his work on behalf of the Soviet Union. She accepted everything for as far as she was concerned – indeed for both of them – it was all in the past, and they undertook to pursue their communist ideals to improve the lot of workers and the underprivileged in the United States.[28] The Soviets, however, were not at all keen for Ted Hall to retire, and pressure was put on him and Sax to keep up the supply of material.[29] Hall agreed, but forwarded information on a much less regular basis.

In 1949 and again in 1950 he made it known that he wanted to stop completely, emphasising his wish to concentrate on domestic political activism. In this period, the Cohens met Ted and Joan Hall twice, and it is likely that Willie was there on at least one of these occasions. Ultimately, Willie could not break the Halls' resolve and

---

* BEK is Kurnakov. CAMP-2 is Los Alamos. ENORMOZ is the Soviet code word for the American atomic bomb project. GYMNAST is an associate of a communist youth organisation. TYRE is New York.

although he made it clear that he understood their reasons, he argued that it would be work on behalf of the Soviet Union that would be of most value in the struggle for socialism, not victories in local or national campaigns.[30] The Halls were not convinced, but they were impressed by the care and understanding with which Willie treated their argument. The Cohens too, although accepting the line of Willie's Soviet thinking, noted his magnanimity. The Halls were lost to the cause, but Ted Hall never confessed his role to the authorities or admitted his role as a Soviet source until nearly at the end of his life in the late 1990s.[31]

Willie Fisher had passed a number of tests since his arrival in the United States but now the pressure became intense. In January 1950 Klaus Fuchs, a German-born anti-Nazi and Communist Party member who had lived in the United Kingdom from the early 1930s, was arrested in London. Fuchs was a brilliant physicist, working on the Tube Alloys Project, the code name for Britain's atom bomb research, and was a senior member of the British team seconded to Los Alamos to work on the Manhattan Project. Whilst there he passed secrets to the Soviets, and continued to do so on his return to England. He confessed to spying over a period of seven years, pleaded guilty at his trial and was sentenced to life imprisonment. Fuchs's confession identified his American contact as Harry Gold, who was arrested in May 1950 and started talking.

But there was other evidence that incriminated some of the Soviet agents, evidence so secret that it could not be presented in court. The awful truth was that after a number of years, the United States Army Security Agency (ASA) was now decoding parts of some of the Soviet encrypted cables from the early and mid-1940s. Since the 1920s, Soviet intelligence had used a 'one-time pad' cipher system. With this system, after each message was sent, its code was destroyed so that it could never be used again. The recipient likewise destroyed his code page after the message was decrypted. In the heat of the Second World War, in 1941 with the German army advancing fast on Moscow, to save time and increase output the NKVD print unit began printing duplicate 'one-time' pads. The practice was soon stopped, but damage had been done.[32] Embassies, consulates, trade organisations, and military and naval intelligence had all received and sent messages using the vulnerable pads. It soon transpired that the United States had acquired copies of hundreds of original messages from the period

1942 to 1946, and from late 1946 the ASA could decrypt parts of some messages in a project codenamed VENONA. To maintain the blanket confidentiality, the CIA was not informed and even President Truman himself was not briefed. In 1947 a Soviet agent in the ASA got a message to the Centre that some decrypts were possible. This was vital information for the Soviets, but although they knew that Fisher's role could not have been discovered, as he had arrived in New York after they had reintroduced their secure one-time pad system, they did not know which cables, or which parts of the messages from the early 1940s, were compromised.[33] The Soviets knew that Gold could identify Lona Cohen as a courier and that Lona knew all the VOLUNTEERS and the new illegal *rezident*, Willie Fisher. Once Gold was arrested and started talking, the Centre had to move at once.

Breaking crucial rules, the legal *rezident* Yury Sokolov travelled quickly to the Cohens' apartment on East 71st Street and ordered them to leave the country without delay.[34] They left promptly, via the Mexico route, for Europe and Moscow. It may well have been that Willie was not available to warn the Cohens because he was already in Mexico arranging their escape. Sokolov's visit was not too soon for on 16 June David Greenglass, a Communist Party member and US Army sergeant based at Los Alamos, was arrested and confessed to passing documents from Los Alamos to a courier, knowing that they would then be passed on to Soviet sources. Greenglass also named his brother-in-law, Julius Rosenberg, as the man who had recruited him.[35] On 17 July Rosenberg and his wife Ethel were arrested. Although the period of Willie's most successful work in America was over, his phlegmatic approach was just what would be required in the next nervous months

13

UNDERCOVER ARTIST

With the departure of the Cohens and the vulnerability of the remaining VOLUNTEERS, Willie continued to establish himself as a New Yorker and consolidate his role as a semi-retired photographer. With his cameras, equipment for enlarging prints and chemicals for developing and printing film, he had good cover, for he was preparing microfilm and microdots for despatch, and miniaturising notes and decrypts with his own orders which he might need to enlarge from time to time. In this 'semi-retirement' he was also required to exploit the interest and skill in drawing and painting that had begun in his childhood, for this too was cover and an opportunity to enter New York cultural circles. His knowledge and love of painting had been used already in his cover as an artist during his time in southern England in the 1930s, and even when he was not obliged to do so by his bosses he pursued his art at every opportunity and encouraged his daughter Evelyn's artistic talents. When she was a child, he had given her a paintbox as a birthday gift. 'But Daddy,' she had said, 'it only has three colours. Your paintbox has lots of colours!' He then showed her how to make all the colours by mixing them.[1] Now, under orders, he had the opportunity once more to develop his artistic talents. Meanwhile, on the broader operational level, the policy of the Centre continued to evolve. Korotkov's illegals' project expanded, and in March 1950 Valery Mikhailovich Makaev arrived in New York to set up another illegal *rezidentura*. Makaev was codenamed HARRY, and his first job would be as case officer to the British Secret Intelligence

Service officer and Soviet mole Kim Philby, then codenamed STANLEY by the Soviets. The courier between the two was Guy Burgess, who was now also in Washington.[2] Once the Korean War started in June 1950, the intelligence from British embassy sources, filched by Philby and Maclean, was of incalculable value. Should the war spread, the Special Period might begin, initiating Willie's task to manage secret saboteurs in the United States.

Like Willie's, Makaev's cover was in the arts, as a musician in his case, and not long after his arrival he was teaching music at New York University.[3] With Willie stretched covering the remaining VOLUNTEERS and awaiting orders to activate the sabotage networks, Makaev was given a more proactive role and seemed destined for success when he got to know the family of US Senator R. E. Flanders.[4] He was doing so well that the Centre made plans to send two new illegals to join his team: Vitaly Lyamin, codenamed DIMA, and Reino Häyhänen, codenamed VIK. However, Makaev's star waned as rapidly as it had waxed. When it became clear to Philby in the spring of 1951 that Donald Maclean was about to be unmasked, he sought assistance from his case officer, but Makaev bungled the task. Neither a message nor funds of $2,000 from the legal *rezidentura*, entrusted to Makaev via a dead-letter drop, reached Philby because Makaev failed to find the location. His *rezidentura* was suspended, Makaev himself was put under Willie's supervision and an inquiry was conducted at the Centre. Here it was discovered that Makaev had lost, or misappropriated, a further $9,000; he was recalled to Moscow and dismissed from Korotkov's section.[5]

Another illegal, Konon Molody, codenamed BEN, who had known Willie as agent ALEC during the war, claimed to have met Willie in New York in the early 1950s:

> I walked casually through Central Park towards a well-known landmark. Nearby was a bench with an old woman sitting on it. Next to her sat ALEC. There was no trace of recognition between us and, as I also sat down on the bench, I remarked to the old woman that it was a fine day. After a little desultory conversation between us she got up and moved off.
>
> 'You are quite right,' ALEC said to me. 'It is a fine day.'
>
> After a few more offhand exchanges of this kind, ALEC began speaking in his quiet, precise, professional manner. He kept it as short

as possible. I was to be his communications deputy, responsible for the smooth functioning of his radio communications and of his courier system. I was also to have certain duties in respect to our old pursuit of former Nazis. I could talk for hours about ALEC. He always seemed to me an exceptionally interesting and in many ways a really remarkable person. This quiet, unhurried and somewhat elderly man never attracted attention by his appearance and easily lost himself in any crowd. At a party he never attracted undue attention, whilst at the same time impressing everyone by his attentiveness and courtesy.

His intelligent and penetrating gaze never stopped for long on any particular object but always noticed everything of real interest. His self-control and tenacity always impressed me ... His nature was such that it is inconceivable that he should be capable of panicky or rash actions...

His self-control and courage were not the only characteristics which I admired in ALEC. He was a man interested in many branches of science and art and his general knowledge was truly encyclopaedic. At the same time he was as clever with his hands as the most skilled craftsman. Despite his reserved and somewhat withdrawn attitude he is nevertheless a very warm-hearted and gentle person...

Ever since I met ALEC when I was nineteen, I tried to follow in his footsteps and took him for my model.[6]

Molody's panegyric is typical of Willie's comrades, but there is no evidence that BEN worked with or for Willie in the United States, or that part of either's mission was to trace former Nazis. However, there were reports that Willie met Molody and Philby in Canada on different occasions in the early 1950s.[7]

Meanwhile, Willie carried on, under increasing pressure. He did not have Makaev's flair for recruiting agents, but he pursued his friendship with Alan Winston, Lona Cohen's former charge. Winston was not a communist, but a young man with liberal, radical ideas, critical of many aspects of mainstream American politics and culture. He was a graduate and, like Willie, an artist, although he sculpted as well as painted.[8] Willie learned much about American life from Winston. In their conversations about art, literature, history and contemporary politics, Willie could escape the confines of ideology and enjoy stimulating intellectual company. Like all good Soviet citizens at the time, Willie was supposed to loathe America and its way of life. It was simply not acceptable for a Soviet citizen who travelled to the

West to speak positively about anything that was found there,[9] and Willie was critical. 'He didn't like the hill-billy music,' remembered Evelyn. 'And the people' – she hesitated, seeking the right words – 'he felt ... they lacked ... breeding.' However, his comment was not that of *Homo sovieticus*, but of an old-fashioned, anti-American, English snob. He felt perhaps that Alan Winston was 'well-bred', which aggravated his disapproval of Alan's lifestyle: his pleasant, well-appointed bachelor apartment and numerous girlfriends. Willie's way of thinking had elements of the paternalism which he had shown in other ways towards Kirill Khenkin and Molody, for he turned out to be prudishly critical of the younger man's attitude to women, or perhaps he was uncomfortable with Alan's success with women. Nonetheless, he pursued the friendship as contacts were important, and even if Winston was not recruited for the Service, he had other uses: for example, he rented a safety-deposit box for Willie at the Manufacturers Trust Company on Third Avenue, in which $15,000 was locked away.[10]

Operationally, Willie was also dealing with the crisis that was threatening the Cohens' VOLUNTEERS group and which had decimated Julius Rosenberg's group. Some members of the VOLUNTEERS ring – their code names SERB, ADEN and ANTA, known from the decrypted VENONA traffic – were not and never have been identified.[11] The group run by Rosenberg (LIBERAL) was utterly exposed. In December 1950 Harry Gold pleaded guilty to all charges and was sentenced to thirty years' imprisonment; in April 1951 David Greenglass was sentenced to fifteen years and another member of the ring, Morton Sobell, protesting his innocence, to thirty years. The Rosenbergs confessed nothing and on 5 April 1951 they were sentenced to death, going to the electric chair on 19 June 1953. The organs were shaken by the executions: 'The fall of Klaus Fuchs, followed by the break-up of the Rosenberg network and the tragic death of our agent and his wife, created a traumatic shock inside Soviet intelligence.'[12] As well as grief, Willie may also have felt a certain relief for he remained undetected despite the fact that Julius Rosenberg had mentioned to Greenglass some years before that 'a new Soviet contact [had] arrived around 1948 "flush" with money', and that Gold reckoned that the new contact 'took over as Rosenberg's superior in the United States'.[13]

In 1951, around the time of the Rosenbergs' sentence, Willie moved to an apartment in Riverside Drive, West 74th Street, overlooking the

Hudson River. Although little is known of him or his work at this time, he was keeping watch in New York as the debris of the Cohen and Rosenberg networks piled up, reacting to events rather than making things happen.

Willie would have been unaware of what was happening in Moscow, including the demotion of his old protector, Andrei Andreev, in 1950 and, in the summer of 1951, the arrest of Viktor Abakumov, the security minister who had watched his departure from the Leningrad Station in Moscow back in 1948.[14] Willie would have been unaware, too, of Leonid Eitingon's arrest in the autumn of 1951.[15] Stalin, just as he had created notions of a plan to wipe out the Politburo in 1936, now fuelled an intrigue known as the Doctors' Plot or the Zionist Conspiracy, which purported to show that Jewish doctors had schemed to poison senior Soviet leaders. As a Jewish Chekist, Eitingon was the victim of a new purge of the organs; he was one of the officers suspected as having 'protected' the doctors. However, Willie would have been very well aware of the death of Josef Stalin on 5 March 1953, from American newspapers, television and radio and conceivably, too, from Radio Moscow broadcasts. He would realise that changes would follow, but could not have known the details. Lavrenty Beria was arrested on 26 June 1953 and Pavel Sudoplatov on 21 August; Eitingon had probably been rearrested a few days before.[16] Beria was shot before the end of the year and Sudoplatov and Eitingon were given long jail sentences.

Immediately after Stalin's death, the organs began to change once more. The KI as the overriding management system for foreign intelligence had withered and Vyacheslav Molotov, whose power was in decline before Stalin's death, became weaker still. At Stalin's death, the intelligence services were subsumed into the Ministry of Internal Affairs, the *Miniserstvo Vnutrennikh Del* or MVD, and within a year were redesignated as the Soviet security and intelligence service, the *Komitet Gosudarstvennoi Bezopasnosti* with the abbreviation by which history would come to know the organs, the KGB. A power struggle was underway, and when Willie learned at the end of 1953 from the American press that Nikita Khrushchev had become first secretary of the Communist Party of the Soviet Union, it is unlikely that he was delighted. Willie had fallen foul of Khrushchev at the time of the Adamovich affair and now that Khrushchev was clearly Stalin's successor, Willie was vulnerable once more. His bosses had been purged and his protector Andreev was dropped from the Soviet leadership. Willie coped by obeying his orders and carrying on with the jobs he had been given. His record in America was good and he had been decorated for his work with the atom spy rings. He had, it could be noted, contributed to the Soviet Union's successful test of its own hydrogen bomb in August 1953 and the Soviet Union was now one of the two world superpowers.

His tasks were mundane. At his Riverside Drive apartment he had set up his short-wave radio receiver with a tape recorder attached to the radio and an aerial running along the ledge from the window.[17] The Centre transmitted his orders on different frequencies and at different times of the week. The call sign for the broadcasts was 'Allo, allo', followed by messages in groups of five-digit numbers, read in English. Willie would record the messages, decrypt them with a page of his one-time code pad and then destroy the page. When the orders in each message had been carried out (including the delivery and receipt of money, equipment, microfilms, orders, messages, letters from home and documents from agents), the tape and any written record would be destroyed.

Towards the end of 1953, he was ordered to establish a second base and to develop his role as an amateur artist. He rented a studio and a storage unit at Ovington Studios, 252 Fulton Street, a seven-storey building in Brooklyn Heights, and found modest residential accommodation in Brooklyn's Hicks Street.[18] It was not until early in 1954 that Willie sought to engage with his fellow artists at Fulton Street. The first neighbour he spoke to was a young painter, Burton Silverman, who was not long out of the army. Burt was a far more accomplished painter than Willie was then or ever would be, but a rare friendship developed between the two men even though Willie was nearly twenty years older than Burt.[19] Like Kirill Khenkin and Konon Molody before him, and for the same reasons, Burt came to admire Willie. For his part, Willie deferred to Burt as an artist and was eager to learn from him. Burt was fascinated by Willie, or Emil, the name he knew him by. His first impression was of the man's height, just under 6 feet, and that he stooped a little. Emil was slim, bald, with aquiline features. He was dressed modestly and informally, with light grey trousers and a grey tweed jacket, and, unlike the mostly young men who rented studios here, he wore a tie. Burt particularly noted Willie's accent: the newcomer spoke with short vowels and rolled his

Rs, but it was not a New York accent, hardly even American.[20] As their friendship developed, they spoke about the accent when Emil told Burt about his childhood. Part of his upbringing had been in Boston, he said, in the home of an aunt and uncle who were Scottish, and he put his accent down to that.[21]

Gradually the other young artists and writers at the Ovington Studios – Burt's friends David Levine, Harvey Dinnerstein, Jules Feiffer, Sheldon Fink, Daniel Schwarz and Ralph Ginzburg – got to know Emil. In the years ahead Burt and his friends would all make names for themselves as fine artists, illustrators, cartoonists, animators and editors – in Feiffer's case as a playwright, too. In 1954 they were young ex-servicemen, graduate art students working to find their individual voices. They were also all radical thinkers, to the left of the American political centre, and David Levine was a member of the Communist Party of the USA for a time.[22]

Willie never recruited any of them, or attempted to, and was hardly even drawn into political conversation with them. When the younger men fumed against the McCarthyite witch-hunts of the time, Willie expressed no opinion. His political comments in any conversation tended to be references to the 1930s. On one occasion Willie was holding forth on his work and travels in his youth, and talked about singing trade union songs in a logging camp in the Pacific north-west. He referred to Big Bill Haywood, the leader of the American Industrial Workers of the World (IWW), known at the time through onomatopoeic acronym as 'The Wobblies'. Of course, Willie had not spent any of his youth in the Pacific north-west, but would have been aware of the Wobblies through the political conversations he had had in England thirty-five years before. And there is every likelihood that he had met Haywood when he was interpreting at Moscow conferences in the 1920s. Haywood had been sentenced under the Espionage Act for agitating against American participation in the First World War, but jumped bail during the appeal and fled to Moscow, where he died in 1928.

Willie had an affinity with the itinerant workers that Haywood had organised in the early part of the century. In effect his father had been an itinerant worker and his own work for the Soviet security service had ensured that his working life, as well as his childhood, had been nomadic. At the studios, Willie spoke disapprovingly of the Bowery 'bums', the New York underclass. This fitted with his ideology and his sense of his own class, the elite working class, but for his young neighbours, despite his wit and character, he was a loner, a man who did not quite fit in. Jules Feiffer confided to Burt, 'Emil gives me the feeling of a guy who's been on the bum. No matter how much of a fat cat they get to be, they never lose that look.'[23]

'Bums' were often the subject of Willie's drawings and paintings too. When Burt Silverman first looked into Willie's studio, 509 on the fifth floor of the Ovington, the first painting that he saw was of three Bowery bums; he was not impressed. He thought that the drawing, the sense of colour and the composition were weak.[24] The feeling, though, was strong, and whilst Burt typified Willie's work as primitive or naïve – his own portrait of Willie was entitled 'The Amateur' – he was taken by it and began to advise Willie on his work. Burt became Willie's tutor and the pupil worked hard, learning from Burt's work, spending time viewing it carefully, and asking questions about technique and materials. With Burt's guidance, he began to paint in oils for the first time.[25] The two men talked about art a great deal with Willie arguing his views about art theory backed up by the well-thumbed books that he kept on his shelves. He was dismissive of the prevailing art criticism of the day and of contemporary abstract art, championing the realist painters of the nineteenth century. 'I like Levitan, a late nineteenth-century Russian painter,' he told Silverman. 'You'd like him, too.'[26]

Willie never mentioned English art of the nineteenth century, particularly not the art of north-east England – the work of Henry Perlee Parker, who painted the coastal workers of Cullercoats in the 1820s and 1830s, for example, or the 1880s' realist paintings of Cullercoats life and landscape by Robert Jobling. He never referred to Ralph Hedley's paintings of the Tyneside and North Sea coastal environment, but his along with other artists' work was lauded in Newcastle's Laing Art Gallery and other galleries that Willie had been able to visit during his teenage years. He would have been able to see the artists George Horton and John Falconer Slater sketching and painting on the cliffs, sands and quays of Whitley Bay, Cullercoats, Tynemouth and North Shields, and he was still living in Cullercoats when Slater founded the North-East Coast Art Club there in 1920. Horton had seen Winslow Homer sketching when the American artist spent his eighteen months in Cullercoats in 1881 and 1882.[27]

Willie had not been able to visit his childhood home since he left in 1921, but he was now living in the city which held collections of

Winslow Homer's Cullercoats pictures, watercolours, etchings and drawings. The Cooper-Hewitt Museum was the recipient of a Homer family bequest and owned a large number of the Cullercoats pictures. Homer's works were also to be found at other New York galleries, including the Metropolitan Museum, the New York Public Library and the Brooklyn Museum, not far from the Ovington Studios. In New York City Willie could see *Men and Women Looking Out to Sea, View of Tynemouth Bay, Fishergirls on the Beach, Cullercoats* and dozens of other images of his home town. He never spoke to Burt about Homer, but Burt related Willie's work to Homer's. 'Yes. That's just the kind of work he would have liked. Yes.'

In the refuge that Willie had at the Ovington not only did his painting improve but he found again a cultural and social life that he missed from his home. There was music here and Burt toyed with the guitar, playing folk music mostly. Willie was impressed with Burt's versatility, but rather like Burt's attitude to his visual art, Willie did not approve of his musical taste. 'That stuff is so banal ... repetitious. And the lyrics are too sentimental,' he remarked.[28] Music was an art in which Willie knew he was Burt's superior. He brought a guitar and a tape recorder to the studios and practised for months until he was playing pieces by Bach. The Ovington boys did not know the other use to which the tape recorder was being put, or that Willie's skills, knowledge and love of music went a long way back. Once, when he and Burt were talking about women, he gave a hint when he talked of a young woman he had courted 'in Boston': 'She played the harp in an orchestra. I learned the harp too, so we would have something in common.'[29] He knew that in creating a legend, elements of truth could help and protect him.

And so Willie's life as retired photofinisher, artist and friend continued on Fulton Street. Meanwhile, his life as *rezident* was changing, with a new code name, MARK, in early 1952 and with the arrival of the illegal Reino Häyhänen on 21 October 1952. It was originally planned that Häyhänen would be a member of Valery Makaev's *rezidentura*, but Makaev's disgrace and recall and the abandonment of the second *rezidentura* had thrown that project into disarray. As a short-term measure, Häyhänen was initially managed by the legal *rezident* Mikhail Nikolaevich Svirin, the first secretary to the Soviet United Nations delegation in New York, but Svirin was given a new diplomatic role in April 1954 and Häyhänen was assigned as Willie's chief assistant.[30] Little knowing then that within months he would be Häyhänen's boss, it is likely that Willie had received, photographed and passed the Centre's message of welcome to VIK in 1952 or early 1953, via a dead drop, as the new illegal was acclimatising to life in and around New York. The welcome was hidden in a hollowed-out 1948 Jefferson nickel. When decoded, in 1957, it read:

> We congratulate you on a safe arrival. We confirm the receipt of your letter, to the address 'V repeat V' and the reading of letter no. 1. For organisation of cover, we gave instructions to transmit to you three thousand in local [currency]. Consult with us prior to investing it in any kind of business, advising the character of the business. According to your request, we will transmit the formula for the preparation of soft film and news separately, together with [your] mother's letter. It is too early to send you the Gammas. Encipher short letters, but the longer ones make with insertions. All the data about yourself, place of work, address, etc. must not be transmitted in one cipher message. Transmit insertions separately. The package was delivered to your wife personally. Everything is all right with the family. We wish you success. Greetings from the comrades. Number 1 3rd of December.[31]

Whereas Willie's first illegal identity was that of a deceased Lithuanian-American, and his second, Emil Goldfus, was that of a native American child who had died in infancy, Häyhänen's identity was that of a live double, Eugene Nikolai Maki.[32] The real Eugene Maki was born in the United States in 1919 and his Finnish-American father had taken him and his family to the Soviet Union in 1927. As a teenager, Eugene became an NKVD informer, and in 1949 the NKVD gave his United States birth certificate to Häyhänen, who was sent to Finland to 'become' Maki as part of his training to be an illegal.[33] As 'Maki', Häyhänen presented himself and his Idaho birth certificate at the US legation in Helsinki on 3 July 1951 and signed an affidavit explaining that he had been residing in Estonia and Finland since his mother's death. A year later he was issued with a United States passport and was in New York by the autumn.

No doubt the Centre thought that a Finnish American would have a good chance of success in recruiting members of his community for espionage work. In the 1920s up to 30 per cent of Finnish-Americans were associated with communist or socialist groups, particularly the IWW.[34] But the appointment and deployment of Häyhänen was a major error on the part of the Service, and a disaster for Willie. Häyhänen was a year younger than the real Maki. He had been born and brought up near Leningrad and became a teacher. Learning Finnish at college he was first used by the NKVD as a translator and interpreter during the Finnish–Soviet War of 1939–40.[35] He became conversant with SMERSH tactics and a member of the Soviet Communist Party in 1943. In 1948 he was brought to Moscow for illegals' training but was utterly unsuited to the life of the illegal. Parted from his Russian wife, he married bigamously in Finland and began drinking heavily. When his Finnish wife, Hannah, joined him in New York, their abusive alcoholic lifestyle continued.

Häyhänen's arrival on the scene coincided with other dangers that began to beset Willie. The FBI had become aware of the 'Allo, allo' broadcasts when their transmission frequencies were discovered and then monitored by the National Security Agency (NSA) signals intelligence experts. The FBI knew that the broadcasts were coming from the Soviet Union, but did not know why, or who they were for.[36] Then, in June 1953, a New York City police detective heard a strange story. One of the officers in his precinct had a teenage daughter whose boyfriend Jimmy Bozart was a delivery boy for the *Brooklyn Eagle*. On his collecting day that week, he had come away from an apartment building in Foster Avenue with a handful of change and dropped a nickel. The coin split apart to reveal a tiny compartment containing a miniature photograph wrapped in tissue paper. The detective called on the boy, took charge of the coin and handed it on to the FBI. Close examination revealed that the coin was constructed from two separate nickels that clipped together and could be opened with a pin inserted into a tiny hole in the lip of the coin. The microphotograph was of ten columns of typed, five-digit numbers.[37] The message would not be decrypted for another four years and would turn out to be Häyhänen's 'welcome note' from 3 December 1952, very likely taken down and photographed by Willie and inserted into a coin that he himself had hollowed and constructed, only for it to be lost or spent as loose change by Häyhänen or Svirin.[38]

From June 1953, the FBI worked hard to discover the meaning of the coin and the microfilm. The man they brought in to tackle the case was 35-year-old Robert J. Lamphere, one of the FBI's most experienced specialist counter-intelligence agents. During the Second World War he had tracked and cornered Nazi agents, and at the end of the war he joined the team working on Soviet espionage techniques. He had worked on the Fuchs and Rosenberg cases and was skilled in the analysis of the decoded VENONA traffic. Within days of its discovery, the hollow coin and its hidden microfilm were on Lamphere's desk. The FBI laboratories confirmed that the nickel had been constructed by an expert and that the numbers on the microfilm had been typed on a Cyrillic-script typewriter. Lamphere sent copies of the microfilm to FBI and NSA cryptanalysts for any leads on breaking the code. He also contacted all United States intelligence agencies, together with agencies in Canada and the UK, to discover what light they could bring to his case.[39] The Royal Canadian Mounted Police (RCMP) were particularly interested for Canada had had recent experience and success in debriefing Soviet defectors. The RCMP officers were cagey, but they indicated various things for the FBI man to consider. They urged him to take seriously the thought that the Soviet Union might have an illegal agent operating in New York, and that the microfilm and the hollow nickel might be linked to the 'Allo, allo' broadcasts.[40]

Lamphere pondered. The US had become wise to Soviet intelligence techniques, having broken the LIBERAL spy ring and rendering inoperative the VOLUNTEERS; the Soviet consulates in New York and San Francisco had been closed down; and Soviet diplomatic and trade missions were under constant surveillance. Lamphere prepared a memo for his New York office chief, arguing that the Soviet Union did have an illegal agent in New York. The nickel, the microfilm and the five-digit numbers were evidence of the communications system, he reasoned. The watch on the Soviet embassy in Washington, and similar watches by the British and the Canadians on the Soviet embassies in London and Ottawa, suggested an alternative route for messages back to Moscow Centre. Lamphere guessed Mexico City, or possibly Paris, as the likely communications link. He also speculated that the illegal might have couriers working for an airline or shipping line. The man had arrived on a false passport, he suggested, and then changed identity papers when he settled in New York. The action Lamphere recommended included the monitoring of suspected couriers on Paris–New York and Mexico–New York journeys. He also proposed a closer FBI liaison with United States Customs, the Immigration and Naturalization Service (INS) and the State Department in the checking of United States passports issued abroad. Lamphere's chief accepted the argument but bemoaned the lack of hard evidence. Without it, the bureau could never countenance the cost and staffing implications of Lamphere's memo, he said, and the proposal was shelved.[41] Two years later, Lamphere left the FBI after a distinguished career and joined the United States Veterans Administration.

Willie was not aware of Lamphere's deductions, but by the summer of 1954 he had as his *rezidentura* assistant the man who had lost the hollow nickel in the first place. However, Häyhänen was not a happy man. He had hoped for a comfortable post in the culturally and politically safe confines of a Soviet embassy.[42] His English was not good and he was coming to loathe the language, so as much as possible he avoided places where he had to speak English and frequented bars used by Poles or Finns. After Svirin's departure, he waited months before he received a message to meet Willie. They met at RKO Keith's Movie Theatre in Flushing, Häyhänen wearing a red and blue striped tie and smoking a pipe for identification. Willie recognised him immediately. Häyhänen's recollection of Willie, whom he knew as MARK, was of a tall, thin man, dressed in clothes similar to those described by Burt Silverman: grey trousers, a shirt with a tie in the hot summer weather, a jacket and a straw hat with a wide band. They walked from the cinema to a café some distance away. Willie took his role as a boss seriously, briefing Häyhänen on the urgency of getting cover work that would still leave him time for his espionage tasks. Willie organised regular meetings and said that he would pay Häyhänen directly, rather than have him paid via the dead drops.[43]

Amongst Häyhänen's early espionage jobs in New York was to pass on a report emanating from a Soviet agent in the UN Secretariat. It was to be collected by the legal *rezidentura* for forwarding to Moscow, but somehow the report went missing and the agent in the UN, frightened of the implications, sought to break his contact with the Soviets.[44] Willie may have been unaware of this particular lapse, but he was certainly aghast at Häyhänen's incompetence. The assistant failed to locate dead drops and, to Willie's particular outrage, did not know the Morse code.[45] His photography was poor, his microdots were inadequate and he was ignorant of the technique to hide them in magazines. Willie went back to the methodology that he had used in the NKVD training department, setting his fellow illegal in the field exercises in microdot preparation; and, if the results were not adequate, like the strictest of schoolmasters he set the exercises again. But unlike his previous pupils – his niece Lidiya, Kitty Harris, Konon Molody and Kirill Khenkin – Häyhänen was neither bright nor committed. Willie's exasperation began to border on the pathological. Why did Häyhänen not recognise his eminence and learn the trade from him? Willie was unaware of the Häyhänens' turbulent marriage, but he was aware that his assistant drank too much. His recurring head colds, chest infections and sinusitis meant that he could not always smell the alcohol on Häyhänen's breath, but he did recognise the hangovers and the unshaven, dishevelled appearance.

Willie did not have the reputation of a party member ready to denounce others, and no KGB records that might show his concerns about Häyhänen have been declassified, but the Centre did react in early 1955 by recalling Willie to Moscow for 'a vacation' and 'reliability checking'.[46] The relevant records have been read by Vasily Mitrokhin, and there is no doubt as to his conclusion:

> It is obvious that the KGB wanted to keep VIK in intelligence work no matter what, regardless of signs that he was in trouble, because they did not want to expose any of their operations, because the training of a replacement would be difficult and time-consuming, and because they regretted wasting so much time and money on VIK.[47]

If Willie was departing for Moscow, there was some work to be done before he left. He knew that he could be away for some time and needed to prepare as best he could for the interim, ensuring that VIK caused as little damage as possible during his absence, and so shortly before he left he was relieved to learn that his assistant had at last acquired some cover. As Eugene and Hannah Maki, the Häyhänens had rented a store and ground floor flat in Newark, New Jersey, and began to set it up as a photographic shop and studio, the type of business that Willie had advised. Willie informed the Centre and then had to ensure that Häyhänen could be communicated with during his absence. He took his assistant to his studio at the Ovington Studios and gave him a short-wave radio receiver. Willie took Häyhänen to Fulton Street twice more in the late spring and early summer of 1955. On these occasions, late at night, he did not take Häyhänen up to the fifth floor, but kept him outside, and brought down printing equipment for the Newark photographic studio and shop. He told Häyhänen that he expected to leave for Moscow in June and gave detailed briefings about what was to be done during his absence. He prepared a pack of instructions about photography, for both business and espionage purposes, and ordered him to continue the microdot preparation exercises. He also ordered him to get out and get acquainted with locals to improve his English.[48] Specific arrangements were made for payments that had to be made. In particular, a sum of $5,000 in cash was to be paid to Helen Sobell, wife of the Morton Sobell who was serving thirty years for his role in the LIBERAL spy ring. Willie took Häyhänen to a remote part of Bear Mountain Park, where they buried Mrs Sobell's money in different hiding places. The Soviet officer who had recruited Morton Sobell wrote a letter, which Häyhänen was to use as identification when he gave the money to Mrs Sobell.[49] These were Häyhänen's final orders.

Next, Willie had to explain his absence to his friend Burt Silverman. Times were hard, he said, so to make ends meet he had invented a piece of equipment that would make multiple prints from a single colour negative. He showed Burt how it would work and said he was off to market it in California, where he had a contact who would get him a good deal on the rights.[50] Willie's final arrangements for departure were made with the Centre, and shortly before he left in June 1955 he was delighted to receive a message that he had been promoted to full colonel in the KGB.[51] However, his greatest joy was that he would be seeing his wife and daughter for the first time in nearly seven years.*

---

* Pavel Sudoplatov, in *Special Tasks*, states that Willie had come to Moscow on an earlier leave, when Viktor Abakumov and Vyacheslav Molotov were still ministers. However, questions and answers on any such visit were not permitted when Evelyn Fisher, accompanied by Russian foreign intelligence staff, was interviewed for *Ogonyok* magazine in 1997.

14

TESTING TIMES

Using one of his Western aliases and sets of documents, Willie Fisher travelled though Mexico, Paris and on to Vienna, where he 'changed his shoes' and picked up from a Soviet office a passport under another name to take him to the USSR.[1] He stayed in Paris for two or three days and whilst there went to see Jacques Tati's film *Les Vacances de Monsieur Hulot*. Back home with family and friends the aesthete Willie Fisher, who loved to talk about painting, literature and music, now talked tirelessly about this film.[2] 'I think', said his friend Kirill Khenkin, 'that he wanted to be like Jacques Tati.'

On the evidence of the film, Willie Fisher *was* Jacques Tati. Like Tati as Hulot, Willie was going on holiday. Willie may have been attracted into the cinema by the film's reputation, but as he watched, he began to see his own life unfold in front of him. The film began with an idyllic coastal vista and cut to the chaos of a mainline railway station thronged with holidaymakers. As the platform announcement spluttered onto the soundtrack above the hubbub of the crowds, Willie knew at once that the film was about him and for him. Critics have interpreted the first sounds from the loudspeaker as the announcement of the film's title character, 'Hulot, Hulot',[3] but for Willie it was the call sign for his radio messages from the Centre, 'Allo, allo'. At the distorted announcements, the travellers swarm from platform to platform. The film's inventiveness and visual comedy carried him along, but increasingly he saw himself in it. Hulot was about his own height and wore a small trilby hat, just as he did. There is an extended scene early in the film where the vacationer Hulot checks in to the seaside hotel. Just before he arrives, the radio in the hotel lobby whistles and squeaks into life with musical entertainment for guests at their leisure. Hulot passes guests who relate to each other, but not to him, and then has problems getting the desk clerk to understand him as he registers. This may be due to the pipe gripped firmly between his teeth, with unlit tobacco trailing. A cigarette smoker like his father, Willie was occasionally required to smoke a pipe for visual contact or signal, or was himself required to look for a pipe smoker who would have a message for him. The exasperated desk clerk has to take the pipe from Hulot's mouth to understand what he is saying. Registered, Hulot adjourns to his anonymous upstairs room and comes down to eat in the hotel's cavernous restaurant, alone. Life in the hotel goes on; radios and gramophones burst into life and stop, an earnest young man assails a companion with a complex political thesis. Hulot himself strolls or drives about the resort and its environs. When the film ends, the holidaymakers return home and the resort is empty.

Les Vacances de Monsieur Hulot was filmed during two summers in the early 1950s, in the French resort of St Marc-sur-Mer. The climate of Brittany's St Marc is warmer than that of Cullercoats on England's north-east coast, but the seascapes are similar. At both resorts it is possible to drive down an incline to a sandy beach, possible almost to step from the village to the beach, and both beaches have quays nearby. In a film of less than ninety minutes Willie could experience once again the life of the seaside resort. The tourists arrive for the summer and leave the resort empty of visitors for the winter. In this film he was both holidaymaker and resident. Sitting in the audience, he was on holiday yet was reminded that neither New York nor Moscow was home. He was seeing his life played out before him and it was no wonder that, although there were some things he could not say to those closest to him, he spoke incessantly about the film when he arrived in Moscow.

Ellie and Evelyn were of course delighted to see Willie. When he had left for New York, Evelyn was barely out of high school and now she was a graduate in a good job as a technical editor, specialising in aeronautical texts, at Moscow's Foreign Language Publishing House. Ellie was still playing the harp at the children's theatre, but the whole family was able to holiday together when Willie returned and they visited Leningrad and other parts of western Russia. Back at home they enjoyed their time at the dacha and entertained family and friends, Rudolf and Alexandra Abel, Willie and Valentina Martens, Kirill and Irina Khenkin. When the Abels visited, or when Rudolf visited on his own, he and Willie would carve wood, or make music. Both men played the guitar and the mandolin, and they would swap instruments as they played duets for their own amusement or to entertain the company. Whilst Willie had been away Rudolf had become proficient on the accordion, and this brought a sound back into the Fisher household's music-making which was reminiscent of Heinrich on the concertina.

Outside the home, in Moscow and in the Soviet Union generally, Willie could not fail to notice a new, more relaxed mood. The trauma of the losses during Stalin's purges and the 1941–5 war had lessened somewhat and there was a perceptible atmosphere of greater hope, for although the new man at the helm, Nikita Khrushchev, had not quite achieved full power he was clearly not Stalin. At the Centre, Willie was irritable about changes in his department – the old disciplines were in decline; new, younger people had been appointed; and he thought that there was gross over-staffing – but the familiar requirements remained in place and Willie was debriefed and briefed anew.[4] With the Korean War over, the policies developing in the context of the Soviet nuclear capability meant that the notion of the Special Period which had underpinned Willie's first missions in the United States was being rethought. Willie's political thinking had to be checked and redirected, and his New York role clarified, but despite the failures, and a tacit awareness of the Häyhänen problem, Aleksandr Korotkov's illegals policy was still intact.

Willie had been successful and had proved reliable in New York. However, he was well into his fifties, and had not been adept in recruiting agents, so perhaps the question arose as to whether he should be recalled permanently. But as far as the Centre was concerned, Willie was their best 'espionage tutor' and, despite the problems he faced with Reino Häyhänen, he had kept him in check. The KGB still refused to confront its error of appointing Häyhänen and sending him to the United States as an illegal in the first place but, if Fisher were withdrawn, they would not only have to find someone else to deal with Häyhänen, they would have to find ways of disposing of the studio and the storeroom at the Ovington, and their contents.[5] On balance, it was decided that it was a case of 'as you were' and that Willie should return to New York. There was also a suggestion that Willie might be used to find Aleksandr Orlov in the United States, given that he knew him well. With Stalin now dead, the tacit deal that Orlov had made was redundant, but the order was not given.[6]

In December 1955, after almost six months in the USSR, Willie returned to the United States. The Soviet Union had changed whilst he had been away, but the United States he returned too was changing as well. Senator Joe McCarthy's anti-communist crusade was fading into history, the spy trials were over, the consumer economy was booming and ideological politics was in decline. This in itself made the recruitment of potential Soviet agents from traditional sources more difficult, but Khrushchev's secret speech to the Twentieth Congress of the Soviet Communist Party made it virtually impossible. The speech, 'denouncing Stalin and his crimes', was made in February 1956, just weeks after Willie returned to New York, and reports of the speech began to appear in the USA from March. The Communist Party of the USA received the official summary of the speech in April and in June the American *Daily Worker* published a full translation of it. Peggy Dennis, wife of the American party's general secretary, read the text just before publication and wept.[7] She was not alone, and in less than two years after the publication of Khrushchev's speech in the West, membership of the Communist Party of the USA had slumped to barely 3,000.[8] Willie Fisher was not oblivious to this, but as a Marxist-Leninist, a full member of the Communist Party of the Soviet Union, a senior KGB illegal and their man in New York, he simply carried on with his job.

It was not until the late spring of 1956 that Willie, as Emil Goldfus, returned to the Ovington Studios. Willie had paid advance rent before he had left nearly a year earlier but he was now well in arrears and the building superintendent had begun to get concerned. If Goldfus did not show up soon, he told Burt Silverman, his studio, 505, would be cleared and relet.[9] Coincidentally, 'Emil' telephoned Burt the next day. He had done the deal on the multiple colour printer in California, he said, but on his way back through Texas he had suffered a heart attack and had been in hospital for four months. Burt was astonished and not a little alarmed, and when Willie arrived at the studios a few days later, Burt showed his concern. Willie played down the worries about his health – he had not wanted to cause anyone any trouble, he said – but Burt persisted. He knew that his friend did not enjoy good health, suffering with chest problems and sinusitis, for there were always laundered handkerchiefs hanging up to dry in Studio 505. Burt remained concerned and found that he was beginning to care for the older man. Burt's father had died from heart trouble just two years before, and there was a hint of the son–father relationship between Burt and Willie now that the older man was back.

Willie had changed, too. He became more gregarious and joined Harvey Dinnerstein and Burt to take photographs in Brownsville and in Washington Market, using some of the prints for paintings. He sought to be closer to the young artists, stopped standing on the outside looking in, as it were, and asked up front if he could join their group. From late 1956 he sat in on the group's sketching sessions and contributed with the rest – Burt, Harvey, David Levine, Sheldon Fink and Danny Schwarz – when they hired a model for life drawing.[10] Burt, David and Sheldon did sketches of the man they knew as 'Emil', Danny photographed him at the studios and Burt painted him in oils. David, the newest of the Ovington Studios tenant artists, got to know 'Emil' well on his return to the studios and they were soon dropping in on each other. Willie had now taken on another room, a storeroom which he turned into a workshop, where he installed a small lathe and started to make silver jewellery and rosewood boxes. Willie had no problem if David, or any of the neighbours, came into his rooms. Apart from the art accoutrements, there were bits of radio receivers and cameras. There were also photographic prints, quite a few of which were dull views of Bear Mountain Park, David noted. By the same token, David was quite relaxed if Willie ever came into his studio. David ran a weekly art class for a local women's group and Willie would call in most weeks with coffee for the women and to join them in conversation, finding that they liked his company.[11]

Willie Fisher was becoming more relaxed and comfortable in his cover life as Emil Goldfus, but as KGB officer codenamed MARK he had Häyhänen and the future of the New York *rezidentura* to deal with. The two illegals did not actually get together again until the summer of 1956 and Willie saw immediately that Häyhänen had deteriorated since they last met. Willie was not to know that Häyhänen had done nothing more to establish the photography business in Newark, nor did he know that the drunken rows with Hannah had turned increasingly violent. He may have known from another source, or worked out for himself, that Häyhänen had pocketed the $5,000 intended for

Helen Sobell, and he could see that the man was a continuing liability. The Centre's plan to get Häyhänen back, and at that point to change the work of the New York illegal *rezidentura*, even to wind it up completely, needed to be activated and Willie informed the Centre that Häyhänen's recall was the only option.[12] So, early in 1957, a message came for Häyhänen promoting him to lieutenant colonel and granting him leave in the Soviet Union.

Realising that he was cornered, Häyhänen prevaricated for weeks, postponing his departure at every opportunity. The travel arrangements that Häyhänen was required to make were typical for a KGB illegal. He was to apply for a passport in the United States, but under a new name. The first part of his journey would be by sea to Le Havre, then through France to West Germany. He would make his way to West Berlin and into East Berlin, where he would exchange his American passport for the Soviet passport that would take him to Moscow.[13] Häyhänen's delaying tactics became more manic. 'The FBI is watching me,' he told Willie. 'Three of them questioned me on the ship and I couldn't leave.' Willie had to take this seriously because it was quite conceivable that this was the case; Häyhänen might have been discovered and even be working for the FBI. Or, the whole saga might have been a very elaborate KGB ruse and a test for Willie, with Häyhänen working for the FBI, but as a double agent. Willie's only course of action was to continue to follow orders and to get Häyhänen onto a ship bound for Le Havre. He gave his inept assistant his travel expenses and Häyhänen did actually board the *Liberté,* which set sail for Le Havre on 24 April 1957.[14]

Whilst Willie was playing out this tense drama as MARK, he was continuing his cultured cover life as Emil Goldfus at the Ovington Studios. He was now discussing art history and theory at length with David Levine. He lent David his copy of Arnold Hauser's *Social History of Art*, and David particularly noted a marginal comment: 'A reflection of the importance of chance (disasters, famine, floods, etc.) in commercial affairs. One day rich, the next reduced to poverty by fortuitous circumstances, then by fortuitous circumstances elevated to richness, etc. etc. etc.'[15] There was also a firm mark around a quotation from Fyodor Dostoyevsky: 'What can be more fantastic and unexpected for me than reality?'[16] Willie also gave David a book of Isaak Levitan's paintings.[17]

Events on each front were moving quickly for Willie. Burt Silverman had married on 2 March 1957 and Willie was invited to the pre-nuptial party. He was suffering particularly badly from sinusitis on the day and his friends were worried about him. He may have to go away to warmer, drier weather for a whilst to help his breathing, he said, probably Arizona. At the party he drank more than was usual for him and stumbled a little. It was an Orthodox Jewish wedding and, like all the men present, Willie was required to wear a yarmulke. He wore it at a rakish angle. 'He must be Jewish, with style like that,' joked some of the guests. They had mused before that Willie might be Jewish; whilst others argued that anyone wearing a yarmulke at that angle could not possibly be Jewish. It was good-natured banter during the evening, which, for some guests, added to the enigma of Emil Goldfus, something else about him that they could not quite place. Willie drank a little more and was the last to leave. Burt and Helen Silverman invited him for supper a few days later, shortly before they left for their honeymoon in Europe and before 'Emil' was due to go to Arizona. He brought a bottle of Liebfraumilch, his favourite wine, with him and was talkative, perhaps a little tense, they thought. Towards the end of April, he paid rent in advance for Studio 505 at the Ovington, took paints, brushes and canvases, and departed for Daytona Beach, Florida.[18]

Whilst he was there, on 1 May 1957 Häyhänen arrived in France, took the train to Paris and made coded telephone contact with Soviet officials as required. There were two further contacts with local KGB officers, the second a visual contact by which Häyhänen confirmed that he would leave for Frankfurt by train the next day. Instead, he went to the United States embassy and informed an official there that he was an officer in the Soviet intelligence service, that he had been working in the United States for five years and that he now needed help.[19] He was frightened to return to Moscow as he had been ordered, he said, and wanted to defect. The US embassy immediately put Häyhänen into the hands of the CIA who questioned him and, convinced that he was genuine, contacted the FBI who on 10 May flew him back to New York, where their agents began their interrogation. They searched the Häyhänens' small house in Peekskill, north of New York City, and found false documents and a hollowed-out Finnish coin. When Häyhänen was questioned about the code systems he used, he gave his personal code, which was enough for the FBI to decrypt the microfilm message found in the hollow nickel almost four years before.[20] Although Häyhänen was continually baffled by New York City geography, forgetting the locations of dead drops for example, after days of interrogation the FBI did manage to glean enough information from him to pinpoint the place where Willie had given him the radio and photographic equipment. Their men headed for 252 Fulton Street, the Ovington Studios, and kept watch.[21]

Quite why Willie came back to New York has never been fully explained, but he was back by 18 May. The most likely explanation would be that the FBI had moved quickly, and that the KGB was not sure that Häyhänen had defected. Häyhänen had been seen in Paris on 4 May prior to his scheduled departure for Frankfurt the next day, but perhaps he had simply missed the train, for the KGB might have recalled that it had taken him weeks to arrange his departure from New York. Perhaps he was lying drunk somewhere, in a ditch or in a hotel room, or perhaps he was genuinely physically ill and in bed or in hospital. In New York, Willie was moving again and arrived at the Hotel Latham on East 28th Street just off Fifth Avenue, registering as Martin Collins.

All this time Willie seemed oblivious to any danger, assuming that if the erratic Häyhänen had done anything foolish the Centre would have notified him by short-wave radio message, sign or dead drop. Another possibility that might have crossed his mind was that the KGB had abandoned him to his fate. On 23 May FBI agents saw a man fitting the description that Häyhänen had given them – height, facial characteristics, typical clothing and dark straw hat with broad white band – when he entered and left the Ovington Studios. They followed him, but lost him. 'I'll bet there was hell to pay on that one,' said Robert Lamphere.[22] On 13 June the FBI had confirmed that the man Häyhänen knew as MARK, and the Ovington artists as Emil Goldfus, was registered as Martin Collins at the Hotel Latham. They had found their man and could make a case that he was a spy, but although the unpredictable and unreliable Häyhänen was sticking by his story, he would not agree to be a prosecution witness in a court of law. He wished to protect his mother, sister and brothers in the USSR, he said, but he failed to mention his Russian wife.[23]

The FBI therefore took a different tack and briefed the Special Investigations Department of the INS in Washington, whose agents travelled to New York with the FBI unit. On the night of 20 June 1957 Willie returned to his room, no. 839, at the Latham Hotel and early in the morning of the following day FBI special agents Ed Gamber and Paul Blasco knocked at his door.[24] Willie opened it and the agents entered, telling him that they wished to speak to him on 'a matter involving the internal security of the United States', at one point addressing him as 'Colonel'. Willie was naked and sat on the edge of his bed whilst the agents fired questions at him. 'We got no co-operation from him whatsoever. He said nothing. He just sat there and looked at the floor. He didn't say a word,' remembered Gamber. The FBI men contacted their base and it was agreed that the INS people should take it from there.[25] INS agents entered and, when Willie identified himself as Martin Collins, they charged him under violation of immigration laws. He was ordered to get dressed and to pack his clothes and belongings, which he did, throwing bits and pieces into the waste bin as he went about his task, including paint containers, a block of wood wrapped in sandpaper, pencil stubs, tissues, some empty pharmaceutical bottles, nasal sprays and a half-empty box of Sheik condoms.[26] He kept asking to go into the bathroom, where he took sips of water, fixed his false teeth and used the WC. The room was full of incriminating evidence. The INS agents could not help but notice the Hallicrafter radio and its aerial strung across the ceiling and out of the bathroom window, but they did miss the piece of paper on which he had taken down his last message from the Centre, and the page from his one-time pad for de-coding it. He had not disposed of them the night before. Desultorily, he dabbed some wet paint on his sketchbook with the papers, palmed them, and flushed them away in the bathroom.[27]

The INS men continued to search the room, looking initially for firearms and personal documents, but it was financial material that drew their attention for in effect they were standing in the New York branch office of the KGB bank. They found a bank deposit book giving a balance of $1,386 and the key to the safe-deposit box at the Manufacturers Trust, which would be found to contain $15,000. There was a large amount of cash in the room itself, $6,500 in notes of fifty and twenty dollars. $5,000 of this was in one bundle to which was attached two passport photographs, one of a man, the other of a woman. On the backs of these photographs were written the names 'Morris' and 'Shirley'.[28] They also noted down the contents of his wardrobe, cupboards and drawers. Amongst the items were five pairs of Daks trouser, two jackets, a considerable collection of prescribed and over-the-counter medicaments, eleven pairs of white socks for his athlete's foot and thirty-three white handkerchiefs.[29] Willie was handcuffed to INS agent Ed Boyle and taken under escort to the INS New York headquarters at 70 Columbus Avenue. He asked, and was allowed, to take his cigarettes with him. Later in the day he was taken to Newark airport and flown to McAllen, Texas, arriving at the alien detention facility in the city just before dawn on the following morning.[30]

Meanwhile, FBI agents took over searching Willie's hotel room and cataloguing its contents, noting a miniature photographic kit including special high-quality film stock[31] and bolts and pencils hollowed out as secret message containers. In a wallet they found some scraps of paper with messages that seemed to be signals for use in Mexico City. The contents of the waste bin were examined and the smooth wood block broke apart to reveal Willie's one-time pad and his signal schedule. The discarded pencils contained microfilmed letters from Ellie and Evelyn, all sent and received after his departure from Moscow in December 1955. Most damning were the Hallicrafter, the radio reception and transmission schedule,[32] the microdot equipment and the money, but none of the finds in themselves were evidence of intelligence gathered. The authorities were aware of this and continued to pressurise Häyhänen to give testimony in court and to pursue the immigration violations.

At the McAllen detention facility Willie was saying little to the INS and the FBI. The FBI was offering him a new life and generous financial support, but he was having none of it. He admitted that he had entered the United States illegally, saying that he had found a cache of American dollars in a ruined blockhouse in Russia. He had bought a forged American passport in Denmark in 1948, he said, and entered the United States from Canada later that year. There was one other thing that he told his interrogators: admitting that Emil Goldfus and Martin Collins were not his real names, he said, 'My name is Rudolf Ivanovich Abel.'[33]

Some years later, back in Moscow, Willie's friend Kirill Khenkin asked him why he had identified himself as Rudolf Abel when he was arrested. 'Well,' said Willie, 'firstly, I knew Rudolf's life story as well as I knew my own. Secondly, I had used this name in my signals to the Centre. And finally, I was testing "The Swede".'[34] Based on this answer, Khenkin inferred that Willie had sacrificed himself and hinted at an elaborate theory which would explain Willie's capture, at the heart of which was Aleksandr Orlov. The Centre had been prevented from seeking Orlov when Stalin was alive, but was free to do so after his death. On his return to the United States, calculated Kirill, Willie's main task was to test Orlov and certainly this had been on Aleksandr Korotkov's mind.[35] Kirill thought that Willie was far too clever to be captured. The black straw hat with the white band was deliberate because Willie knew how to throw off a tail. A technique was, say, to wear a distinctive hat into a church, or a store, or an alley, and then exit by a different route without the hat. However, Willie kept the hat on all the time. The contents of the hotel room gave away nothing that was of great significance. Even the passport photograph of Morris Cohen, with his name written on it, found with the $5,000 was part of the plan. Of course, Orlov knew Willie, his assistant in Europe in the 1930s, very well and he also knew Rudolf Abel. He was one who knew about the Fisher–Abel double act, so knew that Willie Fisher was not Rudolf Abel. Orlov also knew Morris Cohen because he and Leonid Eitingon had trained him in Spain. In the press photographs and the newsreel pictures on his journeys to and from the courtroom during his trial, Willie was looking up; he even looked at the camera. This, Kirill argued, was so that he could be identified. The FBI would have shown the pictures of Willie and Morris to Orlov, but Orlov never let on that he knew their true identities or even that he knew them at all. He did apparently identify Willie as 'a KGB officer', remembering him from the Lubyanka, perhaps, but did not recall his name, or what his job was.[36] Orlov, then, was never a true defector, but had kept the faith of a Chekist.

Kirill's theory provides some detail, but it does not provide enough adequate answers. It seems highly unlikely that the KGB would take such a risk as to put Willie Fisher and Reino Häyhänen into the hands of the Main Adversary. Also, Willie was unaware that Morris and Lona Cohen, and Konon Molody, were now a new illegal ring in London. Even if the KGB was prepared to dispense with the ageing Willie and the unstable Häyhänen, they would not risk a loss of this magnitude. There was also the possibility that Orlov would identify Willie and Morris to the FBI and the CIA, but that the Americans would not use the information in any proactive way. They would simply wait to see what happened next. In his memoirs many years after the events, Pavel Sudoplatov was also dismissive of the idea that

Orlov was never a true defector and remained faithful to the cause. Much more important than Willie or Morris were the Cambridge Five, particularly those who still remained in the West – Philby, Blunt and Cairncross. Orlov knew who they were because he had instigated the policy behind their recruitment and knew their roles. It must be certain that he never revealed this particular information to the American intelligence services for if he had, Philby's defection would have been prevented. As Sudoplatov put it: 'I don't believe that loyalty to the Soviet system was the reason Orlov did not expose the Cambridge group ... Orlov was simply struggling to survive.'[37]

In essence, behind Willie Fisher's capture is a catalogue of mistakes. Häyhänen should never have been put into this work in the first place and when his incompetence was picked up, he should have been recalled immediately. Willie should not have taken him to the Ovington Studios. If Willie had informed the Centre the moment Häyhänen left for France, the KGB should not have lost him in Paris. Willie should not have been allowed, or required, to go to Florida when Häyhänen left, but should have stayed by his radio receiver and watching the signal sites. He should have been informed the moment Häyhänen did not board his train. The possibility of defection should have been suspected immediately and, at that point, Willie should have been ordered to abandon his post and leave the United States. But perhaps there had been an order to this effect, because on 21 May he visited a doctor for a health check and a smallpox vaccination, almost certainly as a requirement for overseas travel.[38] Did Willie make another mistake by lingering in New York? Or was there a delay in preparing the escape route for him? The KGB could not be certain that Willie's American aliases had not been compromised so he could not use passports in the names of Andrew Kayotis, Martin Collins or Emil Goldfus with safety. The KGB *rezidentura* in Ottawa, with the help of the Communist Party of Canada, had acquired a passport for a 54-year-old Canadian, Robert Callan, but Willie did not receive it, or collect it, in time.[39] Given all of these errors, Willie then seems to have responded in a way that was typical of the man and of the system he was wedded to.

He was aware that he was being watched, but was not trying to attract his pursuers: far from it. He was trying to shake them off but, as he said to Kirill on another occasion, the FBI had a lot of men in the field; these agents were in cars and were in constant touch with each other by radio and 'walkie-talkie'.[40] The argument that the hat was used to attract the FBI men weakens when one remembers that Willie was bald. In hot weather, as it was in June 1957, he wore his hat to protect his scalp from the sun for he would not have wanted to add sunburn or sunstroke to his list of ailments. Nevertheless, the distinctive black straw hat with its wide white band remains a riddle and a strong argument in Kirill's case. In his earliest statements to the FBI, Häyhänen was clear and specific about the peculiarity of this hat and each time Willie was spotted during the six-week chase he was wearing the hat, even when he was in his studio.[41] The only answer would seem to be related to money. Not only was Willie parsimonious by nature, but he was working to a tight budget and would have to account for all expenditure. The purchase of a number of hats would have identified him as vain and extravagant, traits of character which were unacceptable in the Chekist. Concerns about money sealed Willie's fate. As the KGB paymaster in New York, Willie had thousands of dollars in his room at the Latham Hotel and needed to make payments to a number of agents, including, it is said, Kim Philby.[42] With the right documentation, it would not be difficult to get the money across the border into Canada. He could, of course, abandon his post and the money, but he would be suspected of taking the money, or of having lived luxuriously on it during his time in America. In 1937 one of the allegations against Reiss was that he had defected with operational funds. Orlov had taken thousands of dollars with him when he defected. He had safeguarded his family by threatening Stalin and Yezhov, and he was in a position to carry out those threats, but Willie's only relatives, Ellie and Evelyn, were vulnerable in Moscow. Makaev had been disgraced after financial irregularities, and the money that he was responsible for was considerably less than the amount Willie now had. Häyhänen too was suspected of misappropriating funds. Without safeguarding the money he had responsibility for, Willie must have realised that his life would not be worth living. Again, Sudoplatov should be listened to:

[Fisher] told me the story of his arrest when he attempted to recover $30,000 hidden in a Brooklyn, New York, safe apartment, for which he would have to account to the Centre. We both agreed that it had been stupid of him to return for the money; it cost a great deal more in lawyers' fees when he was arrested by the FBI. But he feared that if the money were left behind he would be suspected of stealing it.[43]

The truth is that Willie took a risk and was caught, but the way he dealt with his arrest and its aftermath is a major part of what secured his place in history.

TRIAL

Willie Fisher spent his first night at the McAllen Alien Detention Facility on 22 June 1957 and was kept there for six weeks. His cell had an iron-framed window of reinforced glass with a steel grating, and when he looked out into the yard he could see the thick blocks of the cells' outside walls. The door from the cell into the corridor was also set into a steel grating, so he could be observed. Inside the cell he had a military-style bed with a thin mattress and a blanket, a chair and a small sink attached to the wall. Previous prisoners had hacked into the plaster walls of the cell, in places exposing parts of the mesh that matched the steel framework holding the door.[1] The other inmates of his Texas prison were mainly Mexicans who had been picked up near the border. Illegal immigration remained the initial focus of his interrogation, but FBI agents Ed Gamber and Paul Blasco had daily sessions with him during his time at McAllen. Now, he did speak to them and would talk about the weather, or make general conversation, but when they turned to matters of his mission, he gave them no information. 'If we asked him about espionage or his activities, he just clammed up. He said nothing.'[2] He remained unmoved by FBI offers of luxury accommodation and a well-paid job with 'a federal agency' in exchange for his co-operation. The KGB man made an impression on Gamber: 'We tried to break him, but we didn't. You had to admire him.' Willie remained calm and resolute, placing his initial hopes on deportation for illegal entry into the United States. In a letter to the supervisor at McAllen, he asked the Immigration Service to contact the Soviet embassy on his behalf.

As identification to his bosses, a signal and an aide-memoire should the interrogation become heavier, he mixed his and Rudolf Abel's biographies, truth and fiction, and gave an explanation to his captors as to where his ability in English had come from:

> As I have stated to officials of the US Immigration Service, my name is Rudolf Ivanovich Abel, born in Moscow USSR in 1902, July 2. My father, Ivan Ivanovitch [sic] Abel, deceased. My mother, Lubov Karneeva, deceased. Education – elementary and secondary schools in Moscow from 1910 to 1920. I have worked as a translator and teacher of English in secondary schools in Moscow.
>
> ... I request the Immigration Service to contact the USSR Embassy officially, giving all the information on this matter.[3]

He knew that his studio and storeroom at the Ovington had been searched. He wrote to David Levine (Burt and Helen Silverman, he believed, would be honeymooning in Europe by this time) asking him to 'go through my paintings and preserve those you think worth keeping until – if ever – I may be able to get them again'. He enclosed $35 for a month's rent, so that David could do the job at his leisure.

By August it was clear that Reino Häyhänen had agreed to give evidence in court: in fact, the prosecution had made it clear to him that if he did not do so he would be returned to the Soviet Union.[4] This meant that the authorities could pursue espionage charges rather than the lesser crimes associated with illegal entry so Willie was taken back to New York, where he faced three counts: conspiring to transmit military information and details of the nation's atomic energy programme to the Soviet Union; conspiring to gather such information; and conspiring to remain in the United States without registering with the State Department as a foreign agent. If found guilty of the first charge he faced the death penalty, whilst the second two charges carried maximum sentences of ten years and five years in prison. The indictment listed Häyhänen, Mikhail Svirin, Vitaly Pavlov and Aleksandr Korotkov as the co-conspirators. Pavlov had been second secretary at the Soviet embassy in Ottawa in the 1940s and had been named in the VENONA traffic. The grand jury indictment continued, setting down the type of material that was destined for the Soviet Union and the methods of communication used:

[The] defendant would use short-wave radios to receive instructions … the defendant would fashion 'containers' from bolts, nails, coins, batteries, pencils, cufflinks, earrings and the like … suitable to secrete microfilm and microdot and other secret messages … [the] defendant and his co-conspirators would communicate with each other by enclosing messages in said 'containers' and depositing them in … pre-arranged 'drop' points in Prospect Park, Brooklyn, and in Fort Tryon Park, N.Y., and at other places …

It was further part of said conspiracy … [that the] defendant would receive from the Soviet government … large sums of money to carry on their illegal activities … some of which money would be stored for future use by burying it in the ground.

… [The] defendant and certain of his co-conspirators would, in the event of war between the United States and the Union of Soviet Socialist Republics, set up clandestine radio transmitting and receiving posts for the purpose of continuing to furnish … information relating to the national defense of the US, and would engage in acts of sabotage against the US.[5]

Willie was brought to court in New York's Brooklyn, not far from 252 Fulton Street, for trial and held at the Federal Detention Centre in West Street. It was difficult to find a lawyer for the defence, so the judge did what was required in these circumstances and asked the Bar Association to appoint someone. Their decision was swift and apt. James B. Donovan's current work was in insurance law, but as a US navy and Office of Strategic Services (OSS) veteran from the Second World War and an associate prosecutor in the Nuremberg war crimes trials of Nazi leaders in 1946, he was the perfect choice. Indeed, although Donovan was not related to Major General William 'Wild Bill' Donovan, he had been a key member of Wild Bill's staff and had been responsible for drafting Donovan's proposals for the Central Intelligence Agency, which was to take the place of the OSS after the war. He was imbued with his namesake's strong belief in the democratic need to keep separate the roles of secret intelligence and counter-intelligence.[6] Donovan's service record and his eminence as a New York lawyer marked him as the ideal choice for the alleged spy's counsel, and the declassification of documents in the 1990s and at the beginning of the twenty-first century shows that the United States government and its intelligence agencies were thinking along the same lines.[7] The public could not have realised the importance of the decision to appoint Donovan.

When his client's true name emerged in the West many years later, Donovan was dead, so he knew and addressed the man he defended as Rudolf Abel, never as Willie Fisher. Ideologically and politically, the two men represented opposite poles. Professionally, Donovan would represent his client's case to the best of his ability whilst Willie would continue to be true to his oath as an illegal and show the virtues of the Chekist, 'warm heart, cool head, clean hands'.[8] Donovan would be true to the Constitution of the United States and uphold the culture and virtues of the free world. As professionals in their field who had both seen action in wartime and who had interests in art, literature and history, the two men understood and respected each other. Not only that, they had wit and a sense of humour in common. Donovan, however, had not bargained for some of the repercussions after his agreement to take the case. First there were the smart asides, like the social occasion when he was teased by a fellow guest for ordering a Russian dressing with his salad, but these were soon followed by poison pen letters and anonymous phone calls. Professional experience enabled Donovan to grit his teeth and cope with this, but it was often his wife Mary who took the phone calls, so the home number was changed. No longer the wartime naval and intelligence officer, Donovan was now a family man and his young children were sometimes bullied at their elementary school, being told that their father 'defended Commies'. Jim and Mary responded by explaining to them what their father's profession was and what this particular job meant.[9] The family also eased the tension one evening when they improvised a song to the tune of 'Rudolph the Red-Nosed Reindeer', with Jim perhaps subconsciously recalling Willie's recurring sinusitis whilst the children revelled in the name and the tune:

Rudolf Ivanovich Abel
Was a very happy spy,
And wherever spies would gather
They would say, 'What a guy!'

Then one dark and stormy night
Came the FBI:
'Rudolf in our very sight
You did dare to spy tonight!'

Now Rudolf's days are over
But all other spies agree
Rudolf Ivanovich Abel
Will go down in history.[10]

As a multi-lingual journalist working in Moscow in the early autumn of 1957 under the auspices of, if not now for, the KGB, Kirill Khenkin was leafing through a new batch of Western periodicals when he came across the current edition of *Paris Match*. There he found a picture of his friend Willie Fisher, with the accompanying story telling of the arrest and arraignment in New York of a Soviet spy by the name of Rudolf Abel. Kirill sought permission to go home early on the pretext of suddenly feeling ill and rushed to Ellie and Evelyn's apartment. It was he who brought them the news of Willie's arrest, although whilst he was at the apartment an official from Willie's office arrived with the same news.[11] All her married life Ellie had known that the liberty of a Soviet intelligence officer was always at risk, but the new situation was as serious as it could be for not only was Willie on trial for espionage in the United States, there would be other implications if his British nationality was discovered. If the British authorities discovered the real identity of 'Rudolf Abel', they might seek his extradition to the United Kingdom, where he could be charged with treason, a capital offence.

The New York trial began on 14 October and Donovan decided that Willie would not give any evidence in his own defence,[12] a policy which met with Willie's approval and which he had adhered to, telling the FBI nothing since the moment of his arrest. Three years later, when they were arrested in London and facing trial as members of the Portland spy ring, Morris Cohen (VOLUNTEER), now Peter Kroger, and Konon Molody (BEN), now Gordon Lonsdale, spoke briefly to each other. They agreed that they would 'pull a Milt'. '[Molody] knew our name for [Willie] was Milton. "Pulling a Milt" meant that we would say nothing. So we said nothing at all about any of these activities … Nothing at all.'[13] Willie's silence may have been an order from the Centre, or it may have been something he remembered from his father's stories of the cartridge trials. Speaking would have drawn much more attention, and although Gamber and Blasco had not identified any specifically English accent in the speech of the man they had interrogated,[14] his accent would have been more exposed and, of course, he would have been cross-examined. Keeping Willie off the witness stand also allowed Donovan and his assistants Arnold Fraiman and Thomas Debevoise to concentrate the defence on the contravention of Abel's rights under the Constitution of the United States and on their cross-examination of prosecution witnesses. The main prosecution witness was Reino Häyhänen, who appeared in court with dark glasses and his fair hair and moustache dyed black. The prosecution team, Assistant Attorney General William F. Tompkins and his juniors James J. Featherstone and Anthony R. Palermo had worked hard to prepare Häyhänen for his role in the court. Their biggest problem was managing Häyhänen's alcoholism. Without alcohol, Häyhänen simply could not function but if he was drinking too much he was incoherent.[15] His English was still poor and in court he had to have questions repeated, or the judge or lawyers asked him to repeat answers if his voice dropped or they had problems with his accent. He looked a shambles, was overweight and came over as incompetent and pathetic as Donovan exposed him as a bigamist, an abusive partner and a drunkard.[16] Häyhänen revealed for the prosecution that the $5,000 hidden in Bear Mountain Park was for Helen Sobell, thus linking Willie to the Rosenbergs. It was a blow, but Donovan made play with the fact that Häyhänen had never delivered the money to Helen Sobell, making it clear to the jury that Häyhänen was a thief to boot.[17]

Other witnesses included FBI agents, people who had been involved in the discovery of the hollow nickel, the superintendent of the Ovington Studios and a sombre Burt Silverman. Burt identified 'Goldfus-Abel' and the typewriter that 'Emil' had lent him a few months before. Whenever he had registered as Emil Goldfus at an American hotel over the previous two years, Willie had put Burt's name as the person to be notified in the case of emergency. Burt had been Willie's first choice as the person to clear Studio 505, and he had wanted to correspond with Burt after his imprisonment. In a letter addressed to Donovan, Burt had declined, and felt guilty about this for years afterwards.[18] A more sensational witness was Roy Rhodes, a master sergeant in the US Army who had been motor sergeant at the US embassy garage in Moscow between 1951 and 1953. In one of the bolt containers found in the search of Häyhänen's property was a message concerning Rhodes, codenamed QUEBEC. He had been ensnared in a classic espionage honey trap in 1952, admitting in court, 'I woke up the next morning in this bed with this girl in what I had taken to be her room.'[19] Blackmailed, Rhodes had provided the Soviets with information on codes and the nature of his work and the work of other military personnel at the embassy. The Soviets had been trying to reactivate Rhodes since his return to the United States and the note in the bolt contained Häyhänen's orders to attempt another contact. When Donovan's cross-examination of Rhodes was complete, the judge muttered to the lawyers, 'Please notify me if the sergeant is proposed for a commendation.'[20]

On the following day, Donovan issued a statement to the press:

> We have reviewed with Mr Abel all the Government evidence and pointed out to him the advantages and disadvantages of taking the stand as a witness in his own behalf. He is perfectly willing to let the case go to the jury on the Government's evidence. It is his own decision, made after a careful examination of all the testimony, that it would not be to his advantage to take the stand.
>
> We shall not call Mr Abel and we do not plan to call any other witnesses.[21]

Before the final statements, the prosecution had read one paragraph of one of the microfilmed letters found in Willie's hotel room: 'Dear Dad, It's almost three months since you went away. Although it's not so much as compared with eternity, still it is a long time and the more so as there is a great quantity of news to tell you.'[22] The letter was dated 20 February 1956 and used by the prosecution to show that 'Abel' had been at home in Moscow during the autumn of 1955, when he was absent from the Ovington Studios. The prosecution's use of the letter enabled Donovan to read the rest of it, and the five other letters, to the court. Evelyn's letters, apart from one, were in English, whilst Ellie's, signed Yelya, were in Russian. Interestingly, Evelyn's letter continued:

> First of all, I am going to marry. Please don't be astounded. I am much surprised myself, and still it is a fact to be taken for granted.
>
> My future husband seems to be a good guy. He is thirty-four and a radio engineer ...
>
> News number two: we are to get a new flat of two rooms. It is not what we supposed to get but it is a flat for ourselves and it is much better than what we have now.

News number three: I have found a job, engineer referent in aviation ...[23]

In her other letters, Evelyn is witty, but shows increasing doubts about her husband. (The marriage ended two years later.) Ellie's letters are longer and more poignant, writing of her love for her husband and of his for her, the pain of being apart, the flowers and fruit in the garden at the dacha, family friends (whom she did not name) and pets (which she did). She gave Willie details of her health and worried about his. As the letters were read, a journalist noted that Willie's 'face grew red and his sharp, deep-set eyes filled with tears', and that women jurors had tears in their eyes.[24] Willie's emotionless professional façade slipped for a moment. He always found it difficult to talk of love, avoiding talking of his deceased brother, for example, fearing that he would break down,[25] but on this occasion he could not do what he usually did when matters of emotion, sentiment or love came close to him: he could not change the subject, or leave the room.

Two days later, just after noon on Friday 25 October, the jury retired to consider its verdict and returned at 4.50 p.m., finding 'Abel' guilty of all charges. Judge Mortimer W. Byers discharged the jury and gave notice that sentence would be passed on Friday 15 November. In his submission to the judge prior to sentencing, urging him not to consider the death penalty for Abel, the last of five points that Donovan made was:

> It is possible in the foreseeable future an American of equivalent rank will be captured by Soviet Russia or an ally; at such time an exchange of prisoners through diplomatic channels could be considered in the best interest of the United States.[26]

On 14 November the *Literaturnaya Gazeta* in Moscow gave the first Soviet response to the case, describing it as a 'fiction' and a 'hoax' on the American people.[27] The following day Willie was sentenced. He received the maximum prison sentences for counts two and three, and thirty years in prison for count one. He was also fined a total of $3,000, but, most significant of all, he escaped execution. However, despite the ruling that the prison sentences were to run concurrently, for a man of fifty-four (or fifty-five, given the birth date Willie had provided for the American authorities), it was effectively a life sentence.

At Moscow Centre wounds were licked, but it had not been a complete defeat. They had lost one of their best men, but he was at the end of his mission and at the end of his days as an officer in the field; and anyway his *rezidentura* was due to be wound up. It had happened more messily than had been anticipated. Aspects of their tradecraft had been exposed, but not all of these were unique to the KGB. Moreover, they had taken revenge on a backsliding agent without having to dirty their own hands, for Master Sergeant Rhodes was immediately arrested and punished by the Americans. On the larger canvas, since Willie's arrest the Soviet Union had launched their Sputnik satellite and sent a dog into orbit around the earth, demonstrating their lead in space and rocket technology, so they had given the Main Adversary some things to think about. Apart from all this, to the men at the Centre, Willie had exemplified the virtues of the Chekist and been true to each line of the illegal's oath. They could also see that Häyhänen had been exposed in the West as a bigamist, an alcoholic and a thief, not as a man who had defected with honourable motives. On the other hand, from their own observations and from sections of the American press they could see that the loyal Willie Fisher, on the other hand, had impressed his lawyers, court officials and jailers.

Willie's own feelings might be expected to have had a different focus, but the evidence suggests that he took to imprisonment well, almost embracing it. He was proud to have upheld his oath as a Chekist and an illegal. He was also true to his father, for Heinrich had been imprisoned for his Leninist faith. No doubt Heinrich had spoken of his imprisonment with pride when he told Willie about how he had worked for the cause. He would also have told his son how to cope with incarceration, how to keep strong and, again, how to survive. Heinrich knew that a prisoner had to keep his mind active, so reading and learning were important and passing skills and knowledge on to other inmates were part of this strategy. Willie also used these techniques to keep fooling his captors by asking for textbooks and treatises, which he said he needed to sustain his interest in mathematics. But this was also a ploy, for by continually referring to mathematics he was trying to camouflage the real meaning of the groups of five-digit numbers that had been discovered on scraps of paper in his rooms. These were of course his messages from the Centre in code for deciphering, and by doodling tables of figures on any paper that was to hand during his captivity he was attempting to show an obsession with mathematics.

'I'm drawing up logarithm tables,' he would say to prison officers and request more mathematics books.

During his remand in New York and after his conviction, Willie remained in the prison at West Street. Here, because of a shortage of maximum-security cells, he had to share with Vincent J. 'Jimmy' Squillante, a New York mobster arrested for extortion. Squillante objected to sharing with 'a foreigner and a Commie' and, when his request to be moved was turned down, he responded by cleansing the floor and walls of the cell with mop and bucket, a crude gesture designed to demonstrate just what he thought of his cellmate. Rather than showing offence, Willie showed his gratitude and as a thank you started to teach Squillante some French. 'What in heaven's name would a gorilla like Squillante do with a knowledge of French?' Donovan asked on one of his visits to his client. 'Frankly, I don't know,' Willie replied, 'but what else could I do with the fellow?'[28]

Donovan visited Willie regularly, on one occasion taking his young son John with him, with the express purpose of singing the spy their family version of 'Rudolf the Red-Nosed Reindeer'. 'He laughed with the understanding of a family man,' said Donovan, 'but rather quickly changed the subject.'[29] In June 1958 Willie was transferred to the penitentiary at Atlanta, Georgia, and a month later heard that his sentence had been upheld in the Court of Appeals. He settled to serve his sentence in the southern state. (The US Supreme Court upheld the sentence in the spring of 1960.)

Years later when he set off on one of his stories, 'In our prison…', Evelyn would stop him. 'Oh, come on, Daddy. It wasn't a prison. It was a sanatorium.'[30] This was a perceptive comment, because once Willie was sentenced and in prison, the pressure was off. For the first time in nine years he was safe, with his food and shelter provided, in an institution where he could be himself and live the reality of being a convicted spy, imprisoned for his crimes. Nor did he have to improvise a domestic and social life in a foreign country.

Unusually for 'communists' in American prisons, he was not bullied by other inmates or by the prison officers. The wardens regarded him as someone special, almost as a 'prisoner of war' that they had a particular responsibility for. At West Street, Willie drew cartoons for the prisoners' newspaper; then, aware of the overcrowding problem, he used the draughtsmanship skills he had acquired in the Tyneside shipyard drawing office to come up with a series of plans to show how a relocation of the prison laundry would provide extra storage space. Warden Alex Krimsksy forwarded the drawings to the US Bureau of Prisons, but Willie's proposed building works were not carried out, denying him the satisfaction of leaving a legacy of prison architecture in the United States.[31]

Donovan's meetings with Willie at West Street meant that both men had come to know Krimsky quite well and on one occasion, when Donovan was leaving after a consultation with his client, they met Krimsky in the detention room:

> [Abel] immediately asked if he could get more books. He said, 'For me, Warden, cell life is very tedious.' ... I told Abel, in front of the warden, that I thought he would be interested in the book *Labyrinth* on wartime counter-espionage, by Schellenberg of Hitler's staff.
>
> 'Schellenberg claims', I said, 'that at one time during the war the Germans had captured over fifty radio transmitters belonging to Russian agents, and turned them around to feed misleading military information back to Russia.'
>
> Krimsky laughed loudly, but Abel quickly countered, 'Did he tell how many of theirs we grabbed and did the same thing with?'[32]

At the Atlanta penitentiary Willie, prisoner number 80016-A, sketched, painted and started silk-screen printing, which was encouraged by the prison, and in his first winter there Willie's processor was used to print the penitentiary's Christmas cards. In later years Willie designed the cards as well as printing them – Russian winter scenes and the shepherds at Bethlehem – and the Warden there had some of Willie's larger work for his office wall.[33] Willie taught his cellmates to play bridge and kept up his mathematics and his science reading, organising a subscription to *Scientific American*. He kept up a correspondence with Donovan not only about the case, but also about art and mathematics, and his lawyer responded with help in acquiring books for his client.[34]

But the image of 'Rudolf Abel' as a compliant, model prisoner does not tell the complete story. Willie remained obsessively interested in mathematics and science partly to maintain the deception that these were innocent hobbies, rather than the *modus operandi* of a professional spy. He also rooted out other Soviet spies and agents in the penitentiary, such as Morton Sobell, of the Rosenbergs' ring, with whom he played chess.[35] He made contact with prisoner Kurt Ponger, who worked in the penitentiary's dental department and who had been jailed for conspiracy to commit espionage during his time as an American serviceman in Austria after the war. Willie was convinced that the Americans had not turned the Soviet agent and that Ponger was still reliable and committed to the Soviet cause.[36]

Willie also kept a disciplined approach to his rights as a prisoner and continually sought to have overturned the ruling that prevented him from writing to his family.[37] He could, however, receive letters from his family and although these were carefully examined by American intelligence officers before they reached him in Atlanta, they contained primarily family matters and, from Evelyn, news, comments and ideas about art and literature. Back home in Moscow, Ellie was not only unhappy, but also angry with the state that had required years of her married life to be spent apart from her husband. It was now unlikely that she would ever see him again, she wrote to the KGB. The outcome was that she lost her job with the children's orchestra and she now looked forward to her declining years financed by a small pension and the company of her daughter, her niece Lidiya and a small but supportive group of friends and family.[38]

16

EXCHANGE OF PRISONERS

The eventuality that James B. Donovan had foreseen prior to Judge Byers's sentencing of 'Rudolf Abel' in November 1957 occurred just over two years later. Early on the morning of 1 May 1960 the CIA pilot Francis Gary Powers, Frank to his comrades, took off in a U-2 aircraft from Peshawar in Pakistan. His mission – the longest and potentially the most dangerous of the U-2 reconnaissance programme so far – was to fly across the Soviet Union photographing key strategic sites. He would fly over the Baikonur missile-testing site in the desert to the east of the Aral Sea and then over the Soviets' top-secret plutonium production centre some 50 miles north of Chelyabinsk. After continuing north over Sverdlovsk, he was then to fly north-west. On this next section of his route the schedule was to photograph a new missile base at Plesetsk in the far north and the submarine yard at Zhdanov before turning to fly south towards base at Bodø in Norway. The nine-hour, 3,800-mile flight was to be at 70,000 feet, out of the range of Soviet aircraft or missile interceptions.

No one is quite sure what happened over Sverdlovsk. It was in the interests of everyone involved to keep the details secret. One story was that a Soviet agent had managed to attach a bomb to the U-2 in Peshawar and that the bomb detonated over Sverdlovsk, but this was never taken seriously. Another was that the plane suffered a flameout and Powers had had to lose altitude to restart his engine. The story that he told his military and KGB interrogators implied that a missile exploded near the tail of his aircraft at 68,000 feet. He brought the disabled U-2 down to 15,000 feet, where he bailed out and parachuted to safety. This version of the events was the one publicly accepted by Powers's CIA bosses.[1]

The chairman of the Soviet Union's Council of Ministers, Nikita Khrushchev, fumed at the penetration of his nation's defences and air space, but was exultant at such a coup against the Main Adversary. He used the incident to sabotage the painstakingly arranged summit meeting between the United States, the Soviet Union, the United Kingdom and France in Paris later that month. In captivity behind the Iron Curtain, Powers coped well with the interrogation. One of the U-2 team's most experienced and reliable members, aware of the role and purpose of his aircraft and its reconnaissance programme, he managed to convince his captors that he was a simple pilot, not really sure about the complex espionage kit that his plane was carrying. He was tried in Moscow and on 19 August 1960 was found guilty of espionage and sentenced to ten years' 'confinement', three years of imprisonment and seven of hard labour.

So, the opportunity for an exchange of prisoners was now a clear reality, but the preparation for such an exchange had begun well before Powers's conviction. Although all appeals and a request for a rehearing of the Abel case had been exhausted by 16 May 1960, when the United States Supreme Court ruled that the conviction and sentences should stand, Donovan had a communication channel with 'Mrs Abel' in place. She had written as early as February 1959 from an address in Leipzig[2] to thank Donovan for his work on behalf of her husband, and the payment of legal fees was underway. The moment Powers's U-2 was shot down, CIA lawyers started work on a basis for a Powers–Abel exchange: not only was it quite clear to the Agency that the 'Mrs Abel' letters were coming from the KGB, but also that Moscow would be prepared to negotiate through Donovan.[3] Even as early as 11 May 1960, when he first spoke publicly about the Powers case, President Eisenhower had countered the Soviet charges of the United States 'deliberately spying' by reminding them of Colonel Abel and the evidence brought against him in 1957. Just days later, weeks before the Powers trial in Moscow, American newspapers were calling for an Abel–Powers swap and in early June Oliver Powers, the U-2 pilot's father, wrote to Colonel Abel in Atlanta Penitentiary offering to intercede with the State Department and the President of the United States for his release. In return, he asked if Abel would give his blessing and also approach the authorities in his own country for his son's release. Abel was sympathetic to the father's request, but used the opportunity to let Mr Powers know that the United States Department of Justice was not letting him write to his own family. Oliver Powers's and Colonel Abel's letters were available to the American authorities and on 24 June, two months before the Powers trial in Moscow, the US Department of Justice began to allow Abel to correspond with his family.

Dwight D. Eisenhower's presidency was drawing to its close and in November 1960 John Fitzgerald Kennedy was elected President of the United States. Khrushchev welcomed the change and at the time of Kennedy's election signalled to the incoming administration that he felt the U-2 incident should become 'a thing of the past' and hoped that 'a fresh wind will begin to blow'.[4] So Donovan was not surprised to receive a letter from Abel in the first week of January 1961:

In one of her last letters my wife suggested that I appeal to the new President. I stated that I did not think it possible, in the present circumstances, for me to do so but suggested that she do so herself, much in the same way as the relatives of Powers and the others have done ... I would be indebted to you if you could find it possible to offer her some counsel on this matter.[5]

Donovan followed his usual practice and forwarded the communication to the CIA and the Justice Department. He also wrote to Abel's wife advising her to give the new administration a little time and then to send the President a simple letter, petitioning for her husband's release. Just over a month passed before Mrs Abel, writing from Leipzig, sent her appeal. Khrushchev had already released two Americans detained after another incident and it seemed that Mrs Abel's letter was an invitation for President Kennedy to respond with the release of the colonel, but there was no immediate reply. However, there was some action, for a few weeks later FBI officers visited Abel in Atlanta to interrogate him further, no doubt probing to see if he would give them anything before a possible release. Abel gave them nothing. Three months later Mrs Abel wrote to Donovan again, but this time there was something new. A delicate game was being played:

Thinking over the question whether there is something that could be done to precipitate the solution of the question, I remembered of the letter sent to my husband last year by the father of the pilot Powers. I have not read it but if I am not mistaken, he suggested to my husband that some mutual action be taken to help his son and my husband be released. Rudolf wrote to me then that Powers's case had nothing to do with him and I did not consider myself that any benefit could come of it for us or the Powerses...

I wanted to write about it to Mr Powers at once but was afraid that all the affair could be given publicity which would influence unfavourably the fate of my petition. Not knowing how to act, I have decided to ask your advice ... what should be done to accelerate our case? Please, do not leave my letter without reply.[6]

Donovan and the CIA were now convinced that Mrs Abel's letters were from the KBG and that the Soviets were offering a deal – a swap of Powers for Abel. This was indeed the case, for a detailed strategy and tactical plans for an exchange were in place in Moscow. It was no coincidence that Mrs Abel's letters were being sent from Leipzig. Germany was a focus of Cold War activity and the KBG had its major headquarters for German and broader western Europe operations in Potsdam's fashionable Neuer Garten on the banks of the river Havel, close to Cecilienhof where Churchill, Truman and Stalin had met in the summer of 1945. The exchange itself was given the code name LYUTENTSIA by the KGB and co-ordinated by Vladimir Pavlovich Burdin, who had been the *rezident* in Ottawa for much of Willie's time in New York and who was working with 43-year-old Boris Yakovlevich Nalivaiko, a KGB officer with experience in Germany, Austria and Czechoslovakia and who was now heading illegals work in Berlin.[7] There was more correspondence before 'Mrs Abel' wrote again to Donovan in September 1961. Included in the envelope was a letter for Mrs Powers urging her to petition President Kennedy once more to take measures that would secure the release of her pilot husband. The letter to Donovan indicated movement on the part of the Soviet government:

On your advice I visited the Soviet embassy in Berlin and showed them your letter of July 26. I am glad to tell you that as before the Soviet representative showed great understanding of my case and reassured me of their willingness to help...

I gathered from our talk that there is only one possible way to achieve success now – that is simultaneous release of both F. Powers and my husband which can be arranged.[8]

The game of nudges and nuances continued, with the United States and Soviet governments signalling their moves through their intermediaries: Donovan and, on the Soviet side, the East German Wolfgang Vogel. (Vogel was an East Berlin lawyer who acted for the German Democratic Republic in a range of their international dealings. He was to become an expert in cross-border links and exchanges during the Cold War, making himself a considerable fortune in the process.) Meanwhile, Powers and Abel corresponded with their families, and the families with each other, under the watchful eye or the bidding of their respective governments.

By early 1962 the deal was close. Telling friends and colleagues that he was off to the United Kingdom to act for a client involved in an international life insurance merger, Donovan headed for a meeting with Vogel in East Germany. He broke his journey in London, and British intelligence smoothed his secret departure and flight from eastern England to Berlin. After briefings from the CIA, Donovan presented himself at the Soviet embassy on the morning of Saturday, 3 February. He was directed to the consulate next door, where he was greeted by a woman in her mid-thirties, Evelyn Fisher, who introduced herself as Rudolf Abel's daughter. 'Miss Abel' introduced her mother and a male relative, her mother's cousin, Herr Dreeves. Donovan took the taciturn Dreeves to be an East German police officer, but he was actually Yury Drozdov, Willie's KGB boss. At noon, Ivan Schischkin, 'second secretary of the Soviet embassy', entered and the meeting proper, or rather meetings, began. For five days Donovan shuttled between West and East Berlin, and in East Berlin between the Soviet embassy and Vogel's office. The Americans were pushing for two other detainees to be released and the Soviets were exploiting the East German role in the negotiations. Vogel needed to maintain his own government's profile, all the whilst realising that he was in the process of cornering a very specialised international market. The negotiators, with their masters in the background, edged closer together and as Donovan and Schischkin raised their glasses to clinch the deal on 8 February, Donovan knew that Colonel Abel had been moved from the penitentiary in Atlanta to New York in preparation for his flight to Berlin.

Less than twenty-four hours later, it was agreed that the Glienicke Bridge, connecting West Berlin and Potsdam, would be the transfer point and the time of the exchange was fixed for 8.30 a.m. on Saturday 10 February. Abel arrived in West Berlin and Donovan met with his client in the United States military compound early on the Saturday morning. He seemed to have aged since Donovan had last seen him. They chatted informally whilst Abel enjoyed an American cigarette and thanked Donovan for everything he had done for him. They travelled to the Glienicke Bridge in separate cars, Abel under heavy guard. Donovan walked onto the bridge with a West Berlin-based United States diplomat and, in civilian clothes, Brigadier General Leo Geary, the USAF/CIA liaison officer who knew Powers and could identify him. Schishkin approached from the East Berlin side, also accompanied by two men. At 8.45 Schishkin and Donovan shook hands to complete the formalities and signalled Powers and Abel, both under guard, to come onto the bridge. As the observers confirmed the prisoners' identities, Donovan and Schishkin gestured simultaneously and the crossing began. Powers moved first and, after exchanging greetings with Geary, the two men walked into the western sector and off the bridge. Powers was driven quickly to Tempelhof airport, where he and his party were flown to Frankfurt and then on to the United States.

Abel paused at the crossover point and asked for his official pardon from Fred Wilkinson, the warden of Atlanta Penitentiary, who had accompanied his prisoner and stood on the bridge as one of his guards. Wilkinson had made a point of talking regularly with his famous prisoner throughout his captivity and had no intention of missing this historic moment. Abel turned to Donovan, shook his hand for the last time and bade him farewell. He walked off the bridge into East Germany and was driven just a few hundred yards into 'The Forbidden City', the term Potsdam locals used for the KGB headquarters.

A covert KGB unit was sent to West Berlin to keep watch on the Glienicke Bridge from the American side, whilst armed KGB men were hidden in the East German customs office on the bridge and more KGB men commanded the armed Soviet soldiers at the checkpoint.[9] Ellie and Evelyn were staying at a house in the Forbidden City, awaiting Willie's return, but there was a delay so they decided to make the most of their time in Germany and went shopping in Potsdam. When Willie arrived at the house, his wife and daughter were gone, and agitated KGB men rushed out to bring them back. When they returned Willie, Ellie and Evelyn were together again for the first time in more than seven years.[10]

Back in Moscow there was a ceremonial, but secret, welcome for Willie, with the new KGB chairman, Vladimir Semichastny, presiding. Semichastny had been born in 1924 so was only three years old when the returning Willie Fisher had first joined the ranks of the Chekists. Willie had served under ten of Semichastny's predecessors, dating back to Vyacheslav Menzhinsky in 1927. Also in the welcoming triumvirate were Head of the KGB Foreign Intelligence Directorate, Aleksandr Sakharovsky, and Head of Soviet Military Intelligence, General Ivashutin. Khrushchev was not present, but Semichastny suggested to Willie that he ought to write to thank Khrushchev for his work on his behalf, which Willie did, completing the official requirements and duties of his return.[11]

Like most men returning after long prison sentences, he found it difficult to adapt to life at home. Home was the new private apartment on Mir Avenue, heralded in the letters, not too far from the family's previous communal apartment in Vtoroi Lavrsky Lane, but he could not settle. He had developed domestic routines as a man on his own in his series of hotel rooms and in the discipline of prison life. Now he was living as a family man once more, with a wife and an adult daughter. His depression was compounded by the decision he had made with his superiors in 1955 before he returned for the last part of his US mission, that he would give the name of his best friend as the coded signal should he ever be apprehended.[12] What he did not know was that Rudolf Abel had died two weeks after he had left for New York in December 1955. 'It had been a very cold day,' said Evelyn. 'Uncle Rudolf was walking to see friends in Moscow. He had a heart attack in the street and died.' 'If I had known that Rudolf was dead,' Willie said later, 'I would never have used his name.'[13] Privately, he visited Rudolf's last resting place in Moscow's German cemetery, but in public he was required to go by Rudolf's name for the rest of his life. Willie Fisher prided himself as a man who had betrayed no one, but now he felt that he had betrayed his best friend and it compounded the guilt he felt over the death of his brother Henry.

The pressure was even greater when James Donovan published his record and reminiscences of the case in his book *Strangers on a*

Bridge: The Case of Colonel Abel, in 1964. Donovan had come to admire his client and Willie's stock as a heroic Cold Warrior rose higher in the East and in the West. Donovan also reported the death of Reino Häyhänen.[14] The failed and disgraced illegal had apparently been killed in a road accident on the Pennsylvania Turnpike in the United States, although the most likely cause of death was cirrhosis of the liver.[15] To its own personnel the KGB made out that Häyhänen's death was a KGB hit and this too was used to enhance the Abel-Fisher profile in the organs.[16]

The KGB began to see great possibilities in Willie's capture, imprisonment and homecoming, and exploited them to the full. High school students in Moscow and beyond received visits from the heroic 'Colonel Abel', who regaled them with stories of his exploits in the entrails of the Main Adversary and with patriotic statements on the superiority of the Soviet system. In 1965 the writer Vadim Kozhevnikov published a novel entitled *The Shield and the Sword*, based on a version of Willie's life, and in 1966 Willie's short biographical piece for the youth communist newspaper *Trud* was published, under the name Rudolf Abel.[17] Two years later there was an even greater honour, or burden, when he was invited to speak a prologue to Savva Kulish's film *The Dead Season*. The film, a story of a Soviet intelligence officer who gathers information on a former criminal who carried out chemical tests on prisoners of war, was seen by over 100 million people in the Soviet Union in less than a year after its release.[18] Despite a request to have his own name used on the caption that introduced him as he moved to the camera to speak his prologue, again he had to appear as 'Colonel Rudolf Abel'.[19] Significantly on this occasion, despite the importance of his piece – the role of the secret services in protecting the world against the use of weapons of mass destruction, in this case chemical weapons – he looked embarrassed and talked away from the camera. This was in contrast to his fix on the press cameras when he was arrested in New York in 1957 so that the Centre, and Aleksandr Orlov, could identify him.

Willie Fisher was still a KGB employee and now back at the Lubyanka in Dzerzhinsky Square he learned more about the imprisonment of his old bosses, Pavel Sudoplatov and Leonid Eitingon, and of the death of Aleksandr Korotkov.[20] Willie was now part of the Fifth Department of the First Chief Directorate (Foreign Intelligence), still with the illegals, where the new boss was Anatoly Lazarev, but he had no particular job and, as Donovan had predicted, he was never fully trusted again.[21] Ironically, reminiscent of his cell at McAllen, he had a space in a room and a chair, but no desk. From here he was occasionally called to meet superiors, and his opinion on international matters was sought, but privately he was bitter and resentful. Not long after he returned, the GRU officer Oleg Penkovsky was exposed, tried and executed for spying for the West. When Penkovsky's British SIS courier Greville Wynne was sentenced to eight years' imprisonment in 1963, Willie was scornful. 'They should have sentenced him to death, like they did Penkovsky,' he said. 'That would have given the British something to think about.'[22] Wynne, of course, was used to bargain with and was exchanged for 'Gordon Lonsdale', Konon Molody (BEN), a year later. Willie and BEN, as he continued to be called, resumed their friendship, BEN less openly bitter than Willie, but a chronic alcoholic. He was encouraged to write an autobiography of sorts for publication in the West, in which he lauded Willie under the code name ALEC and the book, published in 1965, further enhanced 'Colonel Abel's' reputation.

Willie was sent to brief and train intelligence officers in Hungary and East Germany, where he was lionised. His host there was the head of the East German Foreign Intelligence Service, Markus Wolf. During the 1930s, the Wolf family, who were communists, had been exiled in the Soviet Union, and it is conceivable that the teenage Markus had met Willie in Moscow in the 1930s or 1940s.[23] In the 1960s Wolf was one of those who could snap Willie out of his gloom and he highlighted Willie's German ancestry, spelling the name 'Fischer' once more. The German spelling had fallen into disuse after the family's years in England and then the Russianising of the name in the Cyrillic script. Willie impressed Wolf by speaking of the German's doctor-playwright father and then launching into a discussion on European theatre of the 1920s and 1930s, science and mathematics. '[He] was a modern-day Renaissance man with a lively interest in chemistry and physics and a particular enthusiasm for Albert Einstein,' Wolf wrote in his memoirs.[24]

Wolf's first boss as Minister of State Security had been Ernst Wollweber, Willie's agent during his early days in the United States, but now that Wollweber had fallen from favour the security apparatus was headed by Eroch Mielke, and he too honoured their visitor. At a formal dinner for Willie, there was an empty place which no one paid heed to, until Lieutenant General Kleinung arrived and, seeing him, Willie smiled, stood and embraced the latecomer. Mielke had discovered that Kleinung had been one of Willie's radio trainees in Moscow in the 1930s and had stage-managed the public reunion of pupil and teacher. Willie returned to Moscow with presents of his favourite wine, the German Liebfraumilch, and continued his round of high school visits; many Russians now in their fifties and beyond recall being addressed by the famous colonel.[25]

One morning Willie was walking along the street behind the Lubyanka when he was approached by another man in his sixties. It was his old comrade from the Red Army days, Ernst Krenkel.

'Willie Fisher! How are you? What have you been doing all these years?' asked the delighted Krenkel.

'Haven't you read about me in the newspapers?'

'No. What papers?'

'Ah. I mean the American papers.'

'What are you doing now?' continued Krenkel.

'I work in there,' said Willie, pointing to the Lubyanka.

'What do you do there?' asked Krenkel.

'I'm a museum exhibit,' replied the gloomy Fisher.[26]

The work became harder to bear, but there were compensations at home and Willie began to enjoy family life again. His belongings had been put into crates and had arrived back in Moscow, via East Germany, before he did. He liked his American clothes, particularly his Daks trousers, and continued to wear them, although Evelyn laughed that the Americans had cut out all the pockets.[27] His paintings and prints from his time in the United States had been well cared for and his work was hung at home and at the KGB officers' club. He treasured his books in English, and amongst the art and science books, there were mysteries and detective stories. There were books in the home from when the family was in England in the 1930s, as well as others from Willie's time in America. The family had privileges, too, and could get books in English during the 1960s. Willie read and reread books by Saki (H. H. Munro), J. B. Priestley, Graham Greene, Dashiell Hammett and Raymond Chandler. He read poetry, too, enjoying Shelley, and returning often to Oscar Wilde's *The Ballad of Reading Gaol*. A particular favourite at home was Patrick Quentin's *Death My Darling Daughters*. 'If ever it was put down,' said Evelyn, who read voraciously in English, too, 'there was a fight as to who would pick it up.'

There was music in the home, played by Ellie and Willie on the piano and the guitar, or listened to on the gramophone. Willie enjoyed Bach, Handel, Chopin, Liszt, Greig and Debussy, and he and Ellie went to orchestral concerts and to the opera although Willie was less keen on going to the ballet. He continued to paint and draw and took great pleasure in cooking for the family, particularly at the dacha where he spent as much time as he could, much preferring it to the Moscow apartment. The dacha's plumbing needed a great deal of attention when he returned and he set about replacing the sewerage system. 'He liked jokes about lavatories,' said Kirill Khenkin, who helped his friend and mentor at the work.[28] They also walked their dogs and talked. BEN had a dacha nearby, but Khenkin was not encouraged to drop in when BEN was visiting. In Moscow, BEN and Willie would also call into Lev Heselberg's place on Kuznetsky Bridge Street near the Lubyanka, where they would meet with Eitingon and Sudoplatov, who had both been released from prison in the late 1960s, and other old illegals. Much to the disapproval of their wives, they would stay out late, reminisce and play billiards, a particular joy for Willie who now picked up a reputation as a pool room hustler, the espionage veterans dubbing him with a joke 'code name' or nickname – SHARK![29] They would take the occasional glass, too, but drink was a particular problem for the alcoholic BEN, who survived for only six years after his repatriation and died of a heart attack in October 1970. Willie enjoyed German wine but was never a heavy drinker. His vice was tobacco and he returned with resignation to the Russian Belomors cigarettes after his years of smoking American brands, calling his cigarettes 'coffin nails', the slang term he had learned during his childhood on Tyneside.[30] He also enjoyed being reunited with Morris and Lona Cohen, who came to Moscow via Poland after their release from British prisons in 1969, exchanged for the detained British lecturer Gerald Brooke.

However, Willie never mixed with or even met the other Westerners in the KGB, who had defected to the Soviet Union. Guy Burgess was dead within a few months of Willie's return and Donald Maclean lived outside Moscow. Kim Philby did live in Moscow and gloried in his KGB role, but Willie loathed him and had no wish to meet him. Intelligence officers should keep a low profile, Willie felt, so he disapproved of Philby's pursuit of fame as well as his drinking. He also utterly mistrusted Philby, calling him 'The Traitor', a tag that he along with other intelligence officers used for anyone who betrayed their own side. But in Philby's case, there was something else as well: as an internationalist, Willie felt that he had never betrayed his homeland but had remained constant in his political beliefs, whereas Philby had rejected and scorned everything that his homeland had given him, and this was something Willie could not forgive.[31]

Willie was philosophical in his last years. He was saddened at having to deceive his American artist friends in 1956 and was humbled when he knew of the letter that Burt Silverman left for him when he visited Moscow in 1967 'looking for Emil'. Of course, he was not informed that Silverman was visiting and would not have been allowed to meet him had he known. Burt wrote:

> I have been in Moscow for ten days, and will probably leave this coming Thursday. Before going, and in the hope that this letter does get to you, I should like to tell you a few things more … I'm sorry that I didn't write to you in Atlanta. In defense of that, I can only say that they were different times, and that I was not above fear. I was also counselled by what I thought were wiser heads. Hindsight, and a changed political climate, have made those decisions and that counsel seem excessively cautious or worse. Maybe the reason I'm here now is to make up for that.[32]

Willie regretted giving his life to espionage and would have preferred a career in education, or art.[33] 'If I hadn't gone to work for the foreign section when I did, I'd have been an artist,' he said to Kirill during one of their conversations walking the dogs near the dacha. 'A member of the Academy of Arts.' Then he paused and laughed, 'But I ha' me doots!' On another occasion, in a more gloomy frame of mind, he said, 'If you knew everything that was going to happen to you, you would take a rope and hang yourself.'

17

AN UNQUIET DEATH

The events of December 1938 were revisited upon Willie Fisher in the summer of 1971. When he went to the KGB personnel department to arrange his summer leave, he was informed, 'Leave is irrelevant. We're currently making the arrangements for your retirement.'[1] He saw the decision as a second dismissal and his intellectual and emotional bond with the state and the party was shaken once again. Thinking about what he might do in the future, he toyed with ideas of interpreting and translating, as he had done in his teens and early twenties, and later under Pyotr Kapitsa's patronage at the Patent Bureau, for Willie needed to work to justify his existence to himself and to the world, as well as to eke out his pension. But the moment he retired, he realised that he was feeling unwell, his cough was worsening and his breathing was sometimes difficult: the lifetime of cigarette-smoking was taking its toll. His father had died of pneumonia aggravated by smoking and now Willie was diagnosed with cancer of the lung. He was admitted to the KGB hospital for surgery on 25 October 1971, but his condition deteriorated rapidly. His boss, the head of Directorate S, General Anatoly Ivanovich Lazarev, had Willie's room bugged with the latest directional microphones and listening technology. To the end, the KGB remained suspicious that Willie had been turned by the Americans and needed to keep checking in case, through the pain or the drugs, he might reveal something.[2]

Willie sank quickly and the only information that emanated from his deathbed were his words to Evelyn, in English, 'Don't forget that we're Germans.' What did he mean? 'I don't know,' said Evelyn. Going back to the family lore, it was said that Henry was Lyubov's son and that Willie was Heinrich's son. Heinrich always thought of himself as German and for most of his life in Russia and much of his time in England to be safe he had to conceal this. Willie was present when his father died, so could it be that these were Heinrich's last words as well and that Willie needed to pass them on to his only child, as watch words, a reminder, a warning? 'Remember, this is our ethnicity. Remember, we're strangers here.' In telling the story of the family, as Evelyn had to do many times, she once said, 'I'm the last one.' Willie Fisher died on 15 November 1971 and, as befitted a Chekist hero, his body lay in state in the KGB hall close to the Lubyanka prior to his cremation at the Donskoi and the interment of his ashes in the cemetery there.[3] He had been back in the USSR for nearly ten years when he died and had had publicly to use the name of his dead friend Rudolf Abel throughout that time. Rudolf had been used in death and even now could not rest in peace, as he and Willie were used again, together. In their eulogy of Willie, a group of his comrades used Rudolf's name:

Krasnaya Zvezda, Moscow, 17 November 1971

Colonel Rudolf Ivanovich Abel, one of the oldest Chekists, a well-known Soviet intelligence officer, distinguished employee of the organs of state security, and member of the CPSU since 1931, died after a serious illness in his sixty-ninth year.

R. I. Abel was assigned to work in the organs of the OGPU in accordance with a Komsomol levy in 1927. From then on, for a period of nearly forty-five years, he faultlessly carried out complex tasks in the maintenance of our Motherland's security in various sectors of Chekist activity. Rudolf Ivanovich proved to be a daring, experienced intelligence officer and capable leader. He was always distinguished by love of the Motherland, a high sense of duty, party principle, impartiality and honor.

Being abroad, working there in complicated and difficult circumstances, R. I. Abel displayed exceptional patriotism, tenacity and steadfastness. His high moral character and manly conduct are widely known, evoking a deep response and arousing sympathy throughout the world.

The Communist Party and the Soviet government highly esteemed the services of R. I. Abel, conferring upon him the Order of Lenin, three Orders of the Red Banner, two Orders of the Red Banner of Labour, and the Order of the Red Star and many medals.

Rudolf Ivanovich remained at his combat post until the very last days. He contributed all his strength and knowledge to that honorable cause to which he had dedicated all his magnificent life. He devoted considerable attention to the training of a younger generation of Chekists, transmitting to them his rich experience and indicating the qualities inherent in the first Chekist-Leninist F. E. Dzerzhinsky.

Great personal charm, modesty, simplicity, and a sympathetic nature won Rudolf Ivanovich universal esteem and well-deserved authority.

The bright memory of Rudolf Ivanovich will be preserved forever in our hearts.

A Group of Comrades[4]

The KGB exploited Willie's funeral. Two years before Willie's death, in November 1969, when Aleksandr and Maria Orlov had settled in Ann Arbor, Michigan, the KGB finally tracked them down. A man calling himself Mikhail Aleksandrovich Feoktistov knocked at their door and asked to speak with them, showing a letter purporting to come from a comrade of SCHWED's. It was a gambit to get Orlov to return to the USSR but unsurprisingly the Orlovs were frightened and moved location once more, this time to Cleveland, Ohio.[5] On 10 August 1971 Comrade Feoktistov called at the Orlovs' appartment in Cleveland and met with them, giving them information about events and comrades, and testing once more whether Aleksandr was still sound and if he and Maria could be enticed to Moscow. On each occasion the Orlovs reported the visits and their fears, although not the detail of their conversations, to Edward Gazur, their FBI minder. A few weeks later on 16 November, the day after Willie Fisher's death, Maria died. Aleksandr's daughter Vera had died as a teenager in 1940 and now he was utterly alone. A few days after his wife's death, Orlov called Gazur in some distress, having just seen copies of the *Chicago Tribune* and the *New York Times* of 21 November 1971, which carried similar articles on the Moscow funeral of 'KGB spy Rudolf Abel'. The *Chicago Tribune* article was headed 'Brutality, Terror Emerge in Soviet Spy Apparatus', datelined 20 November 1971 and credited to James Yuenger, chief of the Moscow bureau. It continued:

The death this week of Rudolf Abel, the Soviet master spy, has prompted reliable Russian sources to give a rare glimpse of the brutality and terror which existed at the top levels of the Soviet Union's espionage apparatus.

Ironically, considering the callous nature of that shadowy world, it is a story of honest human resentment at the shabby treatment of men who, on orders, successfully organised two of Josef Stalin's most ambitious schemes, the murder of Leon Trotsky and the theft of America's atom bomb secrets.

The story emerged because three top ex-spies were not permitted to attend the funeral or cremation of their good friend Abel.

It seems, the sources said bitterly, that the current Kremlin leadership wants to leave elements of the Stalinist past – even, in Communist eyes, the most honourable deeds – to the dust of history.

[When Abel returned to the USSR in 1962, he] reportedly was amazed to find two of his old comrades in arms were being held in a maximum security prison at the ancient city of Vladimir, 110 miles east of Moscow.

He quickly organised twenty-three other top agents, all of whom had been designated 'Hero of the Soviet Union', the nation's highest honour. Together, the sources said, they signed a letter of protest to the Communist Party Central Committee.

The letter pleaded that the two men had risked their lives to ensure a Russian victory in World War II and that they did not deserve to be in prison. But the effort was in vain. The two served out their full prison terms. The appeal never received an official answer.

One of the men involved, who was not invited to Abel's funeral (attendance was by special pass only), is a mysterious figure named Leonid Eitingon.

Now an old man, Eitingon was thought before now to have been shot by Stalin's heirs in 1953 along with Lavrenti Beria, Stalin's hated secret police chief. Sources said, however, that after twelve years in prison, Eitingon is alive and working at the International Book Publishing House in Moscow.

Eitingon's name is not known to have turned up in public since 1957, when a Soviet agent named Aleksandr Orlov, who had defected and been a top-ranking official in the secret police, testified before a United States Senate Subcommittee.

Orlov said that Eitingon, using the name of Kotov, was a secret police general who had directed Soviet counter-intelligence during the Spanish Civil War. In the late 1930s, Orlov added, Eitingon selected Ramón Mercader del Rio, son of his mistress in Barcelona, Spain, to carry out the task of assassinating Stalin's archenemy, Leon Trotsky.

Eitingon was close not only to Beria but also to Stalin himself. Stalin is said to have once told him: 'Eitingon, if a hair of your head should fall, Stalin is no longer alive.' He was arrested shortly after Stalin died in 1953.

The other man named in the appeal organised by Abel was one named Pavel Sudoplatov, who was chief of espionage under Beria. Whilst serving a fifteen-year prison term he went blind, but he also could not attend Abel's funeral.

The third man noticeably absent was one known today as Kheifetz – probably not his real name. He knew Eitingon and Abel well, sources said.

An intelligence officer since 1922, Kheifetz served as Soviet vice consul in New York and returned to the USSR in 1946. That was four years before he was identified and indicted *in absentia* as 'Anatoly Yakovlev' – the man who masterminded the atom bomb spy ring which consisted of Julius and Ethel Rosenberg, David Greenglass, Harry Gold and Morton Sobel.

The same year that the Rosenbergs went on trial, 1950, Kheifetz – Yakovlev – was so badly beaten in prison that his spine was broken.

Other than his record, little information is available. There is only a hint from Greville Wynne, the British businessman spy who was imprisoned at Vladimir. After his release in 1964, Wynne wrote that he had seen two of Beria's assistants there.[6]

Orlov was worried first of all that the press reports about his testimony to the Senate subcommittee were inaccurate. He had written to the newspapers, protesting that he had not maligned Caridad Mercader del Rio in his statements to the subcommittee and that he had not named Eitingon, but his demands for retractions had been rejected. He was also convinced that the information in the articles had been specifically released to show him, Aleksandr Orlov, SCHWED, that he had nothing to fear by returning to Moscow. Two men he knew very well, but of whom the West knew nothing, had not been executed so, he felt, it was a signal telling him that he would be safe. There was also the test of Abel's name once more.[7] Again, for the KGB, there was no indication that Orlov had revealed who the 'master spy' really was, so Orlov was still, in their eyes, 'an absolutely decent man'.[8] Orlov was not gullible enough to be enticed back to the Soviet Union but Willie Fisher's last task, a task required of him after his death – to check that Orlov was remaining silent about the true identity of the man the West knew as Rudolf Abel, and the even deeper secret of Blunt, Burgess, Maclean, Cairncross and Philby – was completed successfully.

Like all careers, Willie's had failures as well as successes. Christopher Andrew and Vasily Mitrokhin are right when they draw attention to the barrenness of Willie's last five years as a KGB illegal in the United States.[9] He was simply an operational drudge, shuffling messages, paying people and cleaning up in the wake of inept colleagues, men who never should have been recruited and deployed in the first place. Certainly the changes in post-war politics in the West meant that there was a decline in the supply of potential agents from the now pitifully small national communist parties, and the illegals policy, so effective in the revolutionary and Stalinist periods, was obsolete or at best in need of a drastic overhaul. But as a political type, Willie himself was obsolete too, living in a bygone world of revolutionary fervour and psychologically unable to use tricks, seduction or blackmail to recruit agents. Operationally, he had been kept doing the same thing for too long, the potential of his scientific knowledge and technical skill now wasted in tiny hotel rooms in New York when they might have been used in the KGB training school in Moscow, or refocused for research and development in signals intelligence.

His first years in the United States were of course more successful, with his preparations for sabotage and supply routes in the event of a third world war, and the establishment of radio reception and transmission sites on the West Coast, near the Great Lakes and between New York and Norfolk, Virginia. His work with the VOLUNTEERS atomic spy ring brought him high honour, but here again to a very great extent he was limiting damage and managing retreat. He kept Ted Hall quiet, but was unable to keep him operational; ensured that no one talked out of turn when the Rosenbergs were tried and executed; and helped the escape of the Cohens, thus enabling their re-emergence and new work in England a few years later. All this had to remain secret, of course, which left the failed end of his career for all to see, but paradoxically his final failure could be hailed as a success. Although ambitious former senior officers like Maklyarsky belittled Willie, virtually everyone he met and worked with liked and admired him. His internationalist understanding of his communism enabled him to make friendships across cultures. Morris Cohen and

Konon Molody spoke of him in the highest terms and Kirill Khenkin, who came to loathe and fear the Soviet institutions that Willie served, nevertheless continued to regard him with warmth and respect that sometimes approached awe. In the Soviet Union Willie received help when he needed it from men in opposing camps in Russian culture, Andrei Andreev and Pyotr Kapitsa. Most crucial of all, and certainly for the KGB, Willie was admired by friends like Burt Silverman in America, by his lawyer James Donovan, by FBI officers like Ed Gamber, and even the director of the CIA, Allen Dulles. The American press noted Willie's dignity during his trial, and so the KGB could exploit a defeat and a failure as a triumph and continued to do so for almost ten years from the date of his return to the Soviet Union until his death.

For history, Willie Fisher's great successes were in the 1930s and 1940s, training and mentoring new officers and agents in radio theory, construction, reception, transmission and maintenance. Kitty Harris, who was to be Donald Maclean's case officer[10] as well as an important link in the theft of the West's atomic secrets, passed through his hands at this time. During the same period he was operational in London for the safe return of Kapitsa's family to the Soviet Union.

In the Second World War Willie's radio and espionage skills were used to effect in the defence of Moscow and then in harrying the Nazi army as it retreated west. It is perhaps to this period that Willie himself would look to celebrate his successes. For him, the last ten years of his life were not happy or comfortable. Everywhere he had lived, he lived as a stranger, and although he might have thought that he could be an honest and open man when he returned to Moscow after the years in America, this was only possible at home with his wife and daughter. Even his oldest colleagues would sometimes refer to him as Rudolf or Abel, and he was tortured even further as he came to hate the name of his best friend.

Ellie was determined to do all she could to ensure that her husband was honoured and remembered as William Fisher. Willie was denied the privilege of burial in Moscow's Novodevichy cemetery, which the authorities wanted, because Ellie would not tolerate a public funeral at which she would be required to see her husband buried as 'Rudolf Ivanovich Abel', and then let him rest under a tombstone bearing that name.[11] Ellie had spent much of her married life apart from her husband. She had been punished because of her love for him and her loyalty to him, and now he was dead she could not honour him publicly in his own name. The anger of her grief at his death did not subside and she channelled it into a campaign to have a tombstone bearing his name, which she achieved a year later. In the Donskoi cemetery on the anniversary of his death, a tombstone was erected with the name Vilyam Genrikhovich Fisher engraved in bold Cyrillic letters, and his last code name, his friend Rudolf's name, added in smaller letters beneath. On the side of the stone were added the names of Willie's mother and father.

EPILOGUE

Each chapter ended. Ellie herself died less than three years after Willie, on 13 April 1974. Her ashes were interred near to his, and her name, Yelena Stepanovna Fisher, engraved on the stone at the Donskoi, below the name and engraved likeness of her husband in his later years, bald, spectacled and, in the manner of his own second name, August.

Pavel Sudoplatov and Leonid Eitingon were rehabilitated and engaged in literary work for the rest of their lives, Eitingon dying in 1981 and Sudoplatov at the age of eighty-nine in 1996. Their ashes are interred in the Donskoi Monastery cemetery along with Willie's, Emma Sudoplatova's and Iosif Grigulevich's. Kitty Harris became mentally ill and spent time in a Soviet psychiatric prison hospital before being retired to Gorky (now Nizhny Novgorod), where she died lonely and bitter in 1966. Amongst her few possessions was a small, engraved locket given to her by Donald Maclean in 1937. Willie's old comrade from the Red Army Radio Battalion, Ernst Krenkel, remained a senior Soviet government technical adviser and died in 1985. Ted Hall went to work at the Cavendish Laboratory in Cambridge in 1962 and settled in England with his wife and family, dying in Cambridge in 1999. Lona Cohen died in 1992 and was laid to rest in Kuntsevskoe cemetery, Moscow, her last wish denied, for like Kitty Harris she had yearned to visit her family in the United States again and, when her time came, to be buried with them. Morris died two years later and was interred with Lona in the Kuntsevskoe. Pyotr Kapitsa consolidated his reputation as one of the greatest physicists of the twentieth century. His work on low temperature physics continued, and his institute contributed to the

Soviet success in developing liquid fuel for rockets. He was honoured with Stalin prizes, Orders of Lenin, and the Rutherford Medal, which he was allowed to travel to the United Kingdom to receive in 1966. In 1978 he was awarded a share of the Nobel Prize for Physics. He died on 8 April 1984 at the age of eighty-nine. His sons became scientists, respected in their field, Sergei in physics like his father and Andrei in geography. Aleksandr Orlov died of a cardiac arrest on 7 April 1973 in Cleveland, Ohio. When Edward Gazur carried out his promise to tidy Orlov's apartment after his death, he noticed some items were missing: a bottle of Drambuie, a firearm, Orlov's appointment diaries from the 1930s and his Russian-language version of his book, *The Secret History of Stalin's Crimes*. As the FBI man realised that the apartment had been burgled, he remembered that Orlov had recently become friendly with a Mr Nagy, a Hungarian neighbour, and wondered whether the KGB, unable to secure the return of Orlov himself, had at least managed to acquire two of his most precious documents. After Orlov's cremation, Gazur arranged for some of his ashes to be scattered secretly in Gorky Park, in Moscow.

*

James B. Donovan continued to practise as a lawyer and added the exchange of Cuban prisoners following the Bay of Pigs landing to his portfolio of international cases. He ran as the New York State Democrat for the United States Senate in 1962, but was defeated by Jacob Javits. Donovan suffered a heart attack and died at the age of fifty-three in 1970, not many months before his famous client.

*

On his return to the United States, Francis Gary Powers became a test pilot for the Lockheed Corporation and in 1970 started work as a helicopter pilot for the Los Angeles broadcaster KNBC. He was killed with his cameraman passenger when they crashed in a sports field in the summer of 1977. In 1996 his son, Francis Gary Powers Junior, founded the Cold War Museum at Lorton, Virginia, to 'preserve Cold War history and honour Cold War Veterans'.

*

Kirill Khenkin became active in the 1970s campaigns for Russian Jews to leave for Israel. He and his wife Irina left the Soviet Union in the 1970s and settled in Germany, where Kirill worked as a radio journalist and where his book *Okhotnik vverkh nogami* ('A Hunter Turned Upside Down') was published in 1979.

*

Evelyn Fisher died in a Moscow hospital on 22 February 2008. After her mother's death she lived alone in the Moscow apartment that her father came home to in 1962. 'Marriage was not for me,' she would say, 'I'm better on my own.' In the spring she would spend as much time as she could at the family dacha in the estate of Old Bolsheviks' dachas, thirty minutes by train from Moscow. Her cousin Lidiya, whom Evelyn still called her sister, became a teacher in a secretarial college, married and had a son. The two women continued to see a great deal of each other, Lidiya too spending part of the summer at the Fishers' dacha. After Evelyn appeared in a Russian television programme about her father in the late 1990s, she was contacted by a man by the name of Fisher, from the Rybinsk region. 'I must have many distant relatives in the north,' she said, 'but I have no children. I am the last of the Fishers. The last one.'

*

My conversations with Evelyn Fisher were mostly over the telephone but there were visits to her, one in the summer of 2000. 'I know nothing of Daddy's work,' she said again. 'We only spoke about important things, cooking, art, music, books.' The supply of books in English was important for Willie and Evelyn. 'He had a copy of John Le Carré's *The Spy Who Came in from the Cold*. I found it and when I had read it I said to him, "Daddy, was it like this?" He looked at me with his head on one side. His expression was, "You know better than to ask those sorts of questions," but it was also, "Yes, it was like this."'

'What did you mean, "like this"?' I asked her. 'Did you mean that it was ... sad, or pessimistic?'

'No. Not that. That the bosses were so ... cynical.'

*

'I do think about his life,' she said, 'and I think that for Daddy, yes, there was ideology, but for him it was also a matter of honour, a matter of truth. And he had to be true … to himself.'

*

Willie Fisher loved English wild flowers, and he missed them. In her art work, Evelyn used plants and natural materials so as presents I had taken her some English wild flower seeds.

'What wild flowers did your father like?' I asked.

'He liked harebells. And he liked scarlet pimpernel.'

I gasped, 'Scarlet pimpernel? Surely … the books … you must have read the Baroness Orzcy … this must be a joke.'

Evelyn's face betrayed nothing. The gift was given and the seeds of English wild flowers were scattered in the garden of the Fishers' dacha.

BIBLIOGRAPHY

BOOKS

Albright, J. and Kunstel, M., *Bombshell: The Secret Story of America's Atomic Spy Conspiracy*, Times Books, New York, 1997

Alexander, J. (compiler), *Images of England: Tynemouth and Cullercoats*, Tempus, Stroud, 1999

Andrew, Christopher and Mitrokhin, Vasily, *The Mitrokhin Archive: The KGB in Europe and the West*, Allen Lane, London, 1999

Antonov, V. et al., *Ocherki istorii rossiiskoi vneshnei razvedki, tom 5*, Mezhdunarodnye Otnosheniya, Moscow, 2003

Badash, Lawrence, *Kapitza, Rutherford, and the Kremlin*, Yale University Press, New Haven, 1985

Barke, Mike, *Social Change in Benwell*, Benwell Community Development, Newcastle upon Tyne, 1977

John Barron, *KGB: The Secret Work of Soviet Secret Agents*, Hodder & Stoughton, London, 1974

Beck, Melvin, *Secret Contenders: The Myth of Cold War Counterintelligence*, Sheridan Square, New York, 1984

Becket, Henry S. A., *The Dictionary of Espionage*, Stein & Day, New York, 1986

Beckett, Francis, *Enemy Within: The Rise and Fall of the British Communist Party*, John Murray, London, 1995

Bernikow, Louise, *Abel*, Hodder & Stoughton, London, 1970

Bigger, Philip J., *The Life and Career of James B. Donovan*, Lehigh University Press, Bethlehem, PA, 2006

Brook-Shepherd, Gordon, *The Storm Birds: Soviet Post-War Defectors*, Weidenfeld & Nicolson, London, 1988

Brook-Shepherd, Gordon, *The Storm Petrels: The First Soviet Defectors 1928–1938*, Collins, London, 1977

Bullard, J. and Bullard, M. (eds), *Inside Stalin's Russia: The Diaries of Reader Bullard 1930–34*, Day, Charlbury, 2000

Burke, David, *The Spy Who Came In from the Co-op: Melita Norwood and the Ending of Cold War Espionage*, Boydell Press, Woodbridge, 2008

Challinor, R., 'Gun-Running from the North-East Coast 1905–7', *North East Labour History*, no. 6, 1972

Chion, M., *The Films of Jacques Tati*, tr. Vinas, Monique, Williamson, Patrick and D'Alfono, Antonio, Guernica, Toronto, 1997

Cikovsky, Nicolai, *Winslow Homer*, Harry N. Abrams, New York, 1990

Cooper, Helen A., *Winslow Homer Watercolors*, National Gallery of Art and Yale University Press, Washington, 1986

Costello, John, *Mask of Treachery*, William Morrow, New York, 1988

Costello, John and Tsarev, Oleg, *Deadly Illusions*, Crown, New York, 1993

Dallin, David J., *Soviet Espionage*, Yale University Press, New Haven, 1955

Damaskin, Igor, *100 velikikh razvedchikov*, Veche, Moscow, 2001

Damaskin, Igor with Elliott, Geoffrey, *Kitty Harris: The Spy with Seventeen Names*, St Ermin's Press, 2001

Deacon, R., *A History of the Russian Secret Service*, Frederick Muller, London, 1972

Dienko, A. et al, *Razvedka i kontrrazvedka v litsakh: entsiklopedicheskii slovar' rossiiskih spetssluzhb*, Russkiy Mir, Moscow, 2002

Dolgopolov, Nikolai, *Oni ukrali bombu dlya sovetov*, XXI Vek – Soglasie, Moscow, 2000

Dolgopolov, Nikolai, *Pravda Polkovnika Abelya*, Komsomolskaya Pravda, Moscow, 1995

Donovan, James B., *Strangers on a Bridge: The Case of Colonel Abel*, Atheneum, New York, 1964

Dorril, Stephen, *MI6: Fifty Years of Special Operations*, Fourth Estate, Harper Collins, London, 2000

Encausse, Helene Carriere d', *Stalin: Order Through Terror*, tr. Ionescu, V., Longman, London, 1984

Feiffer, Jules, *Backing into Forward: A Memoir,* Nan A. Talese/ Doubleday, New York, 2010

Feklisov, Alexander, *The Man behind the Rosenbergs,* Enigma, New York, 2001

Figes, Orlando, *A People's Tragedy: The Russian Revolution 1891– 1924,* Pimlico, London, 1996

Fisher, A., *V Rossii i v Anglii: nablyudeniya i vospominaniya peterburgskogo rabochego (1890–1921 g.g.),* Gosudarstvennoe Izdatel'stvo, Moscow, 1922

Fisher, G., *Podpol'ye, ssylka, emigratsiya: vospominaniya Bol'shevika,* Staryi Bol'shevik, Moscow, 1935

Friedman, Richard, A Stone for Willy Fisher', *Studies in Intelligence,* vol. 20, no. 4, Winter 1986

Futrell, Michael, *Northern Underground: Episodes of Revolutionary Transport and Communications through Scandinavia and Finland,* Faber & Faber, London, 1963

Gazur, Edward P., *Secret Assignment: The FBI's KGB General,* St Ermin's Press, London, 2001

Gerdts, W. H., 'Winslow Homer in Cullercoats', *Yale University Art Gallery Bulletin,* Spring 1977

Goldstein, Alvin H., *The Unquiet Death of Julius and Ethel Rosenberg,* Lawrence Hill, New York, 1975

Gordievsky, O., *Next Stop Execution: The Autobiography of Oleg Gordievsky,* Macmillan, London, 1995

Gramont, S. de, *The Secret War,* Dell, New York, 1963

Grant, R., 'British Radicals and Socialists and Their Attitudes to Russia c. 1890–1917', Glasgow University PhD, 1984

Grant, R., 'The Cartridge Mystery of 1907', *North East Labour History,* no. 17, 1983

Grant, R., 'G. V. Chicherin and the Russian Revolutionary Cause in Great Britain', *Immigrants and Minorities,* vol. 2, no. 3, November 1983

Gromushkin, B. (ed.), *Abel: Rossiya i SShA v tvorchestve sovetskogo razvedchika-nelegala Rudol'fa Abel'ya,* Moskovskie Uchebniki i Kartolitografiya, Moscow, 1999

Harrison, Tony, *Winslow Homer in Cullercoats,* rev. ed., Station Press, Port Seton, 1995

Haynes, John Earle and Klehr, Harvey, *Venona: Decoding Soviet Espionage in America,* Yale University Press, New Haven, 2000

Hendricks, G., *The Life and Work of Winslow Homer,* Harry N. Abrams, New York, 1979

Heradstveit, Per Øyvind, *Hemmelige tjenester: etterretning, spionasje og overvåking,* H. Aschehoug, Oslo, 1973

Hollerton, Eric (compiler), *Images of England: Whitley Bay,* Tempus, Stroud, 1999

House, J. W., *Industrial Britain: the North East,* David & Charles, Newton Abbot, 1969

Hunkin, Tessa, *Benwell Urban Trail,* Newcastle upon Tyne, 1976

'Intimate Portrait of a Russian Master Spy', *Life,* 11 August 1957, pp. 123–30

Judge, Mary, *Winslow Homer,* Crown, New York, 1986

Kahn, D., *The Code-Breakers: The Comprehensive History of Secret Communication from Ancient Times to the Internet,* Scribner's, New York, 1996

Kapitza, P. L., *Pis'ma o nauke (1930–1980),* Moskovskii Rabochii, Moscow, 1989

Khenkin, Kirill, *Okhotnik vverkh nogami,* Posev, Frankfurt, 1979

Khrushchev, Nikita S., *Khrushchev Remembers* (tr. and ed. Talbott, S.), Little, Brown, New York, 1970

King, D., *Ordinary Citizens: The Victims of Stalin,* Francis Boutle, London, 2003

Klehr, Harvey and Haynes, John Earle, *The American Communist Movement: Storming Heaven Itself,* Twayne, New York, 1992

Klehr, Harvey, Haynes, John Earle and Firsov, Fridrikh Igorevich, *The Secret World of American Communism,* Yale University Press, New Haven, 1995

Klehr, Harvey, Haynes, John Earle and Firsov, Fridrikh Igorevich, *The Soviet World of American Communism,* Yale University Press, New Haven, 1998

Knight, Amy, *Beria: Stalin's First Lieutenant,* Princeton University Press, Princeton, New Jersey, 1993

Knight, Amy, *The KGB: Police and Politics in the Soviet Union,* Unwin Hyman, London, 1988

Knipe, Tony, *Winslow Homer: All the Cullercoats Pictures,* Northern Centre for Contemporary Art, Sunderland, 1988

Kolpakidi, A. and Prokhorov, D., *Vneshnyaya razvedka Rossii,* Olma Press, Moscow, 2001

Lacquer, Walter, 'From HUMINT to SIGINT', *Times Literary Supplement,* 11 February 1983

Lamphere, R. and Shachtman, T., *The FBI–KGB War: A Special Agent's Story,* Mercer University Press, Macon, GA, 1995

Lee, H. W. and Archbold, E., *Social Democracy in Britain,* Social Democratic Federation, London, 1935

Lenin, V., *'Left-Wing' Communism, an Infantile Disorder,* Lawrence & Wishart, London, 1920

Le Carre, John, *The Spy Who Came in from the Cold,* Victor Gollancz, London, 1963

Lonsdale, G., *Spy: Twenty Years of Secret Service – Memoirs of Gordon Lonsdale,* Neville Spearman, London, 1965

Macfarlane, L. J., 'Hands Off Russia: British Labour and the Russo-Polish War', *Past and Present,* vol. 38, December 1967, pp. 126–52

McCord, Norman, *North East England: An Economic and Social History,* Batsford Academic, London, 1979

Merridale, Catherine, *Night of Stone: Death and Memory in Russia,* Granta, London, 2000

Middlebrook, S., *Newcastle: Its Growth and Achievement,* S.R., Wakefield, 1968

Mitrokhin, Vasily (ed.), *KGB Lexicon: The Soviet Intelligence Officer's Handbook,* Frank Cass, London, 2002

Montefiore, Simon Sebag, *Stalin: The Court of the Red Tsar,* Weidenfeld & Nicolson, London, 2003

Morrell, Gordon W., *Britain Confronts the Stalin Revolution: Anglo-Soviet Relations and the Metro–Vickers Crisis,* Wilfrid Laurier University Press, Waterloo, ON, 1994

Murayova, L. and Sivolap-Kaftanova, L., *Lenin in London,* tr. Sayer, Jane, Moscow Progress, Moscow, 1983

Nalivaiko, B., 'Operation Altglinnike-Brukke', in Karpov, V. et al, *Declassified by the Foreign Intelligence Service,* Olma Press, Moscow, 2003

Newman, B., *Soviet Atomic Spies,* Robert Hale, London, 1952

Ogonyok, no. 4, 4486, 4487, January 1997

Orlov, Alexander, *A Handbook of Intelligence and Guerrilla Warfare,* University of Michigan Press, Ann Arbor, 1962

Orlov, Alexander, *The Secret History of Stalin's Crimes,* Random House, New York, 1952

Orwell, George, *Homage to Catalonia*, Secker & Warburg, London, 1938

Orwell, George, 'Looking Back on the Spanish War', in *England Your England*, Secker & Warburg, London, 1953

Orwell, Sonia and Angus, Ian (eds), *The Collected Essays, Journalism and Letters of George Orwell*, Seeker & Warburg, London, 1968

Pankhurst, R., *Sylvia Pankhurst: Artist and Crusader*, Paddington Press, London, 1979

Pedlow, Gregory W. and Welzenbach, Donald E., *The Central Intelligence Agency and Overhead Reconnaissance: The U-2 and OXCART Programs 1954–1974*, CIA, Washington DC, 1992

Pleshakov, Constantine, *Stalin's Folly: The Tragic First Ten Days of World War Two on the Eastern Front*, Houghton Mifflin Harcourt, New York, 2005

Pocock, Chris, *Dragon Lady: The History of the U-2 Spy Plane*, Airlife, Shrewsbury, 1989

Pocock, Chris, *The U-2 Spyplane: Toward the Unknown*, Schiffer Military History, Atglen, PA, 2000

Pollitt, H., *Serving My Time: An Apprenticeship to Politics*, Lawrence & Wishart, London, 1940

Potts, A., *Zilliacus: A Life for Peace and Socialism*, Merlin Press, London, 2002

Roberts, Sam, *The Brother: The Untold Story of Atomic Spy David Greenglass and How He Sent His Sister, Ethel Rosenberg, to the Electric Chair*, Random House, New York, 2001

Romerstein, H. and Levchenko, S., *The KGB against the Main Enemy: How the Soviet Intelligence Service Operates against the United States*, Lexington, Lexington, MA, 1989

Rothstein, A., *Lenin in Britain*, CPGB, London, 1970

Sakharov, Andrei, *Memoirs* (tr. Lourie, Richard), Hutchinson, London, 1990

Saunders, David, 'The 1905 Revolution on Tyneside', in Smele, J. D. and Heywood A., *The Russian Revolution of 1905: Centenary Perspectives*, Routledge, London, 2005

Saunders, David, 'A Russian Bebel Revisited: The Individuality of Heinrich Matthäus Fischer (1871–1935)', *Slavonic and East European Review*, vol. 82, no. 3, July 2004

Saunders, David, 'Tyneside and the Russian Revolution', *Northern History,* vol. 21, 1985

Schecter, J. and Schecter, L., *Sacred Secrets: How Soviet Intelligence Operations Changed American History,* Brassey's, Washington DC, 2002

Seth, Ronald, *The Russian Terrorists: The Story of the Narodniki,* Barrie & Rockcliff, London, 1966

Sevin, Dieter, 'Operation Scherhorn', *Military Review,* March 1966

Shoenberg, David, 'Kapitza, Fact and Fiction', *Intelligence and National Security,* vol. 3, no. 4, October 1988

Sinclair, Andrew, *The Red and the Blue: Intelligence, Treason and the Universities,* Weidenfeld & Nicolson, London, 1986

Singh, Simon, *The Code Book: The Secret History of Codes and Code-breaking,* Fourth Estate, London, 2000

Slatter, J. (tr.), 'Observations and Reminiscences of a Petersburg Worker: G. M. Fisher in Newcastle upon Tyne', *North East Labour History,* no. 22, 1988

Stephan, Robert W., *Stalin's Secret War: Soviet Counterintelligence against the Nazis 1941–1945,* University Press of Kansas, Lawrence, 2005

Stonor Saunders, Frances, *Who Paid the Piper? The CIA and the Cultural Cold War,* Granta, London, 1999

Sudoplatov, Pavel and Sudoplatov, Anatoly (with Schecter, J. and Schecter, L.), *Special Tasks: The Memoirs of an Unwanted Witness,* Little, Brown, London, 1994

Tarasov, D., *Zharkoe leto Polkovnika Abelya,* Terra, Moscow, 1997

Thorpe, Andrew, *The British Communist Party and Moscow 1920–43,* Manchester University Press, Manchester, 2000

Thorpe, Andrew, 'Comintern "Control" of the Communist Party of Great Britain 1920–43', *English Historical Review,* June 1998

Thorpe, Andrew, 'The Membership of the Communist Party of Great Britain 1920–1945', *Historical Journal,* vol. 43, no. 3, 2000

Trotsky, L., *My Life,* Scribner's, New York, 1930

Trubnikov, V. A. (ed.) et al., *Ocherki istorii rossiiskoi vneshnei razvedki, tom 4,* Mezhdunarodnye Otnosheniya, Moscow, 1998

Van Der Rhoer, Edward, *The Shadow Network: Espionage as an Instrument of Soviet Policy,* Scribner's, New York, 1983

Volkogonov, D., *Stalin* (ed. and tr. Shukman, H.), Phoenix Press, London, 2000

Volodarsky, Boris, *The KGB's Poison Factory: From Lenin to Litvinenko,* Frontline, Barnsley, 2009

West, Nigel, *The Illegals : The Double Lives of the Cold War's Most Secret Agents,* Hodder & Stoughton, London, 1993

West, Nigel, *MI5: British Security Service Operations 1909–1945,* Bodley Head, London, 1981

West, Nigel, *Venona: The Greatest Secret of the Cold War,* HarperCollins, London, 2000

West, Nigel and Tsarev, Oleg, *The Crown Jewels: The British Secrets at the Heart of the KGB Archives,* HarperCollins, London, 1998

Wicks, Harry, *Keeping My Head: The Memoirs of a British Bolshevik,* Socialist Platform, London, 1992

Wilmers, Mary-Kay, *The Eitingons: A Twentieth-Century Story,* Faber 8c Faber, London, 2009

Wise, David and Ross, Thomas B., *The Espionage Establishment,* Jonathan Cape, London, 1968

Wolf, Markus, *Man without a Face: Memoirs of a Spymaster,* Pimlico, London, 1997

Zelnik, Reginald E., 'Russian Bebels: An Introduction to the Memoirs of the Russian Workers Semen Kanatchikov and Matvei Fischer,' *Russian Review,* vol. 35, 1976, pp. 249–89, 417–47

Zelnik, Reginald E. (ed. and tr.), *A Radical Worker in Tsarist Russia: The Autobiography of Semen Ivanovich Kanatchikov,* Stanford University Press, Stanford, 1986

CD-ROM

Rudolf Abel/William Fisher, *Legenda nelegal'noi razvedki,* Veterany Razvedki, Moscow, 2000

WEBSITES

http://members.tripod.com/~RUDOLFABEL/ (accessed 20.12.00; now defunct, but important original source).

http://www.cartage.org.lb/en/themes/Biographies/MainBiographies/k/Kapitza/l.html (accessed 08.8.10).

http://www.fbi.gov/libref/historic/famcases/abel/abel.htm (accessed 08.8.10).

http://www.histlag.pair.com/h_lag_hist2.htm (accessed 8.08.10).

http://www.humanrightsnights.org/2001/index.cfm?language=english (accessed 20.12.01; now defunct).

http://www.lusitania.net (accessed 08.8.10).

http://www.nobel.se/physics/laureates/1978/kapitsa-bio.html (accessed 08.8.10).

http://www.norskfysikk.no/nfs/epsbiografer/KAPITZA.PDF (accessed 10.8.01; now defunct).

http://www.pbs.org/redfiles/kgb/deep/interv/k_int_morris_cohen.htm (accessed 08.8.10).

http://www.pbs.org/redfiles/rao/catalogues/trans/trac/ trac_kapi_l.html (accessed 08.8.10).

http://www.phy.cam.ac.uk/research/ltp/Section7.html (accessed 10.8.01; now defunct).

http://www.suntimes.com/ebert/greatmovies/hulot_holiday.html (accessed 10.8.01; now effectively defunct).

http://www.uncommonjourneys.com/pages/mauretania/ mauretania.htm (accessed 10.8.01; now forwarding elsewhere).

http://www.warwick.ac.uk/services/library/mrc/ead/ 259col.htm#N1255 (accessed 08.8.10).

http://www.washingtonpost.com/wp-dyn/content/article/2009/10/17/AR2009101701821.html (accessed 08.8.10).

http://www.wcml.org.uk/contents/activists/tom-mann/?keywordl=Tom+Mann&keyword2= (accessed 08.8.10).

https://www.cia.gov/library/center-for-the-study-of-intelligence/ kent-csi/vol9no3/html/v09i3al2p_0001.htm (accessed 08.8.10).

STAGE PLAY

Jules Feiffer, *A Bad Friend*, first performed at Lincoln Center Theater, New York City, 9 June 2003. Playscript published by Dramatists Play Service, New York, 2005.

FEATURE FILMS

The Dead Season, dir. Sawa Kulish, 1968.
Les Vacances de Monsieur Hulot, dir. Jacques Tati, 1954.

TELEVISION

Stranger than Fiction, dir. Trevor Hearing, Tyne Tees Television, 1995.
The Illegals, writer/producer Tom Bower, BBC, 1992.

NOTES

I had many meetings, telephone conversations and exchanges of correspondence with Evelyn Fisher (1998–2007), Kirill Khenkin (1998–2007) and David Saunders (since 1995) during the work on this book. Where my source is notes from these communications I have cited them by name only. Where I refer to the published work of Kirill Khenkin and David Saunders, the bibliographical reference is given. References to Home Office and Foreign Office documents in the Public Record Office, Kew, London, are HO and FO respectively. Other interviewees and archives are identified in individual notes.

CHAPTER 1: GERMAN-RUSSIAN BEGINNINGS

1 HO 144/1010/67901.
2 Much of the information about Heinrich Fischer in this chapter came originally from Reginald E. Zelnik's book *A Radical Worker in Tsarist Russia: The Autobiography of Semen Ivanovich Kanatchikov,* 1986, and his article 'Russian Bebels: An Introduction to the Memoirs of the Russian Workers Semen Kanatchikov and Matvei Fischer', 1976. David Saunders obtained the Fischer memoirs for me, outlined them and discussed them with me. Natalya Kovalenko and Yelena Londareva helped me to locate particular passages and explain and translate them. The information about Heinrich's names, and Russian education at the time, is from David Saunders, whose essay, 'A Russian Bebel Revisited: The Individuality of Heinrich Matthäus Fischer (1871–1935)', published in the *Slavonic and East European Review,* vol. 82, no. 3, July 2004, is now the definitive historical work on Heinrich Fischer.
3 Interview with Evelyn Fisher.
4 Khenkin, Kirill, *Okhotnik vverkh nogami,* 1979, p. 119.
5 Ibid.

6 Ibid., p. 120.

7 Tarasov, D., *Zharkoe leto Polkovnika Abelya*, 1997, pp. 41–3.

8 Zelnik, *A Radical Worker in Tsarist Russia*, p. 197.

9 Ibid.

10 Ibid., p. 198.

11 Interview with Evelyn Fisher.

12 Tarasov, *Zharkoe leto Polkovnika Abelya*, p. 43; Zelnik, *A Radical Worker in Tsarist Russia*, p. 365.

CHAPTER 2: NEWCASTLE UPON TYNE

1 Correspondence with Alan Myers.

2 McCord, Norman, *North East England: An Economic and Social History,* 1979, p. 19.

3 Ibid., p. 162.

4 Slatter, J. (tr.), 'Observations and Reminiscences of a Petersburg Worker: G. M. Fisher in Newcastle upon Tyne', *North East Labour History,* no. 22, 1988.

5 Ibid.

6 Interview with David Saunders.

7 HO 144/1010/145334.

8 Hunkin, Tessa, *Benwell Urban Trail,* 1976, p. 16; Barke, Mike, *Social Change in Benwell,* 1977, pp. 8–9.

9 Slatter, 'Observations and Reminiscences of a Petersburg Worker'.

10 HO 144/1010/145334.

11 Slatter, 'Observations and Reminiscences of a Petersburg Worker'.

12 Saunders, David, 'Tyneside and the Russian Revolution', *Northern History,* vol. 21, 1985.

13 Ibid.

14 Interview with Evelyn Fisher.

15 Tyne and Wear Archives, 7344/1/14.

16 Tarasov, D., *Zharkoe leto Polkovnika Abelya*, 1997, p. 44.

17 Ward's Street Directories 1903–6.

18 Rothstein, A., *Lenin in Britain,* 1970, p. 12.

19 Ibid., p. 14.

20 Figes, Orlando, *A People's Tragedy: The Russian Revolution 1891–1924,* 1996, pp. 173–80; Rothstein, *Lenin in Britain*, p. 18.

21 Interview with David Saunders.

22 Ibid.

CHAPTER 3: GUN-RUNNING

1 HO 144/1010/145334/2.

2 Ward's Street Directory 1906; interview with David Saunders.

3 The Fischer correspondence is held at the Public Record Office.

4 Grant, R., 'The Cartridge Mystery of 1907,' *North East Labour History*, no. 17, 1983; Grant, R., 'British Radicals and Socialists and Their Attitudes to Russia c. 1890–1917', Glasgow University PhD, 1984; Futrell, Michael, *Northern Underground: Episodes of Revolutionary Transport and Communications through Scandinavia and Finland*, 1963, pp. 66–84.

5 Grant, 'British Radicals and Socialists and Their Attitudes to Russia', p. 164.

6 Sudoplatov, Pavel and Sudoplatov, Anatoly (with Schecter, Jerrold L. and Schecter, Leona P.), *Special Tasks: The Memoirs of an Unwanted Witness – a Soviet Spymaster*, 1994, p. 31(n).

7 Futrell, *Northern Underground*, pp. 74–8.

8 Potts, A., *Zilliacus: A Life for Peace and Socialism*, 2002, chs 1, 10, 13.

9 Grant, 'British Radicals and Socialists and Their Attitudes to Russia', p. 164.

10 Grant, 'Cartridge Mystery of 1907'.

11 FO 371/322 400. David Saunders found this document and made me aware of it.

12 FO 371/322 402.

13 Ibid.

14 FO 371/322 386.

15 Grant, 'British Radicals and Socialists and Their Attitudes to Russia', pp. 167–8.

16 Lee, H. W. and Archbold, E., *Social Democracy in Britain*, 1935, p.149.

17 FO 371/322 388.

18 Grant, 'British Radicals and Socialists and Their Attitudes to Russia', p. 171; *Newcastle Daily Chronicle*, 15 May 1907.

19 Grant, 'British Radicals and Socialists and Their Attitudes to Russia', p. 116.

20 Lee and Archbold, *Social Democracy in Britain*, pp. 148–9.

21 *Evening Chronicle* (Newcastle), 6 April 1907.

22 Grant, 'British Radicals and Socialists and Their Attitudes to Russia', p. 174.

23 FO 371/322 388.

24 Grant, 'Cartridge Mystery of 1907'.

25 *Newcastle Daily Chronicle*, 20 April 1907.

26 Futrell, *Northern Underground*, p. 224.

27 HO 144/1010 69701.

CHAPTER 4: TO THE COAST

1 Barke, Mike, *Social Change in Benwell*, 1977, pp. 43, 32.

2 Evelyn Fisher.

3 Hollerton, Eric, *Images of England: Whitley Bay*, 1999, pp. 4, 7–8.

4 Evelyn Fisher.

5 HO 144/1010 67901.

6 Ibid.

7 Ward's Street Directories 1915–16, 1920.

8 Evelyn Fisher.

9 Evelyn Fisher. Documents at the Northumberland County Record Office, CES 69/2/1, show that Henry Fischer *(sic)* attended Blyth Secondary School in July 1914 to go to the new Whitley and Monkseaton High School. The admissions register for the High School at this time has not survived.

10 Tyne and Wear archives T133/98-9.

11 Oxford University archives OUA LE109/28.

12 Evelyn Fisher.

13 Interview with Kirill Khenkin.

14 Tyne and Wear archives T133/98-9.

15 Alexander, J., *Images of England: Tynemouth and Cullercoats*, 1999, pp. 19–22; Hollerton, *Images of England: Whitley Bay*, pp. 15, 56; correspondence from Alan Myers, February 2005.

16 David Saunders.

17 McCord, Norman, *North East England: An Economic and Social History*, 1979, p. 203.

18 *Legenda nelegal'noi razvedki*, 2000. Natalia Kovalenko obtained a copy of this source and translated for me.

19 OUA LE109/28.

20 T133/98-9.

CHAPTER 5: RETURN TO RUSSIA

1 Beckett, Francis, *Enemy Within: The Rise and Fall of the British Communist Party*, 1995, p. 28.

2 Pollitt, H., *Serving My Time: An Apprenticeship to Politics*, 1940, ch. 8.

3 Beckett, *Enemy Within*, p. 9; Pollitt, *Serving My Time*, p. 125.

4 Beckett, *Enemy Within*, p. 12.

5 CPGB circular to branch secretaries, 5 August 1920, quoted in *Weekly Worker* 404, 18 October 2001.

6 *Communist,* vol. 1, no. 3, 19 August 1920, quoted in *Weekly Worker* 404, 18 October 2001.

7 Macfarlane, L. J., 'Hands Off Russia: British Labour and the Russo-Polish War', *Past and Present,* vol. 38, December 1967, pp. 126–52.

8 David Saunders.

9 University of London matriculation pass lists for 1920; University of London Library.

10 Tarasov, D., *Zharkoe leto Polkovnika Abelya,* 1997, p. 70.

11 FO 610 156.

12 Pollitt, *Serving My Time,* pp. 137, 139, 140.

13 Evelyn Fisher; Tarasov, *Zharkoe leto Polkovnika Abelya,* p. 58; interview and exchange of correspondence with George Falkowski, Rosa Prokofiev's son, November 2001.

14 Evelyn Fisher.

15 David Saunders; Evelyn Fisher.

16 David Saunders.

17 Evelyn Fisher.

18 Thorpe, Andrew, 'Comintern "Control" of the Communist Party of Great Britain, 1920–1945', *English Historical Review,* June 1998.

19 Costello, John, *Mask of Treachery,* 1998, pp. 94, 102–3.

20 Thorpe, Andrew, *The British Communist Party and Moscow, 1920–1943,* 2000, pp. 12–13.

21 Costello, *Mask of Treachery,* p. 101.

22 King, D., *Ordinary Citizens: The Victims of Stalin,* 2003, p. 26.

23 Evelyn Fisher.

24 Evelyn Fisher; David Saunders.

25 Evelyn Fisher.

CHAPTER 6: RECRUITMENT

1 'Colonel Abel about Himself', *Trud, Molodoi Kommunist,* February 1966; reprinted in RDCD 00669. I am particularly grateful to Natalia Kovalenko for her translation of this article.

2 Kirill Khenkin.

3 Interview with George Falkowski, spring 2002.

4 See George Orwell, 'Notes on Nationalism', in *The Collected Essays,*

Journalism and Letters of George Orwell, vol. Ill: As I Please 1943–1945, eds Sonia Orwell and Ian Angus, 1968, Item 101.

5 Evelyn Fisher.

6 RDCD 00669.

7 There are discrepancies between Willie's CVs published in RDCD 00669 and the account given by Tarasov, D., *Zharkoe leto Polkovnika Abelya*, 1997, pp. 49–50.

8 'Colonel Abel about Himself'.

9 RDCD 00669.

10 From telephone interviews with Eric Hollerton in the Local Studies Section, North Tyneside Central Library and Arthur Andrews of Cullercoats.

11 Willie's description of his early days as a radio enthusiast are taken from the *Molodoi Kommunist* article, but the author is grateful to members of the Defence Electronics History Society, the Bournemouth Radio Society and Professor Sean Street for guiding him through the technical vocabulary and this period in the history of radio communications.

12 RDCD 00669; Kirill Khenkin; Evelyn Fisher.

13 RDCD 00669.

14 Evelyn Fisher.

15 Ibid.

16 RDCD 00669.

17 Evelyn Fisher.

18 Ibid.

19 Ibid.

20 David Saunders.

21 Evelyn Fisher; Tarasov, *Zharkoe leto Polkovnika Abelya*, p. 55.

22 Evelyn Fisher.

23 *Molodoi Kommunist*, February 1966.

24 RDCD 00669.

25 Andrew, Christopher and Mitrokhin, Vasily, *The Mitrokhin Archive: The KGB in Europe and the West*, 1999, p. 31.

26 Figes, Orlando, *A People's Tragedy: The Russian Revolution 1891–1924*, 1996, pp. 641–2.

27 Andrew and Mitrokhin, *Mitrokhin Archive*, p. 30.

28 RDCD 00669.

29 Evelyn Fisher.

30 Tarasov, *Zharkoe leto Polkovnika Abelya*, p. 70.

31 PRO FO 610/289; Passport 78/1931.

CHAPTER 7: SCANDINAVIAN MISSION

1 Orlov's story is told in Brook-Shepherd, Gordon, *The Storm Birds: Soviet Post-War Defectors*, 1988; Costello, John and Tsarev, Oleg, *Deadly Illusions*, 1993; and Gazur, Edward P., *Secret Assignment: The FBI's KGB General*, 2001.

2 Costello and Tsarev, *Deadly Illusions*, pp. 13–17; Gazur, *Secret Assignment*, pp. 3–4.

3 Costello and Tsarev, *Deadly Illusions*, p. 19; Gazur, *Secret Assignment*, pp. 5–11.

4 Costello and Tsarev, *Deadly Illusions*, pp. 30–31, 42–3.

5 Gazur, *Secret Assignment*, p. 13.

6 Interview with Kirill Khenkin.

7 Kirill Khenkin; Costello and Tsarev, *Deadly Illusions*, pp. 70–71, 91, 103; Gazur, *Secret Assignment*, pp. 14–15.

8 Costello and Tsarev, *Deadly Illusions*, p. 71.

9 Ibid., pp. 111–13, 115, 159.

10 Orlov, Alexander, *A Handbook of Intelligence and Guerrilla Warfare*, 1962, quoted in Gazur, *Secret Assignment*, pp. 577–9.

11 Gazur, *Secret Assignment*, p. 579.

12 See also Andrew, Christopher and Mitrokhin, Vasily, *The Mitrokhin Archive: The KGB in Europe and the West*, 1999, pp. 73–85.

13 The sources for material on the Fishers in Oslo are Heradstveit, Per Øyvind, *Hemmelige tjenester: etterretning, spionasje og overvåking*, 1973; correspondence and telephone interviews with Knut Jacobsen, Frode Jacobsen and Nina Westgaard (formerly Mohr), childhood neighbours of the Fishers in Golia.

14 Friedman, Richard, 'A Stone for Willy Fisher', *Studies in Intelligence*, vol. 20, no. 4, Winter 1986; Kirill Khenkin. In both cases the role is referred to, but not the location.

15 Interview with confidential source.

16 Heradstveit, *Hemmelige tjenester*, p. 15; Evelyn Fisher.

17 Frode Jacobsen; Evelyn Fisher.

18 Costello and Tsarev, *Deadly Illusions*, p. 50; RDCD 00669.

19 Wicks, Harry, *Keeping My Head: The Memoirs of a British Bolshevik*, 1992, pp. 148–58.

20 Khenkin, Kirill, *Okhotnik vverkh nogami*, 1979, pp. 112–13; interview with Kirill Khenkin; Sakharov, Andrei, *Memoirs* (tr. Lourie, Richard), 1988; Sudoplatov, Pavel, and Sudoplatov, Anatoly (with Schecter, Jerrold L. and Schecter, Leona P.), *Special Tasks: The Memoirs of an Unwanted Witness – a Soviet Spymaster*, 1994, p. 180(n); Shoenberg, David, 'Kapitza, Fact and Fiction', *Intelligence and National Security*, vol. 3, no. 4, October 1988.

21 Shoenberg, 'Kapitza, Fact and Fiction'; *The Times* obituary, 11 April 1984.

22 Sinclair, Andrew, *The Red and the Blue: Intelligence, Treason and the Universities,* 1986, p. 26; http://www.nobel.se/physics/laureates/1978/kapitsa-bio.html.

23 Montefiore, Simon Sebag, *Stalin: The Court of the Red Tsar,* 2003, p. 146.

24 Quoted in Sinclair, *Red and the Blue,* pp. 27–8.

25 Kirill Khenkin.

26 Sinclair, *Red and the Blue,* p. 49.

27 Tarasov, D., *Zharkoe leto Polkovnika Abelya,* 1997, p. 70.

28 Interview with Boris Labusov and Oleg Tsarev, November 1999.

29 Shoenberg, 'Kapitza, Fact and Fiction'.

30 RDCD 00669.

31 Kapitsa, P. L., *Letters about Science,* 1989, p. 27.

32 Interview with Nina Westgaard, autumn 2003.

33 Heradstveit, *Hemmelige tjenester,* p. 18.

34 Antonov, V. et al., *Ocherki istorii rossiiskoi vneshnei razvedki, tom 5,* 2003, p. 165.

35 Nina Westgaard.

CHAPTER 8: HOME AGAIN – MOSCOW AND LONDON

1 Costello, John and Tsarev, Oleg, *Deadly Illusions,* 1993, pp. 71–2.

2 Damaskin, Igor with Elliott, Geoffrey, *Kitty Harris: The Spy with Seventeen Names,* 2001, p. 4.

3 Evelyn Fisher.

4 See Damaskin and Elliott, *Kitty Harris.*

5 Ibid., p. 42.

6 Ibid., p 137.

7 Evelyn Fisher.

8 Damaskin and Elliott, *Kitty Harris,* p. 138.

9 Evelyn Fisher.

10 Sinclair, Andrew, *The Red and the Blue: Intelligence, Treason and the Universities,* 1986, p. 52.

11 Ibid., p. 53.

12 Ibid.

13 Ibid., pp. 54–5.

14 Shoenberg, David, 'Kapitza, Fact and Fiction', *Intelligence and National Security,* vol. 3, no. 4, October 1988, p. 50.

15 Sinclair, *Red and the Blue,* p. 55.

16 See ibid., p. 52.

17 Costello and Tsarev, *Deadly Illusions*, p. 159.

18 Andrew, Christopher and Mitrokhin, Vasily, *The Mitrokhin Archive: The KGB in Europe and the West*, 1999, p. 73.

19 Costello and Tsarev, *Deadly Illusions*, p. 134.

20 Andrew and Mitrokhin, *Mitrokhin Archive*, p. 74.

21 West, Nigel and Tsarev, Oleg, *The Crown Jewels: The British Secrets at the Heart of the KGB Archives*, 1998, p. 106; Friedman, Richard, A Stone for Willy Fisher', *Studies in Intelligence*, vol. 20, no. 4, Winter 1986.

22 West and Tsarev, *Crown Jewels*.

23 Ibid., pp. 106, 273–4.

24 Gazur, Edward P., *Secret Assignment: The FBI's KGB General*, 2001, p. 579.

25 Andrew and Mitrokhin, *Mitrokhin Archive*, p. 77.

26 RDCD 00669.

27 Evelyn Fisher.

28 Khenkin, Kirill, *Okhotnik vverkh nogami*, 1979, p. 30.

29 Tarasov, D., *Zharkoe leto Polkovnika Abelya*, 1997, p. 73; Evelyn Fisher.

30 Tarasov, *Zharkoe leto Polkovnika Abelya;* Andrew and Mitrokhin, *Mitrokhin Archive*, p. 192.

31 Dolgopolov, Nikolai, *Oni ukrali bombu dlya sovetov*, 2000, p. 47.

32 Khenkin, *Okhotnik vverkh nogami*, p. 36.

33 Dolgopolov, *Oni ukrali bombu dlya sovetov*, p. 47; Khenkin, *Okhotnik vverkh nogami*, p. 36.

34 Evelyn Fisher.

CHAPTER 9: THE GREAT PURGE

1 Costello, John and Tsarev, Oleg, *Deadly Illusions*, 1993, p. 249.

2 Dolgopolov, Nikolai, *Oni ukrali bombu dlya sovetov*, 2000, p. 49.

3 Costello and Tsarev, *Deadly Illusions*, p. 248.

4 Gazur, Edward P., *Secret Assignment: The FBI's KGB General*, 2001, pp. 129–31.

5 Costello and Tsarev, *Deadly Illusions*, pp. 267–92.

6 Gazur, *Secret Assignment*, pp. 441–72.

7 Ibid., pp. 196–201.

8 RDCD 00669.

9 Grant, R., 'G. V. Chicherin and the Russian Revolutionary Cause in Great Britain', *Immigrants and Minorities*, vol. 2, no. 3, November 1983.

10 Ibid.

11 J. V. Stalin, 'The Immediate Tasks of the Party in the National Question: Theses

for the Tenth Congress of the R.C.P.(B.), Endorsed by the Central Committee of the Party', in J. V. Stalin, *Works,* 1953, vol. 5, pp. 16–30; www.marx2mao.net/PDFs/StWorks5.pdf.

12 www.pbs.org/redfiles/rao/catalogues/trans/trac/trac_kapi_l.html.

13 Evelyn Fisher.

14 Costello and Tsarev, *Deadly Illusions,* p. 249.

15 Ibid., p. 285.

16 Ibid., p. 206.

17 Damaskin, Igor with Elliott, Geoffrey, *Kitty Harris: The Spy with Seventeen Names,* pp. 235–6.

18 Sudoplatov, Pavel, and Sudoplatov, Anatoly (with Schecter, Jerrold L. and Schecter, Leona P.), *Special Tasks: The Memoirs of an Unwanted "Witness – a Soviet Spymaster,* 1994, p. 47; Brook-Shepherd, Gordon, *The Storm Petrels: The First Soviet Defectors 1928–1938,* 1977, pp. 155–6.

19 Andrew, Christopher and Mitrokhin, Vasily, *The Mitrokhin Archive: The KGB in Europe and the West,* 1999, pp. 106–7.

20 Sudoplatov et al., *Special Tasks,* p. 64.

21 Ibid., p. 40.

22 Khenkin, Kirill, *Okhotnik vverkh nogami,* 1979, p. 36.

23 Andrew and Mitrokhin, *Mitrokhin Archive,* p. 106.

24 Knight, Amy, *Beria: Stalin's First Lieutenant,* 1993, p. 86.

25 Ibid., p. 88.

26 Sudoplatov et al., *Special Tasks,* p. 40.

27 Khrushchev, Nikita S., *Khrushchev Remembers* (tr. and ed. Talbott, S.), 1970, p. 96.

28 Sudoplatov et al., *Special Tasks,* p. 59.

29 West, Nigel and Tsarev, Oleg, *The Crown Jewels: The British Secrets at the Heart of the KGB Archives,* 1998, p. 112.

30 Costello and Tsarev, *Deadly Illusions,* p. 79.

31 Evelyn Fisher.

32 Ibid.

33 Tarasov, D., *Zharkoe leto Polkovnika Abelya,* 1997, pp. 79–80.

34 David Saunders.

35 Khrushchev, *Khrushchev Remembers,* p. 236 5(n).

36 Tarasov, *Zharkoe leto Polkovnika Abelya,* p. 80.

CHAPTER 10: SPECIAL TASKS

1   RDCD 00669.

2   Knight, Amy, *Beria: Stalin's First Lieutenant,* 1993, p. 93.

3   Ibid., p. 106.

4   RDCD 00669; Tarasov, D., *Zharkoe leto Folkovnika Abelya,* 1997, p. 82.

5   Sudoplatov, Pavel, and Sudoplatov, Anatoly (with Schecter, Jerrold L. and Schecter, Leona P.), *Special Tasks: The Memoirs of an Unwanted 'Witness – a Soviet Spymaster,* 1994, pp. 7–9.

6   Ibid., p. 24.

7   Ibid., pp. 56–7.

8   Ibid., p. 57.

9   Ibid., pp. 58, 61–3.

10 Ibid., p. 68.

11 The full story of Leonid Aleksandrovich Eitingon is now to be found in Mary-Kay Wilmers, *The Eitingons: A Twentieth-Century Story,* 2009.

12 Andrew, Christopher and Mitrokhin, Vasily, *The Mitrokhin Archive: The KGB in Europe and the West,* 1999, p. 113.

13 Ibid., pp. 114–16.

14 West, Nigel and Tsarev, Oleg, *The Crown Jewels: The British Secrets at the Heart of the KGB Archives,* 1998, pp. 112–13.

15 Knight, Beria, p. 112.

16 Sudoplatov et al., *Special Tasks,* p. 127.

17 Andrew and Mitrokhin, *Mitrokhin Archive,* p. 112; Sudoplatov et al., *Special Tasks,* pp. 58–9.

18 Khenkin, Kirill, *Okhotnik vverkh nogami,* 1979, p. 27.

19 Sudoplatov et al., *Special Tasks,* p. 58; see also Wicks, Harry, *Keeping My Head: The Memoirs of a British Bolshevik,* 1992, pp. 72–4.

20 For the beginning of the Cheka's interest in poisons and poisonings, see Volodarsky, Boris, *The KGB's Poison Factory: From Lenin to Litvinenko,* 2009, pp. 32–3.

21 Andrew and Mitrokhin, *Mitrokhin Archive,* p. 54; Khenkin, *Okhotnik vverkh nogami,* p. 26.

22 Andrew and Mitrokhin, *Mitrokhin Archive,* pp. 95–6.

23 Sudoplatov et al., *Special Tasks,* p. 135.

24 Ibid., p. 126; Kirill Khenkin.

25 Sudoplatov et al., *Special Tasks,* p. 135.

26 Kirill Khenkin.

27 Khenkin, *Okhotnik vverkh nogami,* p. 42.

28 Kirill Khenkin.

29 Khenkin, *Okhotnik vverkh nogami,* p. 32.

30 Ibid., p. 37.

31 Kirill Khenkin.

32 Sudoplatov et al., *Special Tasks,* pp. 153–4.

33 Ibid., p. 155.

34 For the fullest account of the Soviet deception games, see Stephan, Robert W., *Stalin's Secret War: Soviet Counterintelligence against the Nazis, 1941–1945,* 2005, particularly pp. 153–90.

35 Ibid., p. 158.

36 Sevin, Dieter, 'Operation Scherhorn', *Military Review,* March 1966.

37 Sudoplatov et al., *Special Tasks,* pp. 158–60.

38 Kirill Khenkin.

39 Evelyn Fisher.

40 Evelyn Fisher.

41 Andrew and Mitrokhin, *Mitrokhin Archive,* p. 177; Khenkin, *Okhotnik vverkh nogami,* p. 105.

42 Stephan, *Stalin's Secret War,* p. 175

43 Sudoplatov et al., *Special Tasks,* p. 168.

44 The most detailed sources for Operation Berezino, also known as Operation Scherhorn, are Trubnikov, V. A. (ed.) et al., *Ocherki istorii rossiiskoi vneshnei razvedki, tom 4,* 1998; Stephan, *Stalin's Secret War;* and Sevin, 'Operation Scherhorn'. I am grateful to Geoffrey Elliott, who supplied me with a copy of Trubnikov's Russian text, to Natalia Kovalenko for her translations, and to Dieter Sevin, with whom I corresponded about the research he undertook in the 1960s.

45 Sudoplatov et al., *Special Tasks,* p. 168; Trubnikov, *Ocherki istorii rossiiskoi vneshnei razvedki,* pp. 108–28.

46 Sevin, 'Operation Scherhorn'.

47 Ibid.

48 Trubnikov, *Ocherki istorii rossiiskoi vneshnei razvedki,* pp. 108–28.

49 Sevin, 'Operation Scherhorn'.

50 Sudoplatov et al., *Special Tasks,* p. 169.

51 Sevin, 'Operation Scherhorn'.

52 Trubnikov, *Ocherki istorii rossiiskoi vneshnei razvedki,* pp. 108–28.

53 Sevin, 'Operation Scherhorn'.

54 Stephan, *Stalin's Secret War,* p. 176.

55 Trubnikov, *Ocherki istorii rossiiskoi vneshnei razvedki;* Sudoplatov et al. *Special Tasks,* p. 168, says the cash figure was ten million roubles.

56 Sudoplatov et al., *Special Tasks,* p. 168.

57 West, Nigel, *The Illegals: The Double Lives of the Cold War's Most Secret Agents,* 1993, p. 180.

58 Lonsdale, G., *Spy: Twenty Years of Secret Service,* 1965, pp. 47–8.

CHAPTER 11: TRAINING FOR A NEW ASSIGNMENT

1   Dolgopolov, Nikolai, *Oni ukrali bombu dlya sovetov,* 2000, pp. 51–2.

2   Ibid., p. 52.

3   Andrew, Christopher and Mitrokhin, Vasily, *The Mitrokhin Archive: The KGB in Europe and the West,* 1999, p. 190.

4   Sudoplatov, Pavel, and Sudoplatov, Anatoly (with Schecter, Jerrold L. and Schecter, Leona P.), *Special Tasks: The Memoirs of an Unwanted Witness – a Soviet Spymaster,* 1994, p. 238.

5   Andrew and Mitrokhin, *Mitrokhin Archive,* pp. 191–2.

6   Sudoplatov et al., *Special Tasks,* p. 244(n).

7   Ibid., p. 244; Costello, John and Tsarev, Oleg, *Deadly Illusions,* 1993, p. 79.

8   Sudoplatov et al., *Special Tasks,* pp. 240–42.

9   Van Der Rhoer, Edward, *The Shadow Network: Espionage as an Instrument of Soviet Policy,* 1983, p. 94; Khenkin, Kirill, *Okhotnik vverkh nogami,* 1979, p. 119.

10 Khenkin, *Okhotnik vverkh nogami,* pp. 121–2.

11 Sudoplatov et al., *Special Tasks,* p. 242.

12 Andrew and Mitrokhin, *Mitrokhin Archive,* p. 191.

13 Evelyn Fisher.

14 Costello, John, *Mask of Treachery,* 1998, p. 102.

15 Andrew and Mitrokhin, *Mitrokhin Archive,* p. 192.

16 Bernikow, Louise, *Abel,* 1970, p. 16.

17 RDCD 00669.

18 Andrew and Mitrokhin, *Mitrokhin Archive,* pp. 10–11.

19 Khenkin, *Okhotnik vverkh nogami,* p. 122.

20 Ibid., p. 123.

21 Van Der Rhoer, *Shadow Network,* p. 102; Andrew and Mitrokhin, *Mitrokhin Archive,* p. 193.

22 Andrew and Mitrokhin, *Mitrokhin Archive.*

23 Bernikow, *Abel,* p. 16. Bernikow's book and James Donovan's *Strangers on a Bridge: The Case of Colonel Abel* (1964) are the key secondary sources from the American perspective which explore how Willie Fisher entered, settled and lived in the United States.

24 Andrew and Mitrokhin, *Mitrokhin Archive,* p. 193.

25 Ibid.

CHAPTER 12: FIRST US MISSIONS

1 Kirill Khenkin.
2 West, Nigel, *The Illegals: The Double Lives of the Cold War's Most Secret Agents,* 1993, p. xii.
3 Andrew, Christopher and Mitrokhin, Vasily, *The Mitrokhin Archive: The KGB in Europe and the West,* 1999, pp. 187–8.
4 Sudoplatov, Pavel, and Sudoplatov, Anatoly (with Schecter, Jerrold L. and Schecter, Leona P.), *Special Tasks: The Memoirs of an 5 Unwanted Witness – a Soviet Spymaster,* 1994, p. 242.
5 Ibid., p. 243; http://members.tripod.com/~RUDOLFABEL/ (20.12.00).
6 Schecter, J. and Schechter, L., *Sacred Secrets: How Soviet Intelligence Operations Changed American History,* 2002, pp. 57–8.
7 The Soviet policy of preparing these dumps is covered by Andrew and Mitrokhin, *Mitrokhin Archive,* see particularly pp. 467–8.
8 Sudoplatov et al., *Special Tasks,* pp. 24–5, 243.
9 Wolf, Markus, *Man without a Face: Memoirs of a Spymaster,* 1997, pp. 65–6; Damaskin, Igor with Elliott, Geoffrey, *Kitty Harris: The Spy with Seventeen Names,* 2001, p. 241.
10 Schechter and Schechter, *Sacred Secrets,* pp. xxvi, 207.
11 www.pbs.org/redfiles/kgb/deep/interv/k_int_morris_cohen.htm.
12 Albright, J. and Kunstel, M., *Bombshell: The Secret Story of America's Atomic Spy Conspiracy,* 1997, p. 197.
13 Ibid., p. 26.
14 Ibid.
15 Costello, John and Tsarev, Oleg, *Deadly Illusions,* 1993, pp. 276–7.
16 Albright and Kunstel, *Bombshell,* p. 31.
17 Ibid., p. 33.
18 Ibid., pp. 47–8.
19 Ibid., p. 33.
20 Ibid., p. 181.
21 Sudoplatov et al., *Special Tasks,* p. 209.
22 Albright and Kunstel, *Bombshell,* p. 198.
23 Bernikow, Louise, *Abel,* 1970, pp. 16–17.
24 Albright and Kunstel, *Bombshell,* pp. 244, 247.

25 Evelyn Fisher; Andrew and Mitrokhin, *Mitrokhin Archive,* p. 227; http:// members. tripod.com/~RUDOLFABEL/ (20.12.00).

26 Albright and Kunstel, *Bombshell,* pp. 93–6.

27 Ibid., p. 98.

28 Ibid., pp. 171–4.

29 Ibid., p. 191.

30 Ibid., pp. 200, 221–2.

31 Ibid., pp. 288–9.

32 *The Guardian,* 13 February 2002.

33 Andrew and Mitrokhin, *Mitrokhin Archive,* pp. 188–9.

34 Albright and Kunstel, *Bombshell,* pp. 4–6.

35 Schechter and Schechter, *Sacred Secrets,* pp. 174–5.

CHAPTER 13: UNDERCOVER ARTIST

1 Evelyn Fisher.

2 Andrew, Christopher and Mitrokhin, Vasily, *The Mitrokhin Archive: The KGB in Europe and the West,* 1999, pp. 204–5.

3 Ibid., p. 205.

4 Ibid., p. 206.

5 Ibid., p. 209.

6 Lonsdale, G., *Spy: Twenty Years of Secret Service,* 1965, pp. 62–4.

7 Confidential source.

8 Bernikow, Louise, *Abel,* 1970, pp. 19–20, 120.

9 Khenkin, Kirill, *Okhotnik vverkh nogami,* 1979, pp. 185–6.

10 Bernikow, *Abel,* p. 120.

11 Albright, J. and Kunstel, M., *Bombshell: The Secret Story of America's Atomic Spy Conspiracy,* 1997, pp. 132, 193.

12 Feklisov, Alexander, *The Man behind the Rosenbergs,* 2001, p. 316.

13 Roberts, Sam, *The Brother: The Untold Story of Atomic Spy David Greenglass and How He Sent His Sister, Ethel Rosenberg, to the Electric Chair,* 2001, p. 452.

14 Knight, Amy, *Beria: Stalin's First Lieutenant,* 1993, p. 157.

15 Wilmers, Mary-Kay, *The Eitingons: A Twentieth-Century Story,* 2009, p. 386.

16 Knight, *Beria,* pp. 196–200; Sudoplatov, Pavel, and Sudoplatov, Anatoly (with Schecter, Jerrold L. and Schecter, Leona P.), *Special Tasks: The Memoirs of an Unwanted Witness – a Soviet Spymaster,* 1994, p. 131; Wilmers, *Eitingons,* p. 399.

17 Van Der Rhoer, Edward, *The Shadow Network: Espionage as an Instrument of Soviet Policy,* 1983, p. 107.

18 Bernikow, *Abel,* p. 21.

19 Ibid., pp. 22–3.

20 Interview with Burt Silverman, winter 2000.

21 Bernikow, *Abel,* p. 30.

22 Interview with Jules Feiffer, February 2009.

23 Bernikow, *Abel,* p. 28; Feiffer, Jules, *Backing into Forward: A Memoir,* 2010, pp. 224–31.

24 Ibid., pp. 25–6.

25 Evelyn Fisher.

26 Bernikow, *Abel,* p. 24.

27 Knipe, Tony, *Winslow Homer: All the Cullercoats Pictures,* 1988, p. 27.

28 Bernikow, *Abel,* p. 33.

29 Ibid., p. 37.

30 www.fbi.gov/libref/historic/famcases/abel/abel.htm; Andrew and Mitrokhin, *Mitrokhin Archive,* p. 223.

31 www.fbi.gov/libref/historic/famcases/abel/abel.htm.

32 Andrew and Mitrokhin, *Mitrokhin Archive,* p. 224.

33 Ibid.

34 Klehr, Harvey and Haynes, John Earle, *The American Communist Movement: Storming Heaven Itself,* 1992, p. 19.

35 www.fbi.gov/libref/historic/famcases/abel/abel.htm.

36 Lamphere, R. and Shachtman, T., *The FBI–KGB War: A Special Agent's Story,* 1995, p. 276.

37 www.fbi.gov/libref/historic/famcases/abel/abel.htm.

38 Kahn, D., *The Code-Breakers: The Comprehensive History of Secret Communication from Ancient Times to the Internet,* 1996, pp. 668–71.

39 Lamphere and Shachtman, *FBI–KGB War,* p. 270.

40 Ibid., p. 271.

41 Ibid., p. 272.

42 Van Der Rhoer, *Shadow Network,* p. 112.

43 Bernikow, *Abel,* pp. 62–4.

44 Andrew and Mitrokhin, *Mitrokhin Archive,* p. 224.

45 Bernikow, *Abel,* p. 65.

46 Khenkin, *Okhotnik vverkh nogami,* p. 144; http://members.tripod.com/-RUDOLFABEL/ (20.12.00).

47 Andrew and Mitrokhin, *Mitrokhin Archive,* p. 226.

48 Bernikow, *Abel,* pp. 66–7.

49 Van Der Rhoer, *Shadow Network,* p. 113.

50 Bernikow, *Abel,* p. 41.

51 Van Der Rhoer, *Shadow Network,* p. 113.

CHAPTER 14: TESTING TIMES

1 Van Der Rhoer, Edward, *The Shadow Network: Espionage as an Instrument of Soviet Policy,* 1983, p. 113.

2 Kirill Khenkin; Evelyn Fisher.

3 Chion, M., *The Films of Jacques Tati,* 1997, p. 43.

4 Khenkin, Kirill, *Okhotnik vverkh nogami,* 1979, p. 144.

5 Van Der Rhoer, *Shadow Network,* p. 114.

6 Sudoplatov, Pavel, and Sudoplatov, Anatoly (with Schecter, Jerrold L. and Schecter, Leona P.), *Special Tasks: The Memoirs of an Unwanted Witness – a Soviet Spymaster,* 1994, p. 243.

7 Klehr, Harvey and Haynes, John Earle, *The American Communist Movement: Storming Heaven Itself,* pp. 143–4.

8 Ibid.; Klehr, Harvey, Haynes, John Earle and Firsov, Fridrikh Igorevich, *The Secret World of American Communism, 1995,* p. 72.

9 Bernikow, Louise, *Abel,* 1970, p. 71.

10 Ibid., p. 75.

11 Ibid., pp. 82–6.

12 Van Der Rhoer, *Shadow Network,* p. 115.

13 Ibid., pp. 115–16.

14 Ibid., p. 115.

15 Bernikow, *Abel,* p. 86.

16 Ibid., p. 88.

17 Ibid., p. 86.

18 Ibid., p. 90.

19 www.fbi.gov/libref/historic/famcases/abel/abel.htm.

20 Ibid.

21 Lamphere, R. and Shachtman, T., *The FBI–KGB War: A Special Agent's Story,* 1995, p. 273.

22 Ibid.

23 Bernikow, *Abel,* p. 103.

24 Ibid., p. 106.

25 Interview with Ed Gamber, June 2003.

26 Bernikow, *Abel,* pp. 109–13; Gramont, S. de, *The Secret War: The Story of*

International Espionage since 1945, 1963, pp. 201–3; Van Der Rhoer, *Shadow Network*, p. 115; West, Nigel, *The Illegals: The Double Lives of the Cold War's Most Secret Agents*, 1993, p. 119.

27 'Colonel Abel about Himself', *Trud, Molodoi Kommunist*, February 1966; RDCD 00669.

28 Bernikow, *Abel*, p.1ll; Van Der Rhoer, *Shadow Network*, p. 117.

29 Bernikow, *Abel*, pp. 110–12.

30 Ibid., pp. 112–15.

31 Interview with Anthony Palermo, June 2010.

32 Anthony Palermo.

33 Bernikow, *Abel*, pp. 116.

34 Khenkin, *Okhotnik vverkh nogami*, pp. 16–17.

35 Sudoplatov et al., *Special Tasks*, p. 243.

36 Kirill Khenkin; Costello, John and Tsarev, Oleg, *Deadly Illusions*, 1993, p. 372.

37 Sudoplatov et al., *Special Tasks*, p. 46.

38 Andrew, Christopher and Mitrokhin, Vasily, *The Mitrokhin Archive: The KGB in Europe and the West*, 1999, p. 805 n75; Bernikow, *Abel*, p. 97.

39 Andrew and Mitrokhin, *Mitrokhin Archive*, pp. 365–6, 834 31(n).

40 Kirill Khenkin.

41 Anthony Palermo.

42 Van Der Rhoer, *Shadow Network*, p. 117.

43 Sudoplatov et al., *Special Tasks*, p. 241.

CHAPTER 15: TRIAL

1 'Colonel Abel about Himself', *Trud, Molodoi Kommunist*, February 1966; RDCD 00669.

2 Interview with Ed Gamber.

3 Bernikow, Louise, *Abel*, 1970, p. 119.

4 Interview with Anthony Palermo, June 2010.

5 Donovan, James, *Strangers on a Bridge: The Case of Colonel Abel*, 1964, pp. 21–3; Khenkin, Kirill, *Okhotnik vverkh nogami*, 1979, ch. 16.

6 Donovan, *Strangers on a Bridge*, p. 59.

7 https://www.cia.gov/library/center-for-the-study-of-intelligence/kent-csi/vol9no3/html/v09i3al2p_0001.htm; http://www.washingtonpost.com/wp-dyn/content/article/2009/10/17/AR2009101701821.html.

8 Khenkin , *Okhotnik vverkh nogami*, p. 181.

9   Donovan, *Strangers on a Bridge,* pp. 50–52.

10 Ibid., p. 67. The ditty also appeared, with its electronic jingle, on http:// members. tripod.com/~RUDOLFABEL/ (20.12.00).

11 Kirill Khenkin.

12 Gramont, S. de, *The Secret War: The Story of International Espionage since 1945,* 1963, p. 211.

13 http://www.bombshell-l.com/archives/doc2.txt (12.03.01).

14 Ed Gamber.

15 Anthony Palermo

16 Donovan, *Strangers on a Bridge,* pp. 227–8.

17 Ibid., pp. 153–7.

18 Ibid., pp. 182–4; Bernikow, *Abel,* pp. 311–12.

19 Donovan, *Strangers on a Bridge,* p. 190.

20 Ibid., p. 207.

21 Ibid., p. 207.

22 Ibid., p. 213.

23 Ibid., p. 213.

24 Ibid., p. 214.

25 Evelyn Fisher.

26 Donovan, *Strangers on a Bridge,* p. 253.

27 Ibid., p. 251.

28 Gramont, *Secret War,* pp. 206–7; Donovan, *Strangers on a Bridge,* pp. 273–4.

29 Donovan, *Strangers on a Bridge,* p. 67.

30 Kirill Khenkin.

31 Donovan, *Strangers on a Bridge,* p. 259.

32 Ibid., pp. 72–3.

33 Gramont, *Secret War,* p. 223.

34 Ibid., p. 223.

35 http://members.tripod.com/~RUDOLFABEL/ (20.12.00); interview with Jules Feiffer, February 2009.

36 Andrew, Christopher and Mitrokhin, Vasily, *The Mitrokhin Archive: The KGB in Europe and the West,* 1999, p. 227.

37 Donovan, *Strangers on a Bridge,* p. 348.

38 Andrew and Mitrokhin, *Mitrokhin Archive,* p. 228.

CHAPTER 16: EXCHANGE OF PRISONERS

1   Pocock, Chris, *Dragon Lady: The History of the XJ-2 Spy Plane,* 1989, pp. 33–58;

Pocock, Chris, *The U-2 Spyplane: Toward the Unknown*, 2000, pp. 184–91. See also Whittell, Giles, *Bridge of Spies: A True Story of the Cold War*, forthcoming.

2 Donovan, James, *Strangers on a Bridge: The Case of Colonel Abel*, 1964, pp. 298–9.

3 https://www.cia.gov/library/center-for-the-study-of-intelligence/kent-csi/ vol9no3/html/v09i3a12p_0001.htm.

4 Donovan, *Strangers on a Bridge*, p. 359.

5 Ibid.

6 Ibid., p. 363.

7 Andrew, Christopher and Mitrokhin, Vasily, *The Mitrokhin Archive: The KGB in Europe and the West*, 1999, pp. 227–8; RDCD 00669; Evelyn Fisher.

8 Donovan, *Strangers on a Bridge*, p. 367.

9 Andrew and Mitrokhin, *Mitrokhin Archive*, p. 228.

10 Evelyn Fisher.

11 Andrew and Mitrokhin, *Mitrokhin Archive*, p. 227.

12 Interview with Sergei Kondrashev, spring 2003.

13 Evelyn Fisher.

14 Donovan, *Strangers on a Bridge*, pp. 179–80.

15 Andrew and Mitrokhin, *Mitrokhin Archive*, p. 227.

16 Ibid., p. 478.

17 Wise, David and Ross, Thomas B., *The Espionage Establishment*, 1968, pp. 21(n).

18 http://www.humanrightsnights.org/2001/index.cfm?language=english (20.12.2001).

19 *Ogonek*, no. 4, January 1997.

20 Sudoplatov, Pavel, and Sudoplatov, Anatoly (with Schecter, Jerrold L. and Schecter, Leona P.), *Special Tasks: The Memoirs of an Unwanted Witness – a Soviet Spymaster*, 1994, p. 244 9(n).

21 Gordievsky, O., *Next Stop Execution: The Autobiography of Oleg Gordievsky*, 1995, p. 141; Donovan, *Strangers on a Bridge*, p. 343.

22 Khenkin, Kirill, *Okhotnik vverkh nogami*, 1979, p. 148.

23 Ibid., p. 265.

24 Wolf, Markus, *Man without a Face: Memoirs of a Spymaster*, 1997, p. 95.

25 Independent observations from Yelena Londareva, Natalia Kovalenko, David Saunders.

26 Interview with Oleg Gordievsky, autumn 2000; Evelyn Fisher.

27 *Ogonek*, no. 4, January 1997.

28 Kirill Khenkin.

29 Sudoplatov et al., *Special Tasks*, p. 428; http://members.tripod.com/~RUDOLFABEL/ (20.12.00).

30 Khenkin, *Okhotnik vverkh nogami,* p. 267.

31 Evelyn Fisher; Kirill Khenkin.

32 Bernikow, Louise, *Abel,* 1970, p. 311.

33 Evelyn Fisher; Kirill Khenkin.

CHAPTER 17: AN UNQUIET DEATH

1 Khenkin, Kirill, *Okhotnik vverkh nogami,* 1979, p. 261.

2 Gordievsky, O., *Next Stop Execution: The Autobiography of Oleg Gordievsky,* 1995, p. 140; interview with Oleg Gordievsky.

3 Friedman, Richard, 'A Stone for Willy Fisher', *Studies in Intelligence,* vol. 20, no. 4, winter 1986.

4 Facsimile reprinted ibid.

5 See Gazur, Edward P., *Secret Assignment: The FBI's KGB General,* 2001, Part 4, pp. 357–438.

6 Ibid., pp. 424–6.

7 Ibid., p. 428.

8 Costello, John and Tsarev, Oleg, *Deadly Illusions,* 1993, p. 372.

9 Andrew, Christopher and Mitrokhin, Vasily, *The Mitrokhin Archive: The KGB in Europe and the West,* 1999, pp. 192, 226, 256.

10 Damaskin, Igor with Elliott, Geoffrey, *Kitty Harris: The Spy with Seventeen Names,* 2001, pp. 168–81.

11 Evelyn Fisher.

INDEX

INDEX

INDEX

Swan Hunter shipyard 44, 44n

Tarasov, Aleksandr 57n, 77
Tati, Jacques 156
'Throne' organisation 112–13
trade unions (England) 13–14, 33, 47
Trotsky, Leon
    accused of conspiracy 93
    assassination attempts on 98–9,
      102, 106–7
    influence on young people 58
    murder of 102, 107, 132–3, 197–8
    support for Georgy Chicherin 97
    visits Denmark 74
Trud (newspaper) 189
Truman, President Harry S. 140
Tsar Nicholas II *see* Nicholas II, Tsar
Tsarev, Mikhail 60
Tube Alloys Project 139
Twentieth Century Press 16
Tyne (river) 9, 10, 12, 41

U-2 reconnaissance programme 182–3
Ukrainian Communist Party 120
Ukrainian Nationalist Organisation
    102, 105
Ulbricht, Walter 133
United Nations 124, 134

Vacances de Monsieur Hulot, Les (film)
    156–7
VENONA project 140, 144, 152, 171
Vladimir Province 59
Vogel, Wolfgang 186
Volga (river) 51
Volkonsky, Prince 1
Vologda 52, 53, 67
VOLUNTEERS network 133–4, 136, 140,
    144, 199

Wallsend shipworks 44, 45
West Street Federal Detention Centre
    172, 179–80
Whitley Bay 33–6, 38, 41
Whitley Bay and Monkseaton High
    School 38–9
Wilkinson, Fred 187
Winston, Alan 135, 137, 143–4
Wissel, Kurt 133–4
'Wobblies' (IWW) 147, 151
Wolf, Markus 190

Wollweber, Ernst 133, 190
Workers' Socialist Federation (WSF)
    46–7
Wright, Chief Constable J. B. 19, 21–2,
    27, 37
Wynne, Greville 190, 198

Yagoda, Genrikh 80, 95, 99, 126
'Yasha Group' 109
Yekaterinburg 24n
Yezhov, Nikolai 95–6, 99, 100–101,
    105–6
'Yezhovshchina' 105 Yuenger, James
    196

Zamyatin, Yevgeny 43n
Zarya ('Dawn' – journal) 15–16
Zhidov, Vasily 7
Zhidova, Lyubov Vasilyevna (mother of
    Willie Fisher)
    marries Heinrich Fischer 7
    birth of sons 14–15
    moves to Whitley Bay 35
    middle-class lifestyle of 38, 41
    relationship with sons 39, 40, 51–2,
      56, 62–3, 66, 82, 195
    returns to Russia 49–50
    health of 52, 54, 93
    becomes Social Secretary to Old
      Bolsheviks 52
    relationship with granddaughter
      (Evelyn) 66
    relationship with Kapitolina
      Lebedeva 81–2
    moves to Kuibyshev 109–110, 114
    death of 115
Zhukov, Marshal Georgy 113
Zilliacus, Konni 21–3, 21n
Zilliacus (jnr), Konni 21n, 23
Zinoviev, Grigory 93, 94, 95, 99

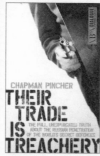